CHRISTIAN MISSION & ECONOMIC SYSTEMS

The book makes a significant contribution in rethinking the relationship between Christian mission and economics. The studies introduce fresh approaches like reciprocity in economic understanding, learning from Islam's approach to free-market capitalism, the moral logic explaining "bribes" in some cultures, and the economic struggles of pastors in the developing world. The studies set a benchmark for empirically grounded, theoretically informed research about the contexts of Christian mission. Its innovative research approaches are a good model for those researching Christian mission.

Vinay Samuel, founder and director emeritus of the Oxford Centre for Mission Studies

This book is a treasure chest filled with information providing invaluable help for understanding the laws, folkways, and mores governing economic practices cross-culturally. It also enables us to gain perspectives on our own capitalistic systems and to judge them according to Scripture. Those who believe that missionaries are obligated to contextualize the essential gospel message, while avoiding the tendency to impose Western socioeconomic values on those in other cultures, will find this book extremely helpful. I read these essays twice and still did not distill all the gems they hold.

Tony Campolo, speaker, evangelist, and founder of the Evangelical Association for the Promotion of Education

An important contribution by gifted scholars and practitioners to our understanding of how economics intersects with every aspect of Christian mission. A better grasp of the crucial issues raised in this book will greatly strengthen and improve contemporary missions.

Ronald J. Sider, president of Evangelicals for Social Action and author of *Rich Christians in an Age of Hunger: Moving from Affluence to Generosity*

Christian Mission and Economic Systems is a grand world tour of the fiscal and relational realities of the world's amazing diversity in how transactions are made, how enterprise is financed, and how communities thrive. This book is an indispensable research volume for people undertaking cross-cultural mission.

R. Paul Stevens, professor emeritus of marketplace theology, Regent College, and author of *Doing God's Business: Meaning and Motivation for the Marketplace*

The present book is an amazing combination of profound scholarship interacting with authentic, longtime cross-cultural experience of its authors. The diversity of nationalities, cultural and scholarly backgrounds of the writers, and the variety of themes investigated by them opens the eyes and the mind for realities that lie well beyond the classic and simplistic capitalism versus socialism and/or communism debates of the last century.

Martin Hartwig Eitzen, professor of missiology and intercultural studies, Universidad Evangélica del Paraguay, and director of the Instituto Aquila y Priscila

A desire to bring a spiritual influence does not cancel the impacts of economic forces on one's activities. A simple default response to diverse extant economic dynamics is inadequate. The wide-ranging contributions from multiple authors alert us to this basic truth, but also encourage us to understand and respond intelligently to dominant Western economic systems. *Christian Mission and Economic Systems* is vital reading for those concerned with mission who want to see beyond the blinkers of their cultural presuppositions on economic issues.

Jim Harries, professor of religion, Global University (Assemblies of God), and founder of the Alliance for Vulnerable Mission

This collection is pointing to a missing link—that transitional form that should be found between the enterprise of mission as we know it and the primordial jungle of economic realities, where life and ministry began in simplicity before climbing out of the dark waters and onto the shores of ministerial reality. Herein is an evolutionary call to do partnership better, do patronage better, and even bribe "better." Furthermore, we are called to have evolved vision to see the ministry world through economic eyes and to see economics through kingdom eyes. A part of this new vision includes seeing the realities of Majority World friends who are not really experiencing "life more abundantly." In this regard Christian NGOs are called upon to continue becoming what they are, i.e., Christian. This is an important volume, especially in terms of asking hard questions as mission continues integrating kingdom values with life as it is.

Frampton F. Fox, Associates in Community Training Solutions

CHRISTIAN MISSION & ECONOMIC SYSTEMS

A Critical Survey of the Cultural
and Religious Dimensions of Economies

John Cheong & Eloise Meneses
Editors

WILLIAM CAREY
LIBRARY

Published by William Carey Library
1605 E. Elizabeth Street
Pasadena, CA 91104 | www.missionbooks.org

Andrew Levin, editor
Brad Koenig, copyeditor
Alyssa E. Force, design

Cover Image: iStockPhoto

William Carey Library is a ministry of the
U.S. Center for World Mission
Pasadena, CA 91104 | www.uscwm.org

Printed in the United States of America

18 17 16 15 14   5 4 3 2 1 BP 300

Library of Congress Cataloging-in-Publication Data

Christian mission and economic systems : a critical survey of the cultural and religious dimensions of economies / John Cheong and Eloise Meneses, editors.
   pages cm
Includes bibliographical references and index.
ISBN 978-0-87808-075-5 -- ISBN 0-87808-075-9 1. Missions. 2. Economics. 3. Economics--Religious aspects--Christianity. I. Cheong, John, editor.
BV2063.C47 2014
261.8'5--dc23
                                                    2014037294

To the memory of

PAUL HIEBERT

a father to his family,
a mentor to his many students,
and a pioneering thinker and
writer in missiology

CONTENTS

FOREWORD

With this book, evangelical missiology enters a "brave new world." *Economic systems* is a subject category rarely broached in either the theory or the practice of Western evangelical missions. Influenced by the subversively pervasive economic ideologies in which we and our defining institutions live and move and have our being, conservative Christian missiologists have been loath to acknowledge—let alone wrestle with—the ethical-missiological implications of economic *systems*.

It is a risky and potentially embarrassing thing for missiologists to venture into the realm of entrenched economic custom, as we see in the response of experts to Jesus's apparently naive understanding of economics. "You cannot serve both God and money," Jesus said—to which "the Pharisees, who loved money" (and could pride themselves on their more sophisticated grasp of economic realities), responded by "sneering at Jesus" (Luke 16:14). Sneers and snickers—often from the seemingly most pious—continue to deflect piercing kingdom truth on economic questions. That is why the editors and publishers of this book are to be thanked for making the subject the focus of serious missiological reflection.

While all nine essays in this volume (including Priest's introduction) are worth reading, several seem to me to be groundbreaking. I will comment primarily on the chapter by John Cheong, the chief editor and originator of the book. Islamic banking and economic practices are more consistent with biblical teaching than those characterizing the West, he argues (chap. 3). Because religious principles rather than bald economic interests constitute the bottom line for banking institutions infused with Qur'anic and *hadith* values, they tend to be more responsible to local communities and relatively less myopically focused on profit. Entitled "Islamic Banking and Economics: A Mirror for Christian Practices and Mission in Muslim Contexts," this essay should be required reading not just for missionaries, but for earnest Christians serving within the power structures of Western financial institutions and businesses. If it seems ironic that Islam could help us to repent and get our banking practices back in line with biblical ethics, there is ample precedent to be found throughout the biblical record, where God's recalcitrantly disobedient people are shown the path of obedience by their nemeses. In the biblical account, God's people almost never embark on the humbling path of repentance. Perhaps evangelicals in North America are different, and will listen to what God is saying, whatever his medium of communication?

While each chapter in this volume deserves more acknowledgment and response than is possible in this space, two other essays are striking for their originality and penetrating insights into the "real" world of everyday economic life. Such is the chapter by Douglas Wilson, "Western Mission–established Churches and Ministry in Mali's Collectivist Economy" (chap. 6), and Eloise Meneses' "Exchange, Relationships, and Reciprocity: Living as a Christian in a Capitalist World" (chap. 1). Both essays exemplify the "boots on the ground" empathy requisite to incarnational ministry.

It is deeply satisfying to see evangelicals at last begin to develop a vocabulary of economic analysis, a language that enables them to notice and reflect on the theological implications of economic systems. Although no one can live by bread alone, physical survival requires bread, and bread requires the economic means to both produce and procure it. Thus economics is to physical survival what religion is to the spiritual. It is hard to imagine one without the other.

Paul Hiebert, to whose memory the book is dedicated, would be honored, proud, and encouraged were he to read this timely book. To be remembered for student mentoring and groundbreaking thinking is honor enough for most teachers; to have a long neglected theme of such fundamental significance addressed so substantially by those he mentored would make him proud!

As one who has taught and mentored for most of his life, it is my strong recommendation that the essays in this book be required reading in missiological training across the globe.

JONATHAN J. BONK

author of *Missions and Money: Affluence as a Missionary Problem*
executive director emeritus, Overseas Ministries Study Center

ACKNOWLEDGMENTS

Editing a book is not an easy process, in no small part because there are so many moving parts—sending, receiving, and mailing materials, proofreading, editorial corrections, document handling, legal advice, and so on. To this end, we want to thank the following people for their part in making this book happen.

To Jeff Minard and William Carey Library: Thank you for your willingness to consider our book when we were first exploring uncharted territory in evangelical missiology on the subject of Christian mission and economic systems. Your editorial board review comments and feedback encouraged us to see that the kernel of the idea we had was worthy of growth and development. It allowed us to pursue what we had to say with confidence. *Muchas gracias!* To Andrew Levin: Your detailed review, with insightful and incisive comments on the draft (on matters we thought were clear but actually were not so!) was a tremendous help to us. Without them, this would have been a lesser book in its final form. You taught us to be better editors. To Wendy Hayes: Thanks for staying in touch with us through the many emails as we worked across two continents in our globalized world. We are especially grateful to you for your patience and graciousness in the early phase of the proposal when we might have despaired of the process.

To Melissa Hughes: thank you for your help and advice on the legal, contractual, and logistical aspects of publishing.

To our reviewers and endorsers: We feel very privileged that you took the time to read and comment on this book. We have learned much in the past from you that has contributed to our own growth as missiologists and Christian writers. We humbly hope that this book has stimulated or broadened your own thinking on the subject of mission and economic systems. May the Lord use this work to further your own ministry among Christian businesspeople, tentmakers, missionaries, mission executives, and the marginalized and economically disempowered of this world in ever more creative and missiologically informed ways.

To our fellow writers and contributors: Thank you for coming on board when we first broached the subject of this book with you. Through the process of reading your chapters, we discovered that your passion and conviction on this subject was just as strong as ours! We are grateful also that you stayed with us through thick and thin, through the many months of writing, editing, revising (and then revising over and over again) in what must have seemed an endless process. We hope you are satisfied with the finished product and can now see the fruit of your own labor. To Bob Priest: Thank you for your willingness to write the introduction for us, and for providing encouragement and experienced comments along the way. We consider you the literary equivalent of Adam Smith's "invisible hand," assisting us at key moments in the shaping of this material.

Lastly, to our spouses and children: You have been patient and have made many sacrifices to support us in our writing and ministry endeavors. We are sorry for the late dinners (and leftover meals), all-nighters, or bleary-eyed mornings because we have had to attend to this project (or another) along the way. Thank you for your grace, love, and prayers for us. We love you!

JOHN CHEONG & ELOISE MENESES
August 2014

CONTRIBUTORS

LINDY BACKUES has worked for eighteen years (1989–2007) in the design and implementation of holistic community development projects in Bali and Java, Indonesia. Dr. Backues' work has been in the integration of development theory, religious aspiration, and on-site grassroots development practice, to the end that such holistic approaches to development practice might result in greater understanding, deeper appreciation of local resources and local community aspirations, and deeper impact in relation to tangible local needs. Since 2007 Dr. Backues has taught economic development at Eastern University in St. Davids, Pennsylvania. At present he is associate professor of economic development and teaches at both the undergraduate and graduate levels. He has an MDiv from Asbury Theological Seminary, an MSc in economic development from Eastern University, and a PhD in community development from the University of Leeds.

DAVID BRONKEMA has been involved in international development, justice, and environmental concerns for over twenty years. He has been a consultant for the Harvard Institute for International Development in El Salvador and the National Center for State Courts in Guatemala and has worked with the Eastern Research Group on worldwide environmental enforcement. For eight years he was program coordinator for the Latin American and Caribbean region with the American

Friends Service Committee. Dr. Bronkema now holds the Templeton Chair for Christian Service through Entrepreneurship in the School of Leadership and Development at Eastern University, where he has served as chair and directs the master's program in international development. He has a PhD in anthropology and an MA in international relations from Yale University.

JOHN CHEONG is from Southeast Asia and has served in various church planting ministries for six years in a Muslim environment that pioneered the modern Islamic banking system. He holds a PhD in intercultural studies from Trinity Evangelical Divinity School and has published articles on the socioreligious and economic aspects of globalization and migration among Muslims and on the dynamics of mission in globalization and emerging global megaregions. He has also sat on his church mission board, which oversees the funding and support for missions. He currently collaborates with the Global Diaspora Network and teaches missiology and intercultural studies in a Southeast Asian seminary, specializing in globalization, Islam, work, and money and mission.

MARY LEDERLEITNER, PhD, is a consultant for the Wycliffe Global Alliance. She has written the book *Cross-cultural Partnerships: Navigating the Complexities of Money and Mission* (InterVarsity Press, 2010) and has contributed chapters to other missiological publications. She has been a certified public accountant and has served as a tax examiner for the Internal Revenue Service and for the city of Cincinnati (USA), as well as serving as the Asia area finance manager and head of international audit for Wycliffe and SIL International. At present she also serves as a researcher and adjunct professor at Trinity Evangelical Divinity School. She is also a conference speaker and serves on the advisory board of the *Evangelical Missions Quarterly.*

ELOISE MENESES is professor of cultural anthropology in the Department of Missions and Anthropology at Eastern University in the Philadelphia area. She has done research on the lives of Dalit ("untouchable") women, which is published in the book *Love and Revolutions: Market Women and Social Change in India* (University Press of America, 2007). She has also served as a board member for the Mennonite Central Committee, a relief and development agency of the Mennonite churches, for ten years. Presently she teaches in the areas of poverty, global economic systems, India, women's experience, linguistics, race and ethnicity, and faith and science.

MIKE NJALAYAWO MTIKA is originally from Malawi, where he worked first as an agricultural extension and rural development officer in the Ministry of Agriculture for eight years. Later he worked for World Vision for six years, beginning as a projects coordinator, moving on to director of technical services and finally operations (projects) director. Upon completion of his PhD in sociology at Washington State University in the USA, he taught sociology at the University of Alaska in Anchorage. He is currently professor of sociology at Eastern University in Philadelphia, and engages in community development research and practice in Malawi. He has published several articles on AIDS, the political economy, and food security in Malawi, and is author of *Social Relations and Cultural Demands in Economic Action: AIDS, Food Security, and Change in Peasant Societies* (Lambert Academic, 2010).

ROBERT J. PRIEST is president of the American Society of Missiology (2013–14), professor of mission and anthropology, and also G. W. Aldeen Professor of International Studies at Trinity Evangelical Divinity School, where he has served since 1999. Prior to coming to Trinity, Dr. Priest served nine years as a professor at Columbia Biblical Seminary and Graduate School of Missions. He has served in a variety of ministries, including the roles of youth director and assistant pastor. Born to career missionaries, he was raised in Bolivia and eventually returned to South America, conducting nearly two years of anthropological field research among the Aguaruna of Peru, focusing both on traditional religion and on conversion to Christianity. Among his publications are *This Side of Heaven: Race, Ethnicity and Christian Faith* (Oxford University Press, 2007), coedited with Alvaro Nieves, and the edited volume *Effective Engagement in Short-term Missions: Doing It Right!* (William Carey Library, 2009).

JASON RICHARD TAN is from the Philippines and earned his PhD in intercultural studies from Trinity Evangelical Divinity School. Reverend Tan previously served as academic dean for the Great Commission Missionary Training Center and taught pastoral studies and theology at All Nations College of Ministry and Mission and at the Alliance Graduate School, as well as being a senior pastor in Manila. His interest in the study of bribery and extortion practices arose from his former experiences as a sales manager, where he was exposed to the complexities of financial transactions in the Philippines and forced to reflect upon his Christian faith in the midst of an environment characterized by corruption. He has published the article "Missionary Ethics and the Practice of Bribery and Extortion" in the *Evangelical Missions Quarterly.*

DOUGLAS WILSON served as a missionary in Mali from 1990 to 2002, where he was the field director responsible for the distribution and supervision of funds designated by Western donors for Malian pastors and church projects. His concern for the economic difficulties confronting Malian urban pastors, as well as for the positive and negative effects of Western funding, culminated in his doctoral dissertation, "Give Me Neither Poverty nor Riches: Assessing the Material Realities of Malian Urban Pastors and Their Experiences with the Use of Foreign Resources" (Trinity Evangelical Divinity School, 2006). He has been a professor at the Institut Biblique Reed, Faculté de Théologie et Missiologie Évangélique au Sahel, and an instructor at Trinity International University. Currently he is the intercultural ministry specialist for Avant Ministries.

INTRODUCTION

CHRISTIAN MISSION AND ECONOMIC REALITIES

Robert J. Priest

While Christians claim citizenship in heaven, we nonetheless live and minister within the material world. Not only must bodies be fed, clothed, and housed, but everything from travel to education to ministry requires material underpinnings.

And yet missiologists and theologians have often perceived the world through lenses that treat the economic as marginal and insignificant. Such an anti-economics bias is evident, for example, in C. S. Lewis' *Screwtape Letters* (1942, 4), where Lewis has the demon Screwtape tell his nephew Wormwood that university students should be discouraged from studying the physical sciences, since the physical sciences focus on God's creation and thus might have the effect of pointing students to God, but that Wormwood should encourage students to study economics, which presumably more firmly belongs in the devil's camp.

My own early education taught me the value of studying and understanding many human dynamics. As a child of missionary linguists working with the Sirionó, a hunter-gatherer group in the Bolivian rainforest, I grew up in a missionary setting where linguistics—the rigorous study of languages—was highly valued and where missionary linguists like Ken Pike, Esther Matteson, and Eugene Nida were heroes. As a second to linguistics, there was anthropology—the discipline that would help missionaries understand culture. The journal *Practical Anthropology* was widely read, and both of my parents published articles in the *American Anthropologist* (A. Priest 1964; P. Priest 1966). To a degree this anthropology focus did include a tangential appreciation of economic dimensions of traditional culture (see P. Priest 1966), but it featured economics within a traditional setting, not within a world of change and globalization. The rather unusual economic underpinnings of my parents' ministry, based as it was on gift income, further buffered me experientially from consideration of wider economic realities.

When I later attended Bible college and seminary, the social models I learned stressed that belief was the independent variable affecting all other (dependent) variables. My church history classes were essentially classes in historical theology, where doctrine was understood as the engine determining all else. I studied Francis Schaeffer and was introduced to the idea that the order in culture is primarily a cognitive and philosophical order, and that this cognitive order, described as a worldview, is the key to understanding and explaining all else. Diagrams in my classes featured onions—concentric circles—with worldview at the center and economic behaviors on the outer edges. Or they featured platforms, with worldview as the "foundation" of all else, including economic realities that were caused and determined by worldviews. Or they featured images of depth versus surface, where worldview was "deep" and economic realities simply "surface" epiphenomena. Naturally what really needed to be studied was that which was "central," "foundational," and "deep," rather than that which was peripheral or shallow—a secondary byproduct of other, more basic realities.

Over summers I painted houses and worked in construction, as well as on the assembly line of a furniture factory. But my coursework did not help me make sense of these experiences, other than as necessary evils on the route to what really mattered. When I eventually took a pastoral position after seven years of theological education, I knew how to teach and preach Scripture in a way that framed the work of pastors and missionaries as meaningful and important. But I did not know how to help Christians in other work arenas make sense of their own work and vocation as a positive good. Like C. S. Lewis before me, I tended to treat the world of work, of business, and of economics as more properly belonging in the devil's camp.

It is true that my coursework in missiology had touched on economic dimensions of mission. But it did so in a selective and moralizing fashion. Thus, under the rubric of "indigeneity," we learned that healthy indigenous churches should be self-supporting and that local religious institutions should not receive "outside" funds. We were encouraged to be morally judgmental of those that did. Rather than striving through careful research for empathic understanding of the actual material conditions under which local pastors or seminary professors operate, as Doug Wilson has done so marvelously with Malian pastors in his chapter in this book, we were encouraged to moralistic shortcuts, where the right answer was known ahead of time.

While we were briefly introduced to "liberation theology," the Marxist theoretical frame was treated as a philosophy, a "worldview" to be either fully resisted or fully embraced, rather than as a more limited and focused invitation to systematically consider various kinds of economic structures and their possible contributions to social inequality. That is, we were not encouraged to consider as a limited claim the idea that economic structures themselves, and not just belief or worldview, might be independent variables affecting other dependent realities such as inequality. Instead we were encouraged to adopt a moralistic and absolutist stance on liberation theology as ideology. Nothing we read was anything like the fascinating chapter in this book by Mike Mtika, where we learn how changing economic structures in Malawi have contributed to new and more extreme forms of inequality.

When I later pursued graduate work in anthropology, I initially brought with me the assumption that the order within culture was best understood as a cognitive and philosophical order, and that belief was the independent variable affecting all else. Only gradually did I begin to see that people are not primarily philosophers striving for rational abstract coherence and attempting to be faithful to a given philosophy, but that they are motivated by anxiety, guilt, love, lust, hunger, envy, desire for success and approval, and so on. That is, in everyday life, people spend their time and effort on such matters as romance, material well-being, and attempting to achieve honor. They are often only marginally interested in rational abstractions and consistency. Like Pontius Pilate, they are often quite willing to act against what they believe to be true (consider Pilate's words, "I find no fault in him. Take him out and crucify him"), or to embrace ideologies that help them rationalize and justify their behavior or social position. In short, I increasingly learned that the order present within society and culture might be functional, instrumental, economic, political, psychological, and ideological rather than rational and logical. Furthermore, I increasingly learned that the direction of causality can flow in more than one direction. Yes, belief can and sometimes does have an impact on other cultural patterns, including economic patterns (see Weber 1958; or John Cheong, chap. 3 in this book). But economic and psychological and political dynamics can also be independent variables contributing to larger sociocultural patterns, with belief sometimes a dependent variable influenced by other factors, or emerging as a secondary rationalization of some other, more primordial dynamic.

Even if we focus narrowly on the economics of church life, similar issues hold true. While I was taught to consider church history from the vantage point of doctrine, there was no intrinsic reason that this history could not have focused centrally on the material side of life as itself consequential to other church patterns. Churches have varied widely in the methods and structures employed to secure their economic underpinnings. In some cases states have taxed all citizens to pay for church expenses. Naturally such a funding structure, with the state holding the purse strings, impacts church dynamics in many ways. Again, when churches have used "pew rentals" to cover their costs, with the better pews going for higher prices ("better" in the sense of being closer to the pulpit and to the heat in winter), this contributed to a social dynamic where wealth and status were visually evident to all. Again unique dynamics were produced when churches employed *benefices* to support their pastors—where wealthy donors could "endow" a pastoral position, similar to the way one can endow a "university chair," and could then stipulate who had the authority to determine and hire (or fire) a given pastor for the position. Many of these practical strategies for covering costs were not grounded in particular theologies but simply emerged as functional ways of covering costs. But once such patterns were in place, they had their own consequences. Thus pastors who were funded by the benefices of wealthy patrons, or pastors who were visually reminded through seating arrangements of who was paying their salaries, were naturally less likely to preach from the Old Testament prophets against the exploitive sins of such wealthy elite and more inclined to adopt rhetoric that would be appreciated and endorsed by such an elite. Again, even while pew-rental churches might formally read from the book of James as a part of Scripture, such churches were naturally more attractive to those who were wealthy than to the working class—since such funding structures functioned to visually display and ratify social class privilege, while simultaneously marginalizing and stigmatizing the working poor. It is not surprising that the early Methodist practice of a "free pew" might naturally have created a church more appealing to working-class people than the Anglican churches so closely tied to social class hierarchies. Funding patterns are consequential, sometimes adversely affecting the evangelism of specific groups.

In my own life as a missiologist, I've increasingly recognized that whatever topic I am interested in, whether short-term missions or the doing of theology, there is likely to be an economic dimension to it, and that this economic dimension should be explored as part of the analysis. Take theology, for example. Several years ago I listened as a leading missiologist stressed the importance of theology being carried out by top Christian scholars from all over the world, including Africa, Asia, and Latin America as well as Europe and North America. He predicted that the Global South would soon become the center of theological influence for the globe. But then he conceded his disappointment that many from the Global South who receive a PhD in Europe or North America, who are clearly bright and gifted, nonetheless fail to follow through with a life of intellectual leadership through writing. When queried further, he suggested that the problem, at its core, was a failure of a sense of personal commitment to writing and research by such scholars. In my response to him, I suggested he was leaving out an analysis of the economic underpinnings of scholarship. The most prolific and influential scholars, whether theologians or otherwise, generally have jobs with limited teaching loads, generous sabbatical structures, professional development funds for conference participation, access to outstanding libraries, and access to research assistants and research grants. By contrast, even in America, those who make their living as adjunct professors would have to teach thirty or more courses a year to approximate the financial support packages provided to many full professors teaching four to six courses a year. It is not surprising that such adjunct faculty less frequently, if ever, become prolific and influential world-class scholars. Many theological educators in Africa or Latin America live under work conditions approximating those of adjuncts in America, taking on heavy teaching and ministry loads in the struggle to make ends meet financially, having limited access to quality libraries, to research funds, and to sabbaticals. It is certainly possible for a Peruvian or Gambian to become a world-class theological scholar (one thinks of Samuel Escobar or Lamin Sanneh)—but not by living and working within the theological education structures of their home countries. Achieving top intellectual leadership is not merely a result of personal virtue and discipline but requires material support structures as well. And any effort to foster world-class theological leadership in the Global South must attend to the economics of theological education, as well as to the personal virtues and sense of calling that are also required.

Several years ago I taught a graduate course in research methods in Lima, Peru, where most of my students were themselves theological faculty. I used grant funds to help each of them do research on short-term missions. Together we examined a case where two hundred short-term missioners from a megachurch in Minneapolis came to Peru to help put on an evangelistic circus. They stayed at the Sheraton and spent over $400,000 on this trip. Simultaneously we examined the funding of theological education in Peru and calculated that this $400,000 amount was several times the total yearly amount being spent in all of Peru to support Peruvian theological educators. We puzzled over the reality that the largest theological seminary in Peru had less than half as many books in its library as one of my own seminary colleagues privately owned in his basement library. We surveyed several hundred Peruvian pastors and learned that their median annual salary was $1,800—which also happened to be the average amount that US teenagers routinely raised in order to take a two-week mission trip to Peru. Most short-termers were completely oblivious to the economic dimensions of ministry in Peru. Each short-termer might contribute eighty hours of labor to help build a church. The Americans, based on numbers suggested by the Independent Sector, might calculate their labor value at $20 an hour, or $1,600 for eighty hours. But within the Peruvian system at the time, even a professional bricklayer would only receive $1 an hour. Thus, from within the Peruvian value system, eighty hours of labor in helping build a church should be valued at $80. But when each of those same short-termers contributed $285 towards the costs of construction, which within the American frame of reference would seem far less than the value of eighty hours of labor, within the Peruvian frame this represented 285 hours of labor value—a far greater value. Increasingly I have become convinced that any analysis of ministry and missions that fails to understand the economic dimension is one-sided, if not outright misleading.

Western missionaries historically played a strategic role in the expansion of global Christianity. But their own theological training poorly prepared them to address the world of work and of economics, as did their own economic base, which was based on gift income from back home. They were far more interested, and better prepared, to found Bible schools and seminaries across Africa, for example, than to help the new and exploding churches understand the wider world of work and vocation and economics. Furthermore, by not systematically studying the economic dimensions of life, missionaries have simply operated with the taken-for-granted assumptions about economics learned through our own primary socialization. The fact that there are fundamentally different economic orders operating in different settings, with profoundly different ideals as to the ways in which material realities are to function in our moral relations with each other, has largely been misunderstood.

This book provides a needed corrective, a strategic first step towards a missiology that helps us rethink our understandings of economics and mission. The authors draw from a wide range of disciplinary strengths and expertise related to economic realities around the globe to help us forge new and better understandings.

In the first chapter, Eloise Meneses draws on her expertise as an economic anthropologist to help us compare the logic of relations within a capitalist market system with the logic of moral relations present in many traditional societies—where reciprocity norms often directly conflict with free-market capitalist ideals. Her analysis of the positive strengths and weaknesses of each system leads her back to Scripture, where she invites readers to rethink taken-for-granted assumptions about the ways in which material resources best serve moral and spiritual ends.

Partnership is central to global mission involvements today. And of course partnerships commonly involve economic dimensions. In the second chapter, Mary Lederleitner focuses on international partnerships that cross the same economic divides discussed by Meneses. Lederleitner highlights common conflicts emerging from cultural differences between Western ideals of accountability and ideals more common elsewhere, while also discussing power dynamics and the way colonial history has invested these issues with moral freight. She draws from years of experience in helping broker and nurture such partnerships to provide wise advice for others.

In his chapter John Cheong introduces us to another economic system, a system fostered within Islam. He demonstrates how Muslim bankers have resisted pure free-market capitalism, achieving significant economic success nonetheless. Importantly, they have done this in a way that is morally attractive to others, and that has contributed significantly to the success of Islamic missions. He invites Christians interested in global mission to consider whether there is something we should learn through this about our own use of financial resources and about our own relations to free-market capitalism.

One of the most common ethical challenges missionaries report is the challenge of being asked (or extorted) for a "bribe." While missionaries often simply treat this as a matter of sinful corruption, Jason Tan demonstrates how older reciprocity norms—where the line between tips, obligatory gifts, and bribes was seldom clearly marked—sometimes shape current practice in the Philippines. Furthermore, when modern bureaucratic structures are conceptualized as paying an adequate wage (to policemen or customs agents, for example), but in fact often pay less than a living wage, it is not surprising that older reciprocity norms are invoked to help make up the difference. Tan provides a careful analysis of how such "bribes" work in practice and are understood in the moral logic of cultural insiders, how they are intertwined with issues of honor and respect, and provides helpful advice for how such realities should be understood and responded to by Christians and their churches.

Both in New Testament times and in much of the world today, social and economic relations have been structured by patron-client norms—hierarchically organized reciprocities. Lindy Backues explores such hierarchically organized structures of reciprocity in West Java, comparing newer, more exploitive versions of patron-client relations with older versions, while also focusing on the patterns of resistance to exploitation sometimes exhibited by subordinates. He compares and contrasts their response with the New Testament engagement of patron-client relations and suggests how we might best understand and respond to such patterns.

In much of the world, pastors serve in settings characterized by relative material poverty. Normative economic assumptions about pastoral life in the American Midwest, for example, should not be exported unchallenged elsewhere. While missiologists have sometimes gotten stuck debating in moralistic terms issues of "self-support" for local pastors, Doug Wilson has done what others have not. He has done a groundbreaking job of examining the actual material and economic realities experienced by urban Malian pastors, using both quantitative and qualitative research methods. I am unaware of anyone who has ever done comparable research on the topic in non-Western settings. No one who reads this chapter thoughtfully can fail to be moved by the challenges Malian pastors face. While Wilson provides a number of helpful suggestions for addressing the situation, it is clear that the challenges are significant and not easily resolved. This chapter merits wide circulation among all who would wish to understand economic realities for pastors in much of the Majority World.

Around the world people are often caught between traditional economic norms with their built-in social protections and the changing realities and norms associated with free-market capitalism. Mike Mtika provides a superb analysis of economic and moral changes experienced across several generations within his own family and community in Malawi, showing how new capitalist norms created both winners and losers in the new order, with older protections for the more vulnerable increasingly stripped away. He provides both critique and positive theological and practical prescriptions for what is needed.

Increasingly, Christian global involvements are lived out through Christian NGOs with a strong focus on development and poverty alleviation. David Bronkema, himself an expert in development, provides a helpful and practical review of the issues and realities related to cultural dimensions of economics that development workers must understand. This chapter provides a helpful and synthetic conclusion to the wide variety of issues raised by the other chapters of the book.

John Cheong and Eloise Meneses are to be commended for drawing together an excellent collection of essays of consistently high quality, empirically grounded in research, theoretically informed, and practically oriented. Missionaries, development workers, missiologists, and theologians will all find much to appreciate here. Clearly more remains to be done. But this book lays a solid foundation for others to build on.

REFERENCES

Lewis, C. S. 1942. *The Screwtape letters.* New York: HarperCollins.

Priest, Anne. 1964. Method of naming among the Sirionó Indians. *American Anthropologist* 66, no. 5: 1149–51.

Priest, Perry. 1966. Provision for the aged among the Sirionó Indians of Bolivia. *American Anthropologist* 68, no. 5: 1245–47.

Weber, Max. 1958. *The Protestant ethic and the spirit of capitalism.* New York: Charles Scribner's Sons.

EXCHANGE, RELATIONSHIPS, AND RECIPROCITY: LIVING AS A CHRISTIAN IN A CAPITALIST WORLD

Eloise Meneses

[With] the collapse of Marxism as a world power ... the ideology of the free market now has nothing to limit its claims. There is no visible countervailing power. There seems no sign of a check to its relentless advance. And its destructive potential, both for the coherence of human society and for the safeguarding of the environment, are formidable. The ideology of the free market has proved itself more powerful than Marxism. It is, of course, not just a way of arranging economic affairs. It has deep roots in the human soul. It can be met and mastered only at the level of religious faith, for it is a form of idolatry. The churches have hardly begun to recognize that this is probably their most urgent missionary task during the coming century.

Lesslie Newbigin (1995, 94–95)

The syncretization of the gospel with culture can take many forms, but perhaps the most insidious is when it affects Christian praxis. Typically this is unconsciously done. The baseline assumptions of the larger sociopolitical and economic world formulate Christian discourse so thoroughly as to make Christian living seem impractical or unrealistic within the particular context. In the case of capitalism, an

Enlightenment-based theory of human nature legitimizes the notions that actors must involve themselves in self-interested exchange and that "the market" (personified) must be allowed to operate according to its own principles. Yet there is a significant literature in the social sciences to demonstrate that there is nothing inevitable about market exchange or capitalism.[1] The original form of human exchange, reciprocity, weaves together economic with social concerns in ways that mirror injunctions in the Bible to consider one another. In practice, even people in capitalist systems moderate their economic relationships to avoid the harsh social realities that fully marketized exchange would create. Thus, rather than exhibiting a natural element in human behavior, the self-interested and calculating "economic man" proves to be a *product*, rather than a precondition, of capitalism (Mauss 2005, 98).

In the current circumstance of American-dominated globalization, there is a danger that Christians in ministry may unconsciously find themselves promoting a gospel of capitalism together with, or even above, the gospel of Jesus Christ, his church, and his kingdom. This is not to say that there can be no benefit from a selective involvement in the marketplace and in the world of economic development. Christians have always cooperated with human systems, whether social, political, or economic, for the purpose of meeting people's needs. But an open consideration of the fundamental propositions of those systems is critical to maintaining an independent stance as Christians and to involving ourselves in practices that are truly reflective of the kingdom of God. In this chapter I will examine the nature of market exchange, contrast it with reciprocal exchange, and compare the underlying principles of these two types of exchange to biblical ones. A case study on the market women of India will bring out the complexities of living

---

1   The literature on the history of capitalism and the social construction of the market is truly voluminous. It begins with the classic theorists, such as Marx (1992) and Weber (1947, 1978), and extends to contemporary sociologists (Wallerstein 2004), anthropologists (Appadurai 1986; Carrier 1997; Plattner 1983; Sahlins 1972), historians (Polanyi 2001; Tawney 1972), economists (Blaug 1980), and even theologians (Temple 1977). All of the above works demonstrate the contingent nature of people's economic systems and behavior.

between the two types of exchange in a developing economy. The results will be applied to the work of Christians in ministry under capitalism generally, with a view to finding a model for incarnating the economic aspects of the work without abandoning biblical purposes.

MARKET EXCHANGE

At its most basic level, market exchange consists of the transfer of money, goods, or services between two parties according to a negotiated agreement. In the negotiation, both parties are expected to know and represent their own interests, and neither is expected to consider the other's interest where it might interfere with his or her own. The result is an open contest for the price, or the terms of the exchange, between the buyer and the seller. In large markets with standardized goods, this contest is at the aggregate level over time, as consumers choose to buy or not to buy and producers adjust their prices accordingly. But the result is the same—the exchange is determined by a direct haggle for the rates.

This model for exchange is not a simple, practical reality emerging from a natural self-interest. It is an ideal form of the exchange that is commonly transgressed and that must be reinforced lest the transgressions hinder the functioning of the larger system of which it is a part. For instance, if a customer were to offer to pay an additional amount to a store clerk, the result would be confusion and a fear of misdealing. The clerk would almost certainly refuse the extra. Why should this be so, if self-interest is the only principle governing the transaction? The customer would be thought foolish at best, perhaps suspected of a criminal plan at worst, for breaking the first principle of the market exchange—to represent one's own interests. The rules of the game dictate that the seller should bid high and the buyer bid low. To cross over and think of the other is to complicate the interaction with non-utilitarian motives, perhaps to offer a bribe.

Yet people in fact do exactly this. In the simplest example, merchants trying to create long-term relationships with customers will add a small amount to the agreed-upon sale, a "gift" intended to produce further sales by socially obligating the customer to return. In a more significant example, merchants will give their long-term clients a standard cut on the price and clients will forgo shopping elsewhere as signs of their mutual commitment. The purpose here is still economic for both parties, but a social cement is used to seal the deal, including chitchat about families, expressions of concern for one another, and politeness in the bargaining itself. Even high-level business negotiations are promoted with social interaction. Note that few people can manage to sell at full rates to their families. Minimally, they will drop the price for a family member; maximally, they will give away the product or service for free. The moral obligation to avoid a self-interested struggle is so strong with kin that merchants commonly move away from family, and even deny their ethnicity (a form of extended family), in order to avoid going broke (Foster 1977).

Yet market-style exchange is necessary to an economic system built on the ownership of private property, the specialization of skills, and the need to exchange for purposes of utility. Thus the rules of the game (some informal and some codified in law) protect the system by *insisting* that the parties to the exchange behave in self-interested ways. In most American states, lawyers and real estate agents are required for large purchases, lest buyers and sellers either be misinformed or inadequately represent their own interests. Contracts function to solidify agreements partly by *preventing* the eye-to-eye contact that might soften the arrangements.

There is a positive side to the ideal for market exchange: it is that people may represent their own interests, and even defend them vigorously, without fear of social shame or punishment. In traditional societies this is not possible due to strong taboos on the appearance of selfishness. The taboos fall especially hard on subordinate groups such as women, lower castes, younger people, or ethnic minorities. For such people the market can provide a means of economic escape from social oppression through producing and selling goods or finding paid work. Even a focus on the utilitarian advantage of the exchange itself can be liberating to those who have had to always consider the social implications of pursuing their own interests. Furthermore, there are other values associated with market exchange that benefit society, such as honesty, freedom, hard work, and inventiveness. Because the exchange itself requires these values, disclosure and anticorruption laws are developed to enforce transparency and fair play.

Yet, in the main, most people in traditional societies—and many in modern ones—view the naked struggle for personal advantage inherent in market exchange with alarm. This is not because of any perceived natural human goodness that is being destroyed by an evil system. In fact, most traditional societies believe people to be naturally selfish. Rather it is a fear that the social fabric that restrains people's selfishness is being corroded, even destroyed, by a system in which pure economic self-interest outranks moral obligations. In a subsistence agricultural village, for example, the market is only used for the sale of subsidiary goods such as crafts, and these are only sold to outsiders. As the village becomes more and more incorporated into the wider market system, first crops, then labor, and then land become saleable by market exchange. Villagers typically experience this process as demeaning of things formerly considered sacred, especially the land. We, as outsiders, may deride traditional views of the land, but in certain cases we too believe that the market demeans its commodities. A clear example would be the purchase and sale of people. Slavery is the ultimate commodification of a resource. In a lesser example, the shift from "sister-exchange," in which lineages exchange women for women as wives, to bridewealth, in which money is exchanged for wives, has been experienced as demeaning of women even by elder men in West Africa (Bohannan 1959). Money is a convenient means of exchange, but it is also a symbol of the loss of moral relationships in favor of utilitarian self-interest.

Certainly no one can dispute the many material advantages that have been gained, in the aggregate, from the advent of market capitalism. The simplicity, flexibility, and directness of market exchange makes it possible for societies to develop more complex and coordinated forms of specialization. One could say that the loss of social obligation is the gain of economic efficiency and coordination. The result has been an explosive rise in material goods, new technologies, food production, population growth, and the average standard of living. At the local level, where markets come in, seemingly ordinary material goods such as plastic pots for women carrying water or cell phones for children earning a living on the streets can transform people's lives in beneficial ways. New technologies can lighten the load of field and house work, and contact with outsiders made possible by infrastructure can even facilitate the bringing of the gospel to remote regions.

At the same time, the fact that people can directly defend and promote their own self-interest opens up potential assaults and damages to the social fabric that can be very serious for any human community. For example, the warmth and support of an extended family, not to mention that of a whole village, is a high price to pay for the material advantages of modern urban life. Furthermore, the strong tendency for wealth and power to be increasingly concentrated in the hands of a few leaves many people out in the cold of even the material gains. Current estimates are that nearly half the world's population lives on just USD2.50 per day, and a third on USD1.25 per day (United Nations Development Programme 2007), a circumstance that is a fallout from market systems, not a carryover from previous economies. Moreover, there is evidence that the situation is worsening, yielding the terrible irony that capitalism seems to produce both fabulous wealth and horrendous poverty at the same time (McMichael 2004, 296; Townsend and Gorden 2002, 387). It is here that the missing social fabric is most painfully needed. Without moral obligations to hold some accountable and to provide for others in need, society simply cannot care for its people. Both the ideology and the practice of market exchange under capitalism preclude the enforcement of the moral obligations that would temper the worst effects of the system.

All this might be faced directly if it were not for the fact that there are strongly held pragmatic, if not religious, beliefs that underpin the system itself. In the case of capitalism, the beliefs are that people are naturally rational calculators of their own interests, "economic men," and that the pursuit of these interests through direct negotiated exchange will result in the larger good being served, the "invisible hand" of the market. Behind these beliefs lies a grand narrative of human "progress" that assumes the inevitability of the market and the importance of permitting it to function unhindered by government or societal restrictions. Out of this narrative, dire predictions are made of the ill effects of limiting economic growth or regulating people's behavior. This is despite a long history of market collapses due to people's excessive risk taking, short-term thinking, and narrowly self-interested behavior. As the prominent American evangelist Tony Campolo puts it, "If people don't want regulation, they should stop acting like they need it!"[2] Certainly there is regulation that is unnecessary and detrimental to the public good (generally because it serves powerful interests at the expense of less powerful ones). But my purpose here is simply to point out the passion with which Western, especially American, people are inclined to resist any regulation at all—a passion that points to a religious rather than a rational commitment to the ideals of the system.

Finally, the emphasis on a direct, negotiated, and utilitarian exchange produces values such as individualism, consumerism, materialism, and competitiveness that predominate in the culture. These values too have potential benefits, when not held disproportionately with values on community, cooperation, and religious life. They can encourage inventiveness and hard work. But it is in the nature of culture to overemphasize its own chosen values and underemphasize all others (Benedict 1958). In the case of capitalist cultural values the results have been problematic, even going back to the eighteenth century, when Tocqueville ([1835] 2000, 661) wrote,

> In America, I have seen the freest and best educated of men in circumstances the happiest to be found in the world; yet it seemed to me that a cloud habitually hung on their brow, and they seemed serious and almost sad even in their pleasures. The chief reason [is that they] are forever brooding over advantages they do not possess.

---

2   Dr. Campolo has made this point repeatedly in chapel sermons at Eastern University.

The anthropologist Marshall Sahlins (1972, 3) has expressed the same thought:

> Modern capitalist societies, however richly endowed, dedicate themselves to the proposition of scarcity. Inadequacy of economic means is the first principle of the world's wealthiest peoples.... Consumption is a double tragedy: what begins in inadequacy will end in deprivation. Bringing together an international division of labor, the market makes available a dazzling array of products: all these Good Things within a man's reach—but never all within his grasp.

Capitalism's very strength is its weakness. It produces fabulous amounts of wealth and leaves people wanting more. All this should caution any Christian from an overly optimistic view of the system, remembering especially the tendency of wealth to turn people's hearts from God. Watching his own flock of Methodists flourishing under capitalism, John Wesley (quoted in Weber 1976, 175) worried:

> I fear, wherever riches have increased, the essence of religion has decreased in the same proportion. Therefore I do not see how it is possible, in the nature of things, for any revival of true religion to continue for long. For religion must necessarily produce both industry and frugality, and these cannot but produce riches. But as riches increase, so will pride, anger, and love of the world in all its branches.... So, although the form of religion remains, the spirit is swiftly vanishing away.

Even for the beneficiaries of the system, the material gains are at the expense of a healthy dependence on the community and on God.

RECIPROCAL EXCHANGE

There is an enormous literature in anthropology on humanity's first form of exchange, reciprocity, or gift giving (see Gudeman 1998). Technologically simple societies use reciprocal exchange exclusively in their economies, and even modern ones use it significantly. In the United States, as much as a third of all department store sales occur around Christmas time. So how, then, does gift exchange differ from purchase and sale? In both cases there are two parties to the exchange, and money, goods, or services are transferred between them. The difference lies in the nature of the negotiation. Self-interest may well be lurking below the surface, but it is explicitly denied, even lied about, in gift giving (see chap. 4). Here the stated motivation *must* be concern for the other, to the denial of the self, at least in the immediate instance (see chap. 7). This is perhaps clearest with the most commonly given gift around the world, which is food. The symbolic meaning of giving food is the willingness to forgo one's own need for nourishment, for life itself, in the interest of the other person's need.

The primary purpose of the exchange is also different. The purpose of market exchange is explicitly utilitarian, while the purpose of reciprocal exchange is social. Gifts are given in order to establish and maintain relationships. Their *lack* of utility is legendary: the sweater that doesn't fit, the fourth crock pot, or the misshapen hat. Givers of gifts make real efforts to select things that will be appreciated in order to show their particular concern for their friends and family. But receivers of gifts are reluctant to complain lest they offend the givers—a concern that would make no sense in market exchange. People say that "it is the thought that counts," meaning that the relationship is more important than the gift itself. In fact, the purpose of the gift is to *mark* the relationship and its importance to both parties. Thus social life trumps all other concerns in reciprocal societies, including utilitarian needs.

Contrary to the popular view that gifts are given entirely voluntarily, most gifts are given under terms of very high obligation. While market exchange is truly free in the sense that either party can walk away from the transaction, gift giving is not. Times, places, recipients, and even the gifts themselves may be specified by the society. Among Australian Aborigines, if a kangaroo is killed, each of the parts of the animal must be given to specific kin as gifts (Haviland et al. 2011, 195). Among Malaysian fishers of Kelantan and Trengganu, guests at a wedding feast must present gifts of money at the reception door and have the amount called out publicly by an announcer (Firth 1975, 178). In the West, gifts are mandated for all close kin at Christmas gatherings. The obligation to give gifts is simply an assertion of the rights of society over the rights of the individual, expressed as a reminder that we all still need one another. To refuse to give gifts is a rejection of social life itself.

Still, the facade of *voluntary* gift giving must be maintained lest the purpose of the gift, the commitment to relationships, be denied. Once again, dishonesty may be the result as people make flowery speeches about their appreciation for one another as the occasion demands and deny their own interest in the matter. And, of course, genuine heartfelt love may well be expressed through the gift-giving channels that society provides. In any case, reciprocal exchange places a higher value on social needs than on economic ones, and strengthens the social fabric of the community as a whole by its affirmation of the importance of relationships. It is true that the stress on relationships can hold the community back materially. Commonly in villages, for instance, an "image of the limited good" (Foster 1965) creates jealousy and prevents individuals from gaining in comparison to their neighbors. In some American urban neighborhoods, individuals who "succeed" may be considered traitorous to their own family or ethnic group. But the emphasis on a common life ensures that everyone receives a kind of holistic care, including but not limited to material needs.

Yet there is a potentially negative characteristic of reciprocal exchange that must be noted here because of its relevance to Christian charity. In all societies, through the very act of giving a gift, the giver gains at least temporary prestige over the receiver, yielding the proverb "Charity wounds" (Mauss 1967, 63). There are truly no exceptions. The receiver may gain materially, but the giver gains socially from the transaction. Philanthropists, for instance, give large amounts of wealth and receive back the prestige of having their names associated with projects. In established hierarchical relationships, from tribal leaders to corporate bosses, gifts flow downward, signaling not only appreciation for followers and employees but also the higher rank of the givers (even parents are included here). In fact, such givers are under heavy obligation to give in order to maintain their reputation as generous leaders. Receivers are always humbled. But if their lower rank is a stable one, then far from feeling themselves slighted they may claim their position as a moral right. This surprises many egalitarian Americans, who may find that their gifts inspire not gratitude but annoyance if more is not forthcoming. The expectation that leaders must give and followers have a right to receive is simply an acknowledgment that rank exists within a society of common welfare, and it holds higher ranks accountable for the circumstances of lower ranks and for their care (see chap. 2).

Taking a closer look at the matter, in egalitarian relationships the prestige imbalance creates a problem. Even in the warmest of circumstances, the gift places the receiver under obligation to the giver. This creates a situation of gift "debt," which can only be resolved by a return gift, given either at the same time (as with Christmas) or at a later date (as with birthdays). Gift debts are the very fabric of social relationships (Mauss 1967). They are an acknowledgment that the relationship is significant to both parties. Of course, the initial gift can be rejected, or accepted and not returned, but if this is done the message will be clear: "I do not want a relationship with you!" This is particularly evident in courtship due to the tentative nature of the relationship, but it is equally true in other relationships. A one-way flow of gifts means either a hierarchical relationship or a rejected egalitarian one. Hence the return of gifts has a double purpose: to acknowledge and establish the relationship that has been offered and to right the balance of prestige and maintain the relationship's egalitarian nature.

Finally, in societies that are governed by the principles of reciprocity, the rules for borrowing and lending money can be quite different than in the modern capitalized West. David Maranz (2001) identifies the following rules, among others, from Senegal (which I have paraphrased):

1. Those who have resources are expected to be lenders, not borrowers.
2. People receive satisfaction from being asked for financial help.
3. A request for help is a compliment.
4. Friendships are built with gifts.
5. Resources are to be used, not hoarded.
6. Accurate accounting shows a lack of a generous spirit.

Cross-culturally, overly careful accounting implies that the parties to the exchange are strangers, not friends or family. In fact, such accounting is a form of *estrangement* because of its implied concern with self-interest. An unstated and flexible timeframe for the repayment of loans (or gifts) is actually an expression of the trust that cements relationships. An Indonesian man says, "You are in my debt, I am in your heart; I am in your debt, you are in my heart."[3] At its best, such a system of exchange builds cohesive social relationships. At its worst, trust may be abused. Still, without trust all exchanges become purely self-interested and materialistic, and relationships are damaged.

Many Westerners, especially Americans, are uncomfortable with this mix of money and relationships. Modern societies with complex economies sort out relationships into types, such as family, business, work, market, etc., assigning different rules to the different types by their different purposes. But in traditional societies, relationships are multifaceted, with a holistic character. There is no embarrassment about asking for monetary help from friends or coworkers, for instance, and there is a deep expectation that others will *want* to help with generosity. Thus Americans and other Westerners who befriend people abroad commonly find themselves barraged with requests for money. The requests signal not only real needs but also a desire to deepen friendships. If friendship has been offered, people naturally expect that material assistance will follow. If it does not, the significance of the friendship has been effectively denied. In any case, the

---

3   Stated in the film "A Poor Man Shames Us All" in the series *Tribal Wisdom in the Modern World* by anthropologist David Maybury Lewis.

greater ability of Westerners to provide help legitimizes the requests and necessarily elevates Westerners' prestige in the socially complex network of the traditional community.

BIBLICAL PRINCIPLES OF THE ECONOMY

In Western debates over the value of modern capitalism, Christians have taken both sides of the issue and attempted to proof-text their positions with verses from the Bible. Pro-capitalist Christians have pointed to the Bible's affirmation of private property and hard work. Anti-capitalist Christians have reminded the church of the Bible's warnings about wealth and injunctions to care for the poor. But to conduct the debate in this manner is to lose the battle against syncretism at the outset. All cultural systems, including economic ones, have their virtues and their vices. What is needed is a truly independent Christian stance, one that is neither afraid to criticize the system nor simply interested in destroying it.

To begin, the Bible assumes both the reality and the value of the material world. This is in contrast to the claim found in Eastern religions such as Hinduism that the material world is illusory and that only the spiritual world is real. Such gnosticism also has a history in the West. In contemporary American society, there is a belief in the sovereign power of the mind and a deep ambivalence over the body, which can cause Christians to be functioning dualists, associating the body exclusively with sin. But the Bible affirms the value of our material existence, from the account of God's creation of us from the dust of the earth to the declaration of Christ's bodily resurrection and hence our own. It was our attempt to escape our creaturely status, to become like God who is Spirit alone, which was the essence of our first disobedience. When human beings are living as they should, they acknowledge their physical as well as their spiritual dependence on God, who provides for them richly. Furthermore, while there are austerities such as fasting mentioned in the Bible, by far the emphasis is on the enjoyment of creaturely life, so long as it is rooted in a relational network with God and one another. It is this acknowledgment of the value of material life that has caused Christians to care for their own and other people's physical needs down through the centuries. No other world religion has come close to Christianity in charitable giving. Missionaries have built hospitals and schools, provided work and food, and assisted in the full variety of types of relief and development being done today.

Yet the materialistic philosophy and cultural practice of the West goes well beyond the Christian affirmation of creation. Most detrimentally, it measures the prestige of the person by accumulation of wealth—a practice that is clearly denounced in the Bible (see the book of Amos). Furthermore, the wasteful consumption of material goods in the West, which is at the expense of the environment and the poor, is a kind of careless living that is also condemned. Our creaturely status is supposed to cause us to turn in gratitude to our Creator and to look to him for every need. Instead, the comforts we have produced with our economic system have caused us to imagine ourselves to be completely independent.

The Bible reminds us repeatedly to value our connection to God and community. Rarely does the Bible admonish us to "stand on your own two feet" or "take care of your own business." Independence is generally viewed as a threat. Dependence on God and interdependence with others are commended. Responsibility is placed on the wealthier and more powerful members of society to care for the poor, with little blame attached to the latter for their circumstances. The value placed on community is perhaps best seen in God's interactions with the chosen people, the nation of Israel, as a whole. There are individuals in the narrative, of course, such as Abraham, Moses, the prophets, and the disciples. But the stories of these individuals' lives are subsumed under the larger narrative of God's saving of his people. Even Jesus' own story is a chapter in the book of God's redemption of humanity. Unlike post-Enlightenment forms of individualism, which take a territorial approach to the rights of the individual, biblical individuals' lives are lived expressly for the purpose of their communities.

This understanding of the relationship between individuals and groups is far clearer in reciprocal societies than it is in capitalist ones. The value on community life found in the Bible mirrors the principles of reciprocity much more closely than those of market-based exchange. Individualism in the West tears friends and family asunder in the pursuit of personal success. The simple willingness of most Americans to move away from family to take a better job makes the point. Social ties have been subordinated to the economy; personal identity, which used to rest in community membership, now rests in jobs (Bellah et al. 2007). Because of its need for labor mobility, capitalism relies heavily on this form of isolating individualism. People entrenched in communities may be unwilling to work long hours or to move to where they are needed, so high pay and the promise of wealth-based prestige are necessary to convince them to give up the support and security of the social fabric. The new form of security is entirely economic and rests in houses, cars, and bank accounts. Not a few anthropologists have demonstrated that such a trade-off is not actually advantageous and that people at the margins of the system know it. Commonly, they must be forced into the global economy through the annexing of their land or the removal of their previous forms of subsistence (Bodley 1999; see also Doug Wilson, chap. 6 in this book).

Most importantly, the Bible subordinates all earthly goods, economic *and* social, to God's own activities in the building of the kingdom of God. Through the church, the material, social, and spiritual well-being of humanity is promoted as creation is restored to its right and harmonious relationship with its Creator. This is to say that the separate pursuit of these goods, either material wealth or social prestige, results in distortion, even idolatry. It is the restoration of the integral network of relationships between God, people, and the earth that is the goal of the kingdom and that produces the truest happiness (Wright 2004). Sin is fundamentally about cutting ourselves off from God and others in order to pursue our own ends. Capitalism very nearly makes this a virtue, encouraging people to pursue their own interests without consulting anyone. On the other hand, reciprocal systems subordinate people so heavily to traditional human authorities that they can make following God's authority difficult or impossible. It is worth remembering that one of the most common reasons people do not become Christians is because their families object to it.

The Bible, then, affirms the material world, including our own material nature, places us squarely within the context of communities to which we are held accountable, and subordinates all our concerns to the redemptive purposes of God's kingdom. Jesus' firm reminder is that we should "seek first his kingdom and his righteousness, and all these things will be given to you as well" (Matt 6:33). Our social and material needs are real enough. We should not try to transcend our creaturely status by imagining that we do not have them. But neither should we place our trust in our own abilities, or systems, to provide for us. While the reliance in reciprocity is on the social system, the reliance in capitalism is on the economic system. Both will fail us sooner or later. An acknowledgment of our dependence on God is what is needed, and a lifestyle that matches that dependence.

THE MARKET WOMEN OF INDIA

In point of fact, the majority of people live in between reciprocal and capitalist systems, especially in "developing" countries. In India, as elsewhere, open-air markets for fruits and vegetables dot the landscape and provide people with produce in the absence of refrigerated grocery stores. Such markets are a magnet for the urban poor in search of a living. Marginalized people, such as women and Dalits ("untouchables"), can start up small businesses with little experience or capital. The capital that is needed is obtained through loans from moneylenders at exorbitant rates of interest, but on terms that resemble reciprocal exchange. Lender and borrower have a face-to-face relationship characterized by flexible negotiations on repayment and a moral rather than legal obligation to one another.

In the market itself prices are established by the haggle, which is certainly a procedure based on the open representation of one's own interests. But merchants commonly give little gifts to establish longer-term ties with customers, and customers restrict their purchases to their own patron merchants. Furthermore, the banter that constitutes the haggle is itself filled with moral talk urging the other party to consider the speaker's interest. Merchants commonly describe their own poverty to customers in order to convince them of the need for higher prices. Customers complain that they are being "cheated" in order to bring the price down. The morality of consideration for the other from the social world is used to temper the harsher aspects of a strictly economic negotiation.

Market women in India take up the selling of fruits and vegetables out of poverty and a lack of other opportunities. Their lives are divided between the heavy demands of home and work and circumscribed by the need to feed and provide for their children. At home they have rich connections to extended family, live in neighborhoods with others in their same circumstance, and support one another through times of crisis. The most serious lack is of the support of steady husbands, since husbands often gamble, drink, have other "wives," and are unemployed. At work there is competition for sitting spaces and for customers, but also a good deal of cooperation, assisting one another with loans and even with sales in each other's absence. Their livelihoods are built upon market exchange, but their lives are built upon reciprocity.

In 1994 I interviewed market women in India to study their understanding of the relationship between people and things (Meneses 2007). There were differences of opinion, of course, but a general agreement that both people (social life) and things (economic life) are needed. The women were reluctant to prioritize and often talked as if the two were interchangeable. One woman said,

> What we earn in life is only people. That is our property, money, and everything. If we have people, then we can easily get property. I believe more in people strength than in material wealth. People take care of us when we are in trouble. We need money, [but] money doesn't care about us…. Relatives are themselves [a kind of] property. (159)

And another woman remarked:

> We can get crowds of friends if we have money…. [But then] we easily lose the money which we have earned. If we have a lot of

friends, we are forced to give them money, and then we are in loss. So we don't want to have too many friends. [Still,] we help by giving meals and clothing to the poor and needy. The more we help others, the more our children will be looked after by God. (159)

This kind of holism was typical. Money can be turned into friends through generosity, and friends can be a source of money in times of need. In the long run, relationships are more reliable than material goods, though each is convertible into the other (see Fox 2003).

For these women, life between society and economy was a negotiation, as it is generally. Even in the West we have little admiration for the person who pursues personal material success so heavily that relationships with family and friends are ruptured. But neither do we admire the one who is so bound by social traditions (including the restrictions on women) as to neglect to do what is economically necessary to feed the family. Thus we must not only balance social and economic needs but recognize that they are intertwined. And we must remember our own inadequacy to provide for ourselves ultimately. As Christians we should recognize the biblical character of the words of a Hindu woman who said, "The more we help others, the more our children will be looked after by God."

CHRISTIAN MINISTRY UNDER CAPITALISM

The gospel of capitalism is that through hard work, saving, careful accounting, and, above all else, self-reliance, anyone can become materially wealthy, so long as the system that is based on private property and free exchange is maintained. The recommended procedure is to use the latest agricultural methods, start a small business, or find a job in the industrial complex; harness the flow of money and direct it away from "wasteful" expenditures; and place children in schools so that they will "get ahead" in the next generation with qualifications for better jobs. The handling of money is key. Expenditures on business investment or education are praised; expenditures on weddings or other social events, or on loans to friends and family, are frowned upon. In fact, there is a strong tendency, even a need, for those who are upwardly mobile to reduce the size of their family connections to a minimum, lest the wealth they earn be dissipated across too many people to whom they are obligated.

The thread that holds all of this advice together is that one's social life must be sacrificed to achieve economic success. In its extreme form, the "good news" of capitalism is that you can become wealthy if you are willing to live alone (as Charles Dickens illustrated with his fictional character Ebenezer Scrooge). In reciprocal systems the social and economic aspects of life are closely interwoven, but in market systems a choice must be made between them. We confront such choices daily. Picture the janitor who risks losing his family's house because he does not want to take a higher paying job in a neighboring city away from his extended kin. Visualize the professor who gives up his academic future to care for an ailing mother. Imagine the student who must brave significant criticism from her neighborhood community for leaving them to get a college education. These are all actual cases from my own experience. And in each one the choice was *between* material and social needs. At the larger level, throughout the history of capitalism there have been mass movements of people, from slaves to migrant workers, who have been forced to leave homes, families, and cultures for work. Today there are Filipino women who leave their own children behind to become domestic workers in New York, Mexican men who leave their families to become day laborers in Los Angeles, and young men all over the world who decimate their village communities by leaving in critical numbers to go to cities. Capitalism's need for labor mobility is a continual threat to the social fabric.

Of course, Christians have always understood the value of community life, especially as it is expressed through the church. But the danger is that, in their attempts to provide for people's very real material needs, Christians in ministry may take market-based principles to be incontestable, simply "the way things are," and advocate for a syncretistic adaptation to the gospel of capitalism. Examples from my own experience include a British youth leader in India who single-handedly destroyed a thriving ministry by eliminating the social visits to donors that were a "waste of time," insisting that donors pay to the penny what they had promised according to his accounts book; and an American economic developer in a highly community-oriented culture in Africa who declared in the most absolute terms that all businesses must be privately rather than communally owned if they were to be successful. Such incidents as these are the result of having absorbed the gospel of capitalism so deeply that alternatives to it seem unrealistic. How can Christians possibly approve of the unwillingness to work in a distant place when an income is badly needed, or the use of loaned develop-ment money to help family and friends? It seems completely necessary to cooperate with the larger economic forces and to legitimize eco-nomic behavior with isolated biblical texts while ignoring the Bible's overall themes.

Many Christians in ministry do not question the goal of incorporat-ing the local economy into the global one. They are persuaded of the argument that poverty is the result of the lack of all the good things that the market has to offer. In reality, however, incorporation usually produces mixed results. It is true that it makes certain technologies and products available even to the poor. But it is also true that poor people and communities are nearly always incorporated at the bottom of a system in which real wealth is trickling up to the rich (Bodley 2008; McMichael 2004; Narayan et al. 2000a, 2000b). In the long run, Christians in ministry now may find themselves blamed for the ill ef-fects of capitalism, just as missionaries of the past have been blamed for the ill effects of colonialism.

At a minimum, Christians in ministry must take a holistic ap-proach to poverty. Bryant Myers describes such an approach, which is rooted deeply in the Bible (Myers 2004). Myers describes poverty as a network of poorly functioning systems, including material poverty, vulnerability (lack of reserves), physical weakness, political powerless-ness, spiritual poverty ("broken relationships with neighbor and God"), and isolation (lack of assets, including education) (72). "Poverty is a result of relationships that do not work," he says, "that are not just, that are not for life, that are not harmonious or enjoyable. Poverty is the absence of shalom in all its meanings" (86). Myers' model is one of incorporation, but it does not make the mistake of promoting material development at the expense of social or spiritual growth. In fact, Myers makes a strong case for the value of Christian conversion to bringing holistic development in people's lives.

The good news to this point is that such a biblically based, holistic approach is actually *more effective* than a narrowly financial one, even in economic terms. Contemporary economic development projects, since the advent of the Grameen Bank, have demonstrated that a design strategy that includes social responsibility brings groups out of poverty better than strategies that attempt to bring individuals out in isolation from one another. Grameen Bank loans are given to women in groups of five for the purpose of starting microbusinesses. The women rotate receipt of the loans and hold one another accountable to repay them. Repayment rates are typically as high as 96 to 100 percent, with interest (Yunus 2001, 187). This practice demonstrates the value of social responsibility in financial management. But the bank goes farther. The women must sign a sixteen-point set of "decisions," including commitments to hygiene, family planning, education, and, yes, hard work. The decisions affirm the value of social life: "We shall always be ready to help each other; if anyone is in difficulty, we shall all help him or her"; "If we come to know of any breach of discipline in any centre, we shall all go there and help restore discipline"; and "We shall take part in all social activities collectively." Decision #12 is carefully worded to protect women from traditional forms of abuse (the downside of social life): "We shall not inflict any injustice on anyone, neither shall we allow anyone to do so" (186–89).

Of significance for our purpose here is the fact that principles of holism and social accountability are not only promoted in the policies and practices of the bank; they are found in the very structure of the institution itself. The Grameen Bank is owned by its borrowers, the poorest women of Bangladesh, who are 94 percent of the shareholders and make up the majority of the members of the board of directors. Muhammad Yunus, the founder of the bank, initially tried to arrange loans for poor women through commercial banks. When they refused him, he was forced to create a new *type* of institution for the work to be accomplished. The Grameen Bank has been so successful financially that recently a variety of for-profit banks have begun offering small loans to poor people at extortionary rates of interest (MacFarquhar 2010). If the goal is truly to lift people out of poverty, it would seem that the profit motive is a poor substitute for a community of mutual accountability.

Finally, while as Christians we must address both the social and the economic needs of the people we serve in ministry, we must not forget that God's kingdom purposes are beyond the comforts of this life. Jesus was clear that both wealth and family must be sacrificed to follow him (Matt 16:24; Mark 10:21; Luke 14:26). Christian history is filled with people who have been willing to give up everything to respond to God's call. Sometimes this has involved a lifestyle so radical that an ordinary involvement in society and economy is impossible. Jesus himself set the example (at least in the years of his teaching ministry), followed by the Apostle Paul, St. Francis of Assisi, Mother Teresa, and many others. Contemporary examples include Viv Grigg (1984) and Shane Claiborne (2006). To some degree, all missionaries leave behind the comforts of family and friends, if not material wealth, to follow Christ to new places.

How does the radical call of Jesus fit in with the Christian affirmation of life in creation, our bodily existence, and appreciation for the social and material good? For some Jewish theologians, Jesus' "anti-family" statements lead them to believe that these two views are incompatible! Christians down through the centuries, from the monastic movements to the Mennonites and Amish, have wrestled with the degree to which we should live "in the world" lest it make us "of the world." So how are Christians to live this life? The answer surely has to do with the larger vision and purpose that guides our decision-making processes. It is not that we must eschew all the pleasures of this life for hair shirts and desert isolation. In fact, extreme austerities can be the means of an attempt at self-salvation. It is rather that we must ensure that our decisions are guided by the bigger picture we have of God's purposes for humanity in the context of his restoration of creation, and by the Holy Spirit's specific and particular call upon our own lives.

That bigger picture, or metanarrative, must not be compromised by the metanarratives of the social and economic systems of which we are a part. What I suggest here is that, as Christians living under capitalism, we must appreciate the value of the economic system at hand while not being deluded by its extravagant claims. Equally, we must recognize the deep distortions that are created by the system and work steadily to rectify them, while taking care not to destroy what is good. Lesslie Newbigin writes,

> We are not conservatives who regard the structures as part of the unalterable order of creation … and who therefore suppose that the gospel is only relevant to the issues of personal and private life. Nor are we anarchists who seek to destroy the structures. We are rather *patient revolutionaries* who know that the whole of creation, with all its given structures, is groaning in the travail of a new birth, and that we share this groaning and travail, this struggling and wrestling, but do so in hope because we have already received, in the Spirit, the first fruit of the new world (Rom. 8:19–25). (1989, 209; emphasis added)

Following Jesus under capitalism includes cooperating with the system by promoting education, agricultural innovation, and economic development for the purpose of providing for people's material welfare. It also includes critically analyzing the system and confronting it by joining in advocacy, fair trade, and alternative forms of economic institutions (see chap. 3). To do both requires a third perspective, neither for nor against the system in total, willing to cooperate with its projects when they are constructive but also to stand apart when they are not. With this alternative perspective, Christians in ministry can provide real hope by demonstrating an ability to bring about constructive change as "patient revolutionaries" representing the gospel of Jesus to complex human systems.

REFERENCES

Appadurai, Arjun. 1986. *The social life of things: Commodities in cultural perspective.* New York: Cambridge University Press.

Bellah, Robert N., Richard Madsen, William M. Sullivan, Ann Swidler, and Steven M. Tipton. 2007. *Habits of the heart: Individualism and commitment in American life.* Los Angeles: University of California Press.

Benedict, Ruth. 1958. *Patterns of culture.* Boston: Houghton-Mifflin.

Blaug, Mark. 1980. *The methodology of economics; or, How economists explain.* New York: Cambridge University Press.

Bodley, John. 1999. *Victims of progress.* 4th ed. Mountain View, CA: Mayfield.

————. 2008. *Anthropology and contemporary human problems.* 5th ed. Lanham, MD: AltaMira.

Bohannan, Paul. 1959. The impact of money on an African subsistence economy. *Journal of Economic History* 19, no. 4: 491–503.

Carrier, James G. 1997. *Meanings of the market: The free market in Western culture.* New York: Berg.

Claiborne, Shane. 2006. *The irresistible revolution: Living as an ordinary radical.* Grand Rapids: Zondervan.

Firth, Raymond. 1975. *Malay fishermen: Their peasant economy.* New York: W. W. Norton.

Foster, Brian. 1977. Mon commerce and the dynamics of ethnic relations. *Southeast Asian Journal of Social Science* 5, no. 1–2: 111–22.

Foster, George M. 1965. Peasant society and the image of the limited good. *American Anthropologist* 67, no. 2: 293–315.

Fox, Frampton. 2003. "Money as water: A patron-client approach to mission dependency in India." PhD diss., Trinity International University.

Grigg, Viv. 1984. *Companion to the poor.* Sydney: Albatross.

Gudeman, Stephen, ed. 1998. *Economic anthropology.* The International Library of Critical Writings in Economics, vol. 99. Northampton, MA: An Elgar Reference Collection.

Haviland, William A., Harald E. L. Prins, Bunny McBride, and Dana Walrath. 2011. *Cultural anthropology: The human challenge.* 13th ed. Belmont, CA: Wadsworth.

MacFarquhar, Neil. 2010. Banks making big profits from tiny loans. *New York Times,* April 13. Accessed April 5, 2013. http://www.nytimes.com/2010/04/14/world/14microfinance.html?pagewanted=all&_r=0.

Maranz, David E. 2001. *African friends and money matters: Observations from Africa.* Dallas: SIL International and International Museum of Cultures.

Marx, Karl. 1992. *Capital: A critique of political economy,* vols. 1–3. New York: Penguin Classics.

Mauss, Marcel. 1967. *The gift: Forms and functions of exchange in archaic societies.* New York: W. W. Norton.

McMichael, Philip. 2004. *Development and social change: A global perspective.* 3rd ed. Thousand Oaks, CA: Pine Forge.

Meneses, Eloise H. 2007. *Love and revolutions: Market women and social change in India.* Lanham, MD: University Press of America.

Myers, Bryant. 2004. *Walking with the poor: Principles and practices of transformational development.* Maryknoll, NY: Orbis.

Narayan, Deepa, Raj Patel, Kai Schafft, Anne Rademacher, and Sarah Koch-Schulte. 2000a. *Can anyone hear us?* Voices of the Poor 1. Oxford: Oxford University Press.

Narayan, Deepa, Robert Chambers, Meera Kaul Shah, and Patti Petesch. 2000b. *Crying out for change.* Voices of the Poor 2. Oxford: Oxford University Press.

Newbigin, Lesslie. 1989. *The gospel in a pluralist society.* Grand Rapids: Eerdmans.

———. 1995. *The open secret: An introduction to the theology of mission.* Grand Rapids: Eerdmans.

Plattner, Stuart. 1983. Economic custom in a competitive marketplace. *American Anthropologist* 85: 848–58.

Polanyi, Karl. 2001. *The great transformation: The political and economic origins of our time.* Boston: Beacon.

Sahlins, Marshall. 1972. *Stone age economics.* New York: Aldine de Gruyter.

Tawney, R. H. 1972. *Religion and the rise of capitalism.* New York: Harcourt, Brace & Company.

Temple, William. 1977. *Christianity and social order.* New York: Seabury.

Tocqueville, Alexis de. [1835] 2000. *Democracy in America.* New York: Bantam Classics.

Townsend, Peter, and David Gordon, eds. 2002. *World poverty: New policies to defeat an old enemy.* Bristol: Policy Press.

United Nations Development Programme. 2007. Eradicate extreme poverty and hunger. MDG Monitor. Accessed June 1, 2011. http:// www.mdgmonitor.org/goal1.cfm.

Yunus, Muhammad. 2001. The Grameen Bank. In *Global studies: India and South Asia,* 5th ed., edited by James H. K. Norton, 186–89. Guilford, CT: McGraw-Hill.

Wallerstein, Immanuel. 2004. *World systems analysis: An introduction.* Durham, NC: Duke University Press.

Weber, Max. 1976. *The Protestant ethic and the spirit of capitalism.* New York: Charles Scribner's Sons.

———. 1947. *The theory of social and economic organization.* New York: Oxford University Press.

———. 1978. *Economy and society.* With a new introduction by Guenther Roth and Claus Wittich. Los Angeles: University of California Press.

Wright, Christopher J. H. 2004. *Old Testament ethics for the people of God.* Downers Grove, IL: InterVarsity Press.

2

CULTURAL DIMENSIONS OF FINANCIAL ACCOUNTING SYSTEMS: A BIBLICAL PERSPECTIVE AND AN APPROACH FOR PARTNERSHIPS IN MISSIONS*

Mary Lederleitner

Many countries are now involved in funding mission around the world, and each has its own legal, cultural, and ethical standards. When working cross-culturally it is a challenge to be fully aware of these differences, let alone comply with and somehow meet multiple standards, without imposing one's own culture upon others. Because of this reality, is it possible for missionaries and mission agencies to adhere to their own ethical and cultural standards regarding financial accountability without fostering neocolonialism while serving in other contexts? In matters of financial partnership, regulations and require-ments in countries such as the United States or Canada pose a serious hurdle for organizations when funding is sent abroad (IRS 2014; Van Cleef 2003; Canadian Revenue Agency 2010). Stringent fiduciary requirements are being imposed in the very mission contexts where colonialism once reigned and past injustices have never fully healed; this raises the question of whether it is possible to partner as "equals" when financial disparities are so enormous and groups with vast sums

*   Sections of this chapter were previously published (Lederleitner 2010a). Used with permission.

of money require in-depth accountability from groups with far fewer financial resources.

This chapter is the reflection of an eclectic mix of academic research in the areas of intercultural communication and cross-cultural conflict, an array of dialogues that have spanned the last fifteen years, theological musings, and my personal training as a professional accountant. Much of my professional experience has been spent straddling the worlds of missiology and financial compliance, where I have felt the internal distress of trying to work in a way that is true to both disciplines. Instead of using financial resources as the trump card that shuts down discussion and demands compliance, I have wondered if a God who values both relationships and accountability might supply answers the global church needs to partner well together. As a result of this journey, I believe examining the tension and complexity through the broader ethical lens of the word of God will provide a place of deeper and more solid agreement. In that place I believe it is possible to find the grace and capacity needed to partner well in this next era of global missions.

WHAT IS NEOCOLONIALISM?

Almost since the beginning of time, foreign governments have conquered near or distant regions of the world and ruled over them. Even Jesus had to deal with this phenomenon (John 19:12–15). Often the invading governments brought with them new laws and different practices. Under colonial rule some forms of progress occurred. At times roads were built, infrastructure was established, and schools were formed. However, what is often referred to as "development" came at the cost of people's freedom. Many who were indigenous to the area being "colonized" lost their voice and their ability to make decisions about what would happen in their own homeland.

A concern in missiology is how there can be effective cross-cultural partnerships without fostering a new form of colonialism now known as "neocolonialism" (Rieger 2004; Cooper 2005; Schwartz 2007). "Neocolonialism" implies that although physical occupation by a foreign power may no longer occur, wealth and resources are provided in ways that enable continued domination of others. This occurs when some on the receiving end of mission funding feel demeaned and controlled by the process; these partners have the sense that they are losing the right to make their own decisions and losing their voice. Neocolonialism raises the concern of whether true partnership, the kind that models genuine mutuality, can even take place between partners in the global church given such vast disparities of wealth.

WHAT HAPPENS IN DIALOGUES INVOLVING FINANCIAL PARTNERSHIP

When mission partnerships form, dialogues about issues of financial accountability can become polarizing. When concerns over excessive control or neocolonialism are expressed by partners who receive funding, wealthy partners can feel unappreciated. The tone of their response can be one of irritation or defensiveness. At other times accusations are hurled that the partners receiving funding are not trustworthy—otherwise they would willingly be "held accountable." For the partners who receive such funds, a different, almost instinctual, response may arise: when funds are received with all kinds of fiduciary requirements, many comment that the requirements are "just another form of colonialism" or "more evidence of neocolonialism." To these recipients, the sense that they are once again being controlled by elite foreign powers returns.

One possible way to explain many of these misunderstandings is through attribution theory (Elmer 2007; Mitchell and Green 2005; Nickerson 1998). When interactions occur between people from different cultures, and when ministry leaders juggle many different responsibilities, it is easy to erroneously attribute negative motivations and character traits to others. One temptation is to assume that an ideology from the past is the cause for current behavior. When this occurs, "yesterday's meaning becomes today's dogma" (Senge 1996, x). When this happens, a vicious loop is created that is hard to escape.

To be sure, with regard to the tension in the global church surrounding the issues of money and financial accountability, often yesterday's meaning does become today's dogma; there seems to be inadequate space for true inquiry, dialogue, and deep reflection. This general lack of awareness erects a barrier to recognizing tacit meanings assigned to financial accountability. In actuality, however, it is the meaning assigned to these financial dealings (Berger 1967, 3–28; Hiebert 1985, 141–69; Mezirow 1991, 1–36) and not financial accountability itself that determines whether such interactions will be a destructive or constructive force in missions. Yet the global mission enterprise often seems anesthetized to such contradictions (Bohm 1996, 5). Great disparities in expectations can arise when affluent churches in countries such as Singapore or Hong Kong fund, for instance, Papuan partnerships. Financial accountability can be assigned, especially by those in the global church with more financial resources, as being a "neutral" issue when it is anything but neutral.

FINANCIAL ACCOUNTABILITY CRITICALLY EXAMINED

Critical thinking is essential if partners desire to serve one another better in global missions, because when "habits of the mind go unexamined, they create limitations and form boxes" (Cranton 2006, 28) that constrain or impede people's ability to work fruitfully together. Joerg Rieger (2004) is a professor at Southern Methodist University whose research deals with issues of religion, theology, and economics. He supplies a starting point for necessary missiological reflection when he writes that "failure to consider our colonial heritage may result in failure to understand who we are today" (202). According to Rieger, "Reading the histories one gets the strong sense that the missionaries meant well…. So why did Christian mission end up as part of the colonial enterprise?" (205). In Rieger's view this happened because colonialism became, for all practical purposes, simply the natural backdrop for life. Many missionaries seem to have been unable to differentiate between "what was" and "what ought to be." Complaints and resistance often arose only when abuses by those in power became especially flagrant (206).

In *African Friends and Money Matters*, Maranz examines money and culture through the lens of cultural anthropology, describing the reasons why Africans and Westerners view money differently. He explains the process of financial accountability under colonial rule, writing that

> during the colonial period African leaders were not accountable to the people under them, but to their colonial masters. These in turn were accountable only to their home governments. The local people were there to be controlled, not informed. Surely this colonial pattern left indelible marks across the continent. (2001, 39)

Current Worldly Standards

Some might say that colonialism is long gone and it no longer influences mission organizations. Partners from wealthy contexts like the United States often like to quickly put the past behind them. Their focus is on what is "new" or "cutting edge." Consequently, many of these partners show little understanding about how financial accountability has been indelibly shaped by colonial practices and how it affects power and status in relationships within specific cultural contexts. For example, when someone with wealth supplies money to another with less wealth (often for altruistic reasons), the latter is now "held accountable" by the person with greater wealth. Almost always the accountability still flows in only one direction. Accountability is most frequently "upward" to those with financial means and not "downward" to those who have fewer resources. As a result, those with greater resources can set the terms and call the shots; those with greater resources set the standards. Proverbs such as "Beggars can't be choosers" or "The one who pays the piper calls the tune" become unexamined "habits of the mind" that guide behavior. Those with significant financial resources have "voice" and the greatest ability to determine outcomes. This value system is the foundation upon which most of the legal requirements regarding financial accountability are based. It is also often the default practice of most wealthy partners, regardless of their nationality, if they are giving funding to someone with fewer financial resources.

Biblical Standards and Values

Scripture sets forth a very different value system. Although Jesus uses parables in which people are held accountable for resources entrusted to them by persons of greater financial means (Matt 25:14–30; cf. Matt 18:23–27; 20:1–15), he also emphasizes that there will be eternal consequences and that everyone will be held accountable for actions toward those with fewer financial resources (Matt 25:40). The letter of James gives a scathing admonition not to show partiality to the wealthy, for it transgresses the Law (Jas 2:1–12). All people are to be treated with dignity and respect. The body of Christ should function in a way that models mutuality and interdependency (1 Cor 12:1–31). Paul explains that all Christians are part of the same body and Christ is the head, forcefully showing that one part of the body cannot say it has no need of another. In a human body, every part has a voice and can impact the whole. In the end, God will hold every partner accountable for each of his or her actions. The searing depth of his judgment will even apply to "every careless word" (Matt 12:36 NASB).

Why Are Partners Surprised?

The secular values governing financial accountability that are currently present in funding policies quite often reflect a very different set of values than those seen in Scripture. Why then are partners surprised when brothers and sisters in Christ feel demeaned by financial accountability requirements? If partners could step back and look at the bigger picture, they would find it odd if people did not feel demeaned by these processes. If accountability only goes upward to those with greater financial means, less wealthy partners may question whether ministry processes will ever model mutuality, dignity, interdependency, and voice for all.

REDEEMING ACCOUNTABILITY PROCESSES

Partners have to comply with financial regulations imposed by governments. If there is no compliance, partners raising funds in contexts such as the United States, Canada, Singapore, Hong Kong, Australia, or Germany, for instance, can incur criminal charges and possibly face jail time. If they do not comply with financial regulations, they will suffer a profound loss of credibility with their donors, their ministries will come to an abrupt halt, and they will severely hinder the witness of Christ. News media outlets will highlight these stories, and that will only cause greater cynicism in the hearts of unbelievers and believers alike. In the spirit of Romans 13:1–8, partners must adhere to the admonition to obey governmental laws regarding accountability. However, Christian love should compel partners to go further than mere compliance with external regulations.

Where Do Partners Begin?

Essential to the act of "redeeming" is trying to discern God's true purpose for something. Before partners can move forward, they need to begin to uncover the positive "meanings" for accountability. If partners start to address the blockages, one of which is the negative or secular meaning of accountability, they can begin to replace them and "create something new" between them (Bohm 1996, 5). Dialogue among partners is the pathway to finding redemptive meanings.

In addition, Satan has distorted the meaning of accountability. His presence is visible in the cross-cultural conflict about financial accountability in global mission. Satan causes partners to think accountability can "mean" only one thing, that those who are wealthier hold those without wealth accountable. However, is that true? Social science research offers a place to begin the search for alternative meanings. Research indicates that accountability is totally necessary for the growth and maturity of individuals in the workplace (Goleman 1998, 268–74). In this sense accountability is something positive. There are also strong parallels to be found in the growth and development of cultural intelligence (Peterson 2004, 89–90). Research also shows that accountability is a critical component in adult transformation (Mezirow 1991; Cranton 2006; Taylor 1994, 2000). Accountability also prepares all believers for the final day when they will stand before God and give an account of their lives (Luke 12:35–48). Biblical accountability means work environments that will foster deep maturity, growth in cultural intelligence, and lasting transformation.

Dialogue also offers a helpful way to begin uncovering better "meanings" for accountability. It fosters different types of questions: for example, as partners look around in the world—in government, in companies, and in the church—does a lack of accountability tend to bring good or bad outcomes? What happens when there is no accountability? People who have seen or been involved in a setting where theft or fraud has occurred know the extreme damage it does to a community of believers and to Christ's witness in a ministry. How might accountability be seen in light of these accounts?

Dialogue about this issue is of utmost importance, because accountability has to be everyone's idea. Financial accountability will not work if one partner assumes it is helpful and other partners believe it is only oppressive and controlling. If left solely to the dogma of each partner's culture, accountability will not be seen in its proper light. Without better meanings, it will be impossible to move forward.

Accountability Processes and Scriptural Values

Someone might ask, "Can accountability processes model scriptural values?" The amazing answer to that question is a resounding yes! Many governmental regulations stipulate that partners have to be able to confirm that funds are being used to accomplish the task or help the people for whom the funds were raised. In theory all partners agree with this or they would not be working together. Despite theoretical agreement, however, if partners seek to only meet that minimal legal objective of financial accountability, their partnerships will not model mutuality, for governmental accountability requirements tend to be in one direction. However, partners have within their power the ability to create a web or system of accountability that can model holistic mutuality.

Covenant/Presbytery Model

An example of a system or approach of holistic mutuality may look something like this: First, the system or approach needs to be designed and developed to fit each specific situation. One size does not fit all. John Rowell writes of utilizing a covenant relationship process in his partnership with Bosnians. In this partnership the parties involved have mutual accountability and mutual voice through a presbytery (2006, 160–61). This model can be helpful for smaller church-to-church or smaller church-to-agency partnerships. Use of this model becomes complicated, however, in a large multinational mission organization that has hundreds of diverse partnerships around the globe. Still, although some basic policies regarding financial reporting are necessary or required in larger agencies, it is feasible for individual regions working closely with indigenous partners to create more comprehensive and God-honoring local accountability structures that facilitate mutual respect and voice.

The key to building accountability processes that model mutuality and foster transformation is to work to level the playing field. In these accountability processes, every person has positions of strength and positions of vulnerability. That means that if one party is bringing funding, he or she needs to be accountable in areas of great vulnerability as well. Areas of vulnerability might include needs for personal maturity in various areas or growth in a professional capacity that the person does not already possess. This broader network of holistic accountability helps to keep everyone honest and to remind everyone in the partnership that all parties are being stretched and are being held to a standard that at times is quite difficult to keep. It is in areas of vulnerability and weakness that partners can pray for one another and stand together as brothers and sisters before their heavenly Father, all in need of growth and maturity.

Mutual Pledges

Partners International is one mission agency that may be highlighted as a positive example of cross-cultural ministry partnerships in many parts of the world. Daniel Rickett, in *Making Your Partnership Work* (2002), outlines some aspects of setting up and working through partnerships that Partners International has found helpful over the years. At the end of the book he highlights a pledge that Partners International makes to its overseas partners (131–38) whereby Partners International tries to convey clearly that it does not see accountability as a one-directional dynamic. They need their partners to be accountable with finances, but Partners International is willing to be accountable in many ways as well. This is an excellent step. Their pledge has been developed over the years in a context of rich and engaging dialogue.

One temptation or concern is that other ministry leaders might take this pledge and use it as a directive—in effect, dictating terms to their partners. Rather than coming together to create mutual account-ability pledges, if not used carefully, this pledge might again become an instance of a wealthy partner dominating the relationship and setting all the terms. Dialogue is utterly critical to mutuality. Documents such as the one developed by Partners International can sometimes be a helpful way to start conversations as mutual pledges are crafted for different ministry contexts.

A Voice for the Most Powerless

In *Walking with the Poor,* Bryant Myers highlights the need for account-ability in all directions. He explains that people "mar the identity of the poor" if there is no way for the latter to have a voice in the process (2007, 130). On the matter of evaluations, for example, which by nature are a part of accountability processes, it is essential that the poorest persons affected by a partnership also be able to hold oth-ers accountable. If the means for this to happen are not built into the process, partners can easily deceive themselves into thinking that their ministries have a greater impact and are more fruitful than they truly are. Also, by including the poor in the process, partners better prepare themselves for the day when God will hold each person accountable for how each partner has treated "the least of these" (Matt 25:40).

HOW DO PARTNERS CONTEXTUALIZE ACCOUNTABILITY PROCESSES?

The field of intercultural communication teaches that the same practice in one setting can have a very different meaning in another (Hofstede and Hofstede 2005; Trompenaars and Hampden-Turner 1998). Partners cannot "plug and play" a set of policies or practices designed for one cultural context and assume they will work effectively in another. "One of the goals of cross-cultural training is to alert people to the fact that they are constantly involved in a process of assigning meaning to the actions and objects they observe" (Trompenaars and Hampden-Turner 1998, 201). Direct and indirect communication, status issues, implications regarding the loss or building of face, tolerances for ambiguity, and the like all impact the meaning ascribed to certain behaviors. Individual personalities, leadership styles, and organizational cultures also vary greatly among partners.

If past behavior is any indication, invariably ministry leaders will want to cut this process short, copy what has been done somewhere else, and just "get on with things." The problem with this mindset is that it circumvents dialogue and substantially increases the likelihood that any new process introduced from the outside will not work or will not be sustainable over the long haul. In missiology, partners seem willing to invest much effort and time to ensure that ministry programs or church planting efforts are contextualized. As a whole, however, they seem to have little patience or awareness that the processes by which partners "do business" or "achieve financial accountability" also need to be contextualized if they are going to foster good meanings and outcomes.

Developing culturally contextualized processes for each partnership will take more time. For instance, in some partnerships it might be possible for partners to speak directly to one another. In other partnerships it might be wise to have many third-party go-betweens in place so voices from people with differing levels of power can truly be heard. In some partnerships, accountability processes from wealthier countries may be the best solution. In others, these same processes might encourage fraud because they are largely based upon paper receipts, which are worthless in many parts of the world.

Mutually developed and contextualized processes are much more likely to have redemptive meanings and sustainability, but creating them will not be a quick process. Things will need to be tried, evaluated, adapted, tried again, tinkered with, and then adapted further. Lest partners tire of the process of dialogue and building accountability structures together, they need to realize that they are establishing a process that has the potential to foster genuine unity and profound growth and maturity for everyone involved. Building processes is far more than a money issue. It is changing the way partners work so that the very processes themselves model the teaching found in Romans 12 as well as Romans 13.

WHAT CAN JESUS TEACH PARTNERS?

Matthew 17:24–27 teaches lessons that can enable global partners to weather what at times seem to be unreasonable and illogical financial requirements. In this passage, people begin questioning Peter as to whether Jesus will be paying the temple tax or not. Using the incident as a teaching moment for his disciple, Jesus inquires of Peter, "What do you think, Simon? From whom do the kings of the earth collect customs or poll-tax, from their sons or from strangers?" (17:25 NASB). Peter responds correctly, stating that this tax is for strangers. Jesus affirms that this is indeed the case. The requirement is illogical and should not apply to them. It is what Jesus says afterwards that is amazing: "However, so that we do not offend them, go to the sea and throw in a hook, and take the first fish that comes up; and when you open its mouth, you will find a shekel. Take that and give it to them for you and Me" (17:27 NASB).

Jesus could have responded in many other ways. He could have railed against the people who were requiring financial compliance. He could have argued that the law was not applicable to him because of his deity. He could have made a case that he had more important things to manage. After all, he was training a group of people who would be leading a global movement. He was healing the sick and raising the dead. He was also preparing to become the sacrificial lamb and die for the sins of all humankind. He had many legitimate reasons to not abide by the financial regulation. Yet Jesus did not let this government-regulated accountability requirement shake his confidence. He did not give the externally imposed financial requirement the power to cause him to feel demeaned or disrespected. Jesus stopped what he was doing to address the issue. He seemed to take extra care to "not give offense." Yet in earlier chapters, Jesus did not hesitate to offend others under different circumstances (Matt 15:12–14). He did not seem to waste a moment worrying about whether he was offending the Pharisees. When his disciples asked if he realized he had offended the Pharisees, his response was, "They are blind guides of the blind. And if a blind man guides a blind man, both will fall into a pit" (Matt 15:14 NASB). Jesus seemed indifferent as to whether or not he had offended the Pharisees. However, when it came to an unreasonable financial accountability requirement, he took care not to give offense.

Perhaps Jesus' example might provide global partners with greater capacity in dealing with frustrating financial requirements. Partners should consider whether financial requirements by governments, in and of themselves, have the ability to demean. What role does maintaining an identity rooted in Christ play in this overall debate? What implications do his actions have with regard to what is worth fighting about and what is not? In the end of this story God provides what is needed through a special act of grace. As partners approach the thorny issue of financial compliance, God's grace and provision are also necessary. This passage provides hope that Christ understands the struggles partners face and can help guide them through these challenges.

CONCLUSION

Accountability and fiduciary requirements are not going to diminish anytime in the near future. With a global war on terrorism underway, funds crossing national boundaries are being scrutinized more than ever. Financial regulations will likely increase rather than decrease, and nonprofit organizations and ministries in places such as the United States and Canada will not be able to give large amounts of unaccounted-for funds across national borders. If that is the reality, should partners just stop sharing financial resources? If so, should partners settle for one part of Christ's body to be rich with financial blessings and for other parts to lack the means to meet their most basic needs? Passages such as Psalm 67 (which says that God blesses people so the ends of the earth may know him) and 1 Corinthians 12 (reminding partners to be the "body of Christ") must be read afresh in consideration of such national and global requirements. Even the earliest of believers seemed to understand that resources should be shared to meet needs within the body (Rom 15:26). On the other hand, does a good relationship mean no accountability? If so, what does it mean for believers who are taught they have a close relationship with Christ, yet one where he holds each of them accountable? Can trust grow with no accountability, or does trust grow as partners are mutually accountable and faithful?

A way forward is to begin to redeem accountability processes so that they no longer mirror worldly values but instead reflect the reality of the global church's own relationship with God. Everything in each culture must be brought to the foot of the Cross. If wealthy partners thrust secular methods of financial accountability onto cross-cultural partnerships without crafting a more holistic approach to accountability, partners receiving funding will likely feel demeaned. Secular patterns of accountability alone will likely never mirror the values found in Scripture. Through the use of dialogue and carefully contextualized processes, partners have the power to fashion processes that model the truth of Scripture found in both the Romans 12 and Romans 13 passages. Accountability can serve as a tutor helping everyone to grow in godliness and maturity in Christ. Once partners devote the time and attention needed to craft contextualized processes that reflect the high value God places on accountability and relationship, a new era can finally emerge in global mission where neocolonialism will be only a distant memory.

REFERENCES

Berger, Peter L. 1967. *The sacred canopy: Elements of a sociological theory of religion.* New York: Random House.

Bohm, David. 1996. *On dialogue.* New York: Routledge.

Canadian Revenue Agency. 2010. Charities in the international context. Accessed October 7, 2014. http://www.cra-arc.gc.ca/chrts-gvng /chrts/ntrntnl-eng.html.

Cooper, Michael T. 2005. Colonialism, neo-colonialism, and forgotten missiological lessons. *Global Missiology* 2, no. 2: 1–14. Accessed October 7, 2014. http://ojs.globalmissiology.org/index.php/english/article /view/105.

Cranton, Patricia. 2006. *Understanding and promoting transformative learning: A guide for educators of adults.* 2nd ed. San Francisco: John Wiley & Sons.

Elmer, Duane. 2007. IMCO (Inter-Mission Cooperative Outreach) conference presentations. Saskatchewan, Canada.

Goleman, Daniel. 1998. *Working with emotional intelligence.* New York: Bantam.

Hiebert, Paul G. 1985. *Anthropological insights for missionaries.* Grand Rapids: Baker.

Hofstede, Geert, Gert Jan Hofstede, and Michael Minkov. 2005. *Cultures and organizations: Software of the mind.* 2nd ed. New York: McGraw-Hill.

IRS. 2014. Tax information for churches and religious organizations. Accessed October 7, 2014. http://www.irs.gov/Charities -&-Non-Profits/Churches-&-Religious-Organizations.

Lederleitner, Mary. 2006. The theology of internal controls. *Evangelical Missions Quarterly* 40 no. 4: 516–21.

————. 2010a. An approach to financial accountability in mission partnerships. In *Serving Jesus with integrity: Ethics and accountability in mission,* edited by Dwight P. Baker and Douglas Hayward, 27–47. Pasadena: William Carey Library.

————. 2010b. *Cross-cultural partnerships: Navigating the complexities of money and mission.* Downers Grove, IL: InterVarsity Press.

Maranz, David E. 2001. *African friends and money matters: Observations from Africa.* Dallas: SIL International and the International Museum of Cultures.

Mezirow, Jack. 1991. *Transformative dimensions of adult learning.* San Francisco: John Wiley.

Mitchell, Terence, and Stephen Green. 2005. Attribution theory: Managerial perceptions of the poor performing subordinate. In *Organizational behavior 1: Essential theories of motivation and leadership,* edited by John B. Miner, 184–203. Armonk, NY: M. E. Sharpe.

Myers, Bryant L. 2007. *Walking with the poor: Principles and practices of transformational development.* Maryknoll, NY: Orbis.

Nickerson, Raymond S. 1998. Confirmation bias: A ubiquitous phenomenon in many guises. *Review of General Psychology* 2, no. 2: 175–220.

Peterson, Brooks. 2004. *Cultural intelligence: A guide to working with people from other cultures.* Boston: Intercultural Press.

Rickett, Daniel. 2002. *Making your partnership work.* Enumclaw, WA: Wine Press.

Rieger, Joerg. 2004. Theology and mission between neo-colonialism and postcolonialism. *Mission Studies* 21, no. 2: 201–27.

Rowell, John. 2006. *To give or not to give: Rethinking dependence, restoring generosity, and redefining sustainability.* Atlanta: Authentic.

Schwartz, Glenn J. 2007. *When charity destroys dignity: Overcoming unhealthy dependency in the Christian movement.* Bloomington, IN: Author House.

Senge, Peter M. 1996. Preface to *Bohm on dialogue,* by David Bohm, vii–xiv. New York: Routledge.

Taylor, Edward W. 1994. Intercultural competency: A transformative learning process. *Adult Education Quarterly* 48, no. 1: 34–59.

————. 2000. Analyzing research on transformative learning theory. In *Learning as transformation: Critical perspectives on a theory in progress,* edited by Jack Mezirow, 285–328. San Francisco: Jossey-Bass.

Trompenaars, Fons, and Charles Hampden-Turner. 1998. *Riding the waves of culture: Understanding diversity in global business.* New York: McGraw-Hill.

Van Cleef, Carol R. 2003. The USA Patriot Act: Statutory analysis and regulatory implementation. *Journal of Financial Crime* 11, no. 1: 73–102.

3

ISLAMIC BANKING AND ECONOMICS: A MIRROR FOR CHRISTIAN PRACTICES AND MISSION IN MUSLIM CONTEXTS

John Cheong

On March 2, 2009, in the midst of a global economic recession, Indonesian President Susilo Bambang Yudhoyono called on Islamic banks to take a leadership role in the global economy while speaking at the opening of the World Islamic Economic Forum in Jakarta. There he remarked that it was time for Islamic banks to do some missionary work in the West. Islamic institutions, he said, had not been hit as hard as their Western counterparts because they did not invest in toxic assets. In addition, banks run in accordance with Muslim laws on interest payments and the sharing of credit risks are seen by many as fairer than traditional banks, less focused on profit, and kinder to the communities they work in.

In the past, while the world of Islamic politics and macroeconomics may have seemed only remotely connected to the concerns of Christian mission, today Muslim visions of expanding the witness of Islam as a growing and progressive religion through the realm of Islamic banking cannot be ignored. It raises new questions and presents new challenges to the way in which Christians do mission.

For the most part, there has been little written on the cultural and religious dimensions of economics. Where Christian mission has engaged with the realm of economics, it has dealt with areas such as raising missionary support, business as a form of mission, church partnerships, or ways in which missionaries have used money in other cultures in their everyday life.[1] There have also been written works that examine issues such as uplift of the poor or the problems of giving and aid.[2] But critical Christian examinations of the cultural dimensions of macroeconomics are rarer. If they have been discussed, they have emphasized Christianity's positive relationship to capitalism (Novak 1993; Weber 1963). Even when capitalism has been critiqued, the recommended change has been mostly directed inward towards the church (Budde and Brimlow 2002; Hauerwas 2000).

In this chapter, the economics of Islam in its cultural and religious contexts will be examined. I will illuminate how the ascent and descent of Islam's empire occurred through its commercial management in history, discuss Muslim morality and ethical practices as they are tangibly expressed in economics, and survey Islam's economic relationship to modernity and globalization in the last century. Three aspects of the economics of Islam will be detailed—*zakat* (Islamic almsgiving/tithing), *waqf* (Islamic endowments/trusts), and Islamic banking (interest-free financing).[3] The chapter will conclude that, by using Islam's example as a mirror, Christian mission may be examined and reframed to accomplish two tasks: engaging the greater socioeconomic forces that impinge on its ability to spread the gospel, and responding to a form of Islam that deems Islamic banking as missionary in purpose as well as economic.

---

1   For example, see McKinney-Douglas and Steffen 2008; Rundle and Steffen 2003; Johnson 2009; Maranz 2001.
2   For example, see Schwartz 2007.
3   This omits other aspects of Islamic economics such as the *baitulmal* (an institution that acts as a trustee for Muslims, looking after assets from which Muslim members could benefit), financing of the hajj (Salleh 1985), and the Islamic inheritance system (Powers 1993), an account of which space does not permit here.

AN OVERVIEW OF ISLAMIC ECONOMICS

Islam is a religion that is concerned with and stipulates conduct for every aspect of life and devotion for its followers, including the realm of development and economics. The Islamic ideal of development can be captured by the term *iqtisad,* which means "economy," not just in the technical sense of the term but in the context of thrift, frugality, providence, and moderation. The economic ideal is tied to the "notion of human beings as moral creatures with obligations to God as well as to each other" (Alatas 2005, 212). Such ideals that regulate the conduct and content of economic transactions trace back to Islam's founding in the seventh century (Aggarwal and Yousef 2000, 95).

The Islamic foundations for piety begin in the Qur'an and continue in the *hadiths* (Kuran 2001, 845). At the personal, pietistic level, the goal is to model one's life after Muhammad's. At the societal level, it is to ensure the justice and righteousness of the *ummah* (Islamic community). Philosophically, Islam's idea of development can be seen in four concepts (Alatas 2005, 212):

1. *Tawhid*—the principle of God's unity, which establishes the nature of the relationship between God and man, as well as that between men.[4]
2. *Rububiyyah*—the belief that it is God who determines the sustenance and nourishment of man and it is he who will guide believers to success. It follows that successful development is a result of human work as well as the workings of the divine order.
3. *Khilafah*—the concept of people as God's vice-regents on earth. This defines humans as trustees of God's resources on earth.
4. *Tazkiyah*—the growth and purification of humankind in terms of their relationship with God, their fellow human beings, and the natural environment.

---

4   Because of this unity, Muslims believe people should no longer be selfish. They have to "consider the consumption and production behaviors of others in society." This concept thus finds unacceptable a basic assumption of neoclassical utility theory, that utility functions are independent (Alhabshi 1994, 210).

The sum of these foundational principles results in *falah*—prosperity in this world and in the hereafter. *Tazkiyah* especially "encompasses the spiritual, moral and material aspects of development, and the ultimate aim is to maximize welfare both in this life and in the hereafter" (Alatas 2005, 212). At the practical level, the organization and functioning of the economy are also guided by three economic principles (213):

1. In the principle of double ownership, neither private property nor public or state ownership are fundamental principles of the Islamic economy. Both forms of ownership are acceptable in Islam, but only in their respective areas of the economy.
2. Limited economic freedom: economic activities must take place within the boundaries of both self-imposed and socially enforced Islamic normative order.
3. Social justice: the redistribution of natural and created wealth based on the notion of mutual responsibility and equity.

Arising from these economic principles are some policy goals, all of which would be broadly under the rubric of Islam's philosophy of development (Alatas 2005, 213):

1. Human resource development must be focused on developing the right attitudes, aspirations, character, personality, physical and moral well-being, and efficiency.
2. Production and consumption must be restricted to those goods and services that are deemed useful for people in the value system of Islam.
3. Efforts to improve the quality of life should emphasize employment creation, the institutionalization of *zakat* (Islamic almsgiving), equitable distribution of income and wealth through tax policies, charity, inheritance laws, usury prohibition, etc.
4. Development should take into account regional and sectoral inequalities to achieve balanced development for the Muslim world.

5. Technology should be indigenized in harmony with the goals and aspirations of the ummah without serious social disruption of the Muslim society.
6. Economic dependency on the non-Muslim world should be reduced, and there should be integration within the ummah.

The goal of an Islamic economic system is the "attainment of rapid economic growth, maintenance of overall stability, equitable distribution of income and wealth, savings mobilization for further investments and hence further growth" (Alhabshi 1994, 207). When Muslims make economic decisions, they touch four distinct areas: consumption, production, sources of income or funds, and performing religious rituals (222). Generally Muslims are very particular about consuming only lawful items. Thus an examination of Muslim interactions with the economy would focus on the last three.

Muslims already had in place successful financial management practices that built, sustained, and perpetuated the Ottoman Empire in the Middle Ages. However, by the nineteenth century many of its financial methods strained to adapt to the coming of modernity. By the twentieth century, the empire collapsed as vast portions of it came under Western domination. Subsequently many Muslim economies became dependent on Western capital and technology as most of them accumulated large foreign debts (Khan 1998, 7). Globalization has deepened the crisis in Islam, producing divergent responses (Moten 2005; Muzaffar 1998). Some believe that the problem of underdevelopment in the Muslim world cannot be resolved through the usual Western approach; many economists believe that the problems are actually inherent in capitalism itself (Khan 1998, 9). Some Muslim solutions to the problems have been expressed through "philanthropy, either at the individual level (giving money to the poor) or at the community level (building mosques, hospitals and schools)" (Moten 2005, 246). At the macro-level, some states have integrated more Islamic law (i.e., shariah) into their legislation or pushed for economic or political empowerment on the world stage (247–49). In the following table, a

Muslim outlines the fundamental difference between the Western and Islamic worldviews on the goals and strategy of development (Khan 1998, 9–11).

TABLE 3.1
Western and Islamic worldviews

	WESTERN WORLDVIEW	ISLAMIC WORLDVIEW
SOCIAL PHILOSOPHY	• Secularism, liberalism, materialism • Moral values are divorced from political and economic sphere of society • Absolute human freedom to pursue material gains	• Belief and submission to God (i.e., *tawhid*—man serves God; *sunna*—Muhammad is the model; material gains must lead to sharing and justice) • Spiritual/moral journey in living with material realities
EDUCATION	• Raise human productivity • Higher income produces better living • Money is the source of happiness	• Moral factor in development • Social and economic justice
ECONOMICS	• Enlightened self-interest and capitalism • Permit free markets to maximize personal gain	• Material and spiritual well-being in cooperation • Exhort people to cooperate between markets and people • Sacrifice for the common cause

With respect to Islamic *economics,* in the classical Islamic tradition there were discussions and works on economic institutions and practices in the Muslim world. However, the notion of an Islamic science of economics and a specifically Islamic economy did not exist. Islamic economics is therefore a modern creation.

It emerged as a result of dissatisfaction with capitalist and socialist models and theories of development…. Interest in Islamic economics predates the rise of the modern Islamic states[,] rejects the ideology of "catching up" with the West and is committed to discerning the nature and ethos of economic development from an Islamic point of view. (Alatas 2005, 214)

Thus the "Islamic economic critique of development studies is not directed only at modernization theory but more generally at the entire body of modernist development thought encompassing perspectives from the left to the right" (215). Muzaffar (1998) comments that

money … which for ages has been a medium of exchange, is now a commodity for profit … [and is] a damning indictment of globalisation itself. [It] has also popularized a consumer culture in every nook and cranny of the planet … which thrives upon the incessant stimulation of material wants. (184)

Islam thus proposes a "different outlook on life and the nature of social change known as Islamic economics" (ibid.). The following pages explain this difference.

ZAKAT AND SADAQA: PIETY OF THE MUSLIM AND ISLAMIC STATE IN CHARITY

Zakat, or alms tax, is one of the five pillars of Islam. It is the religious duty to give up a fixed proportion of one's wealth for specified good causes, and is sometimes synonymous with *sadaqa* (the latter meaning a "freewill offering") (Rippin 2006, 111). It is closely linked to prayer and believed "to purify both givers and the wealth which they give" (Benthall 1999, 27). It is a kind of "financial worship," and without its observance the efficacy of prayer is negated (29). However, there are "no penalties set out in the Quran or the *sunna* to enforce payment or impose penalties on defaulters" (33). Thus gradual reliance has come to be placed on the believer's private sense of responsibility and fear of God. It is also justified by sura 2:27: "Those who break Allah's covenant after it is ratified, and who sunder what Allah has ordered to be joined and do mischief on earth: these cause loss (only) to themselves." (All Qur'anic citations are from Yusuf Ali's translation.)

Zakat derives from the verb *zaka*, which means "to purify," with connotations of growth or increase. The understood meaning is that by "giving up a portion of one's wealth, one purifies that portion which remains, and also oneself, through a restraint on one's greed and imperviousness to others' sufferings. The recipient likewise is purified from jealousy and hatred of the well-off" (Benthall 1999, 29). Thus the action of almsgiving has a moral function as well as a practical one in fulfilling people's needs.

The Qur'an is silent as to what to give and when to give it (Rippin 2006, 111). Sura 2:219 notes that "[you] are to spend ... what is beyond your needs," and sura 3:92 says, "By no means shall ye attain righteousness until ye give (freely) of that which ye have." However, it is more specific on the intended recipients: "Zakah is for the poor and the needy and those employed to administer the (funds), for those whose hearts have been (recently) reconciled (to the truth); for those in bondage and in debt; in the cause of Allah; and for the wayfarer: (Thus is it) ordained by Allah" (sura 9:60).

At its core, zakat is intended to level the socioeconomic circumstances of the ummah by spreading the wealth to all. On this point, sura 2:168; 41:10; and 59:7 ("In order that [wealth] may not (merely) make a circuit between the wealthy and you") imply that "growth must be simultaneously accompanied by distribution ... otherwise inequality will definitely set in" (Alhabshi 1994, 215). In addition, Islam condemns "ostentatious consumption and extols the virtues of voluntary giving" (218). Taken as a whole, it implies "equitable distribution and not equal distribution" (216). Also, "extravagance and waste are also frowned upon by Islam" in sura 7:31 (210). The Qur'an does speak positively of economics in Islam (e.g., in sura 2:201; 4:29; 28:77; 62:9,10) and of institutions as being responsible for regulating the interplay of market forces. But aspects of that distribution are to be undertaken deliberately and not left to the market mechanism alone (216).

Still, Islam does "not repudiate profits if profits are linked to genuine entrepreneurial effort" (Muzaffar 1998, 187). Throughout the Qur'an, the general emphasis is on helping the poor, orphans, and widows, and suggests that all such payments should be made discreetly (Rippin 2006, 111). It is "designed to increase the consumption of low income people in Muslim society through transfer payments" (Khan 1998, 13). Those who collect and administer the funds deserve a portion of it too, including charitable institutions (Benthall 1999, 31). Helping "those whose hearts have been (recently) reconciled" is interpreted as "helping those recently or about to be converted, and mollifying powerful non-Muslims whom the state fears, as an act of prudent politics" (30). "Those in bondage" likely means Muslims captured by enemies needing to be ransomed, and those "in the cause of Allah" are the ones "teaching or fighting or in other duties assigned to them in God's cause," which may include missionary education and Muslim apologetics (31). It is also often stated that zakat recipients must be Muslims, but this view is now infrequently held. For example, a British Muslim agency, Islamic Relief, extends zakat funds to non-Muslims in Africa. However, an opposing British Islamic group, Muslim Aid, serves only its fellow adherents (ibid.).

Traditionally, zakat is 2.5 percent of one's assets per year, but there are different proportions for different kinds of wealth (Benthall 1999, 29). The zakat discussed here is that of the Sunni Muslims. Benthall writes that another sect, the Shi'a, has a different religious tax known as *khoms* (one-fifth) that is levied annually on net income and wealth paid to Shi'a *ulamas* (scholars),[5] allowing them (unlike their Sunni counterparts) to remain independent of the state (1999, 39). It was up to the jurists of later centuries to develop a precise system of donation and payment, a development seen in the hadiths (Rippin 2006, 111).

---

5   In theory, half of it should go to the *sayids* (direct descendants of the Prophet) and the needy, and the other half to the leading Shi'a clergy, but in practice Shi'as often send the entire *khoms* to a chosen, trusted cleric for the funding of seminaries, mosques, hospitals, teachers' and students' salaries, poverty relief, etc. (Benthall 1999, 29). The Islamic Republic of Iran has tried to claim the right to both khoms and zakat, so far without success.

Within the developed schools of law, some general figures emerged for certain items. For example, crops of the field, grapes, and dates are liable to zakat on each crop, stipulated as 10 percent of the crop and paid at harvest time. Camels, oxen, and other small domestic animals that are freely grazing are also liable, the amount paid being a portion of the excess over certain stipulated amounts. Of gold, silver, and merchandise, 2.5 percent of the amount held each year is also payable. The amount is payable directly to the recipient, but it is also preferred that the tax be paid to the authorities in charge of its distribution (ibid., 112).

Muslims below a certain threshold did not have to pay zakat. However, there was an "annual requirement on everyone to pay a small *zakat al-fitr* or *fitrah* to the needy at the end of Ramadan" (Rippin 2006, 29). This is because during Ramadan the "exercise of fasting is supposed to remind believers of what it would be like to be poor and hungry and they are called on to be more than usually generous" (ibid.). A significant motivation for almsgiving during this time was that it was "70 times more meritorious than at other times of the year" (Benthall 1999, 29).

For the Muslim, zakat goes beyond personal charity to the fulfillment of obligations to their society and state. Historically the collection method has varied, from being state mandated (in Pakistan or Sudan) to being based on the individual's private conscience (as in Morocco or Oman). Some are in between; in Malaysia, the Islamic banks can collect zakat and redistribute it to orphans, widows, the poor, educational institutions, etc. Benthall (1999) also notes that around Ramadan in Saudi Arabia, individuals and private institutions are officially invited (but in effect required) to contribute zakat funds in place of tax (39). Having said all this, however, in reality zakat was hard to collect in times of high taxation. Whether "the tax was a voluntary one or required contribution to the state frequently reflected the conditions at the time in terms of the state's prosperity" (Rippin 2006, 112). At various times Muslim authorities pushed for the Islamic ideal of voluntary payment of taxes under the term *zakat*. But programs could quickly crumble under the impact of lost revenue (ibid.). At times Islamic authorities could offset this loss by the imposition of the *jizya* (a poll or head tax on subjugated Jewish and Christian minorities); the jizya is based on sura 9:29, and its imposition did reduce some Jewish and Christian communities to extreme poverty (Riddell and Cotterell 2003, 90). It could be levied at an amount higher than the zakat (93), and provided an incentive for non-Muslims to convert to Islam in addition to restoring their lost social status as minorities in a Muslim-dominant setting. Ironically, since the jizya brought in a considerable amount of money to the Islamic authorities, they actively discouraged mass conversions to Islam, though individual conversions were always accepted (73).

In summary, the administration of the zakat has been context dependent, and its ideology has to some extent served the benefactor's interest through blends of religious, political, and welfarist activism, "delivering effective welfare and relief services in certain contexts where the state has been unable or unwilling to provide them" (Benthall 1999, 28). In places where zakat has become part of the state's taxation system, a measure of official corruption can be found (31). However, there have been times when zakat has been completely marginalized due to the lack of a single Islamic state practicing it correctly (i.e., as a system of automatic redistribution).[6]

WAQF: MUSLIM TRUSTS AND THE FINANCING OF THE ISLAMIC EMPIRE

Every society must grapple with the challenge of providing "public goods" (Kuran 2001, 841). In Islam, a popular vehicle for the provision of such goods was the *waqf*, an "Islamic trust" or "pious foundation" (842). According to Kuran, a waqf is an "unincorporated trust established under Islamic law by a living man or woman for the

6   Two examples bear mentioning: (1) When the Asian tsunami killed thousands of Muslims and destroyed vast swaths of property in Muslim areas such as Indonesia, fellow Muslim nations were criticized by their ummah for their slowness of response, the chief culprit being Saudi Arabia. (2) Even the proposal by Crown Prince Hassan of Jordan for an international zakat system whereby the richer Muslim states would help poor Muslims remained on the table and was not taken up by Jordan's richer neighbors (Benthall 1999, 36).

provision of a designated social service in perpetuity. Its activities are financed by revenue-bearing assets that have been rendered forever inalienable" (842).

The waqf is also "an endowment set apart for a charitable or religious purpose" (Shatzmiller 2001, 46). It is considered an expression of piety in that it is "governed by a law considered sacred, not that its activities are inherently religious or that its benefits must be confined to Muslims" (Kuran 2001, 842). The waqf system enabled founders of public projects to earn a return on their investments. For example, in the Islamic Middle East, an individual who converted personal property into a lighthouse was able to shelter some if not all of his remaining wealth from confiscation. Usually this person would also avoid various taxes, acquire testamentary powers, and earn social status along with the satisfaction of having performed a pious service.

In history, the early waqfs had booty and conquered land set aside permanently for the benefit of Muslims (Kuran 2001, 844).[7] Though the Qur'an does not mention waqf institutions nor their legal parameters, from the eighth century onward some dozen Qur'anic passages "have been interpreted as instructing believers to establish foundations serving religious or charitable purposes" (844–45). Among the passages are sura 34:39 ("Whatsoever ye spend for good, He replaceth it") and 58:12 ("O ye who believe! When ye hold conference with the messenger, offer alms before your conference"). At some point after the early decades of the waqf, privately endowed organizations began providing services with the support of money provided by the Islamic state from either property or non-Muslim poll taxes (i.e., jizya), or from taxes collected under the rubric of zakat (Kuran 2001, 845). With the expansion of Islam, the waqf was increasingly used to shelter immovable wealth gained from conquered lands (Shatzmiller 2001, 49) or from taxation and confiscation (Kuran 2001, 846).

In order to establish a waqf under the protection of Islamic law, the founder had to be a Muslim and the act of establishment had to be

---

7   Islamic law also provides for a land tax (*kharaj*), though due to space limitations I will not treat this here.

registered with the shariah court. Under certain circumstances, waqfs could be established by non-Muslims as well. However, any regulations that were adopted would only apply this privilege of wealth protection to Muslims, since it would have amounted to providing benefits to subjugated outsiders and would have dissipated the state's tax base in regions where non-Muslims constituted the majority (Kuran 2001, 851–52). There was, however, no legal barrier to including non-Muslims among the beneficiaries,[8] or to the founder of the waqf also doubling as the manager of it (852, 861). Designated beneficiaries, however, were to be free from adultery, drunkenness, gambling, or dealing in interest, failing which their entitlements would become null and void (852n16).

The rules for establishing a waqf required the endowment to consist solely of immovables and the property itself to be available forever to the designated mission (Kuran 2001, 852). Though the waqf provided advantages to the founder, the land or buildings owners would have also been beneficiaries. Because the waqf was sacred, rulers were loath to confiscate it lest they be perceived as impious (847). During one period, when Arabia was still the seat of power, "analogous privileges were obtained by owners of easily concealed and movable wealth ... held in the form of currency and precious metals to become exempt from *zakat*" (846). A waqf could have been attached to a mosque, but often it was established and administered by people outside the religious establishment (848). However, there was nothing to keep its founder from appointing himself as its first administrator and drawing a hefty salary for his services. In the modern Islamic world, the waqf is a corporation—an "internally autonomous organization that the courts treat as a legal person" (866).

Though the waqf served as a device to enhance material security, it also supplied public goods in a decentralized manner. From a waqf founder's perspective, these two functions conflicted, since wealth

---

8   At one point an Islamic court in Ottoman Jerusalem even "allowed a *waqf* to use its facilities to house monks" and permitted the tenants to recite the New Testament while on the premises (Kuran 2001, 852).

provided for public services was lost to the founder's personal use. Over time the waqf became a "defining feature of Islamic civilization [and] a source of cross-civilizational emulation [with] indications that it influenced the development of unincorporated trusts in Western Europe much later" (Kuran 2001, 848).[9]

The waqfs financed the expansion of the Islamic civilization along with the provision and maintenance of its public goods and facilities. They ranged from soup kitchens to hostels, shops, water municipal systems, pensions, agricultural projects, *madrassas*, orchards, and animals (e.g., endowing a cow to provide milk for the poor) (Shatzmiller 2001, 47n12, 51). In this way these "worldly *waqfs*" transferred income from politically and militarily dominant Muslims to Christians and Jews as well (Kuran 2001, 852).

In medieval Islam, the rich commonly set aside a portion of their wealth to draw near to God and secure for their souls a place in heaven (Kuran 2001, 853). Thus Muslim piety in the form of a desire to do good works added to the immensity of the waqf system.[10] When a waqf was established, the *mutawallis* (managers or trustees) or successors (who were appointed by the founder) would hire employees to

9   According to Shatzmiller, "Unlike the medieval European state, the Islamic state enjoyed very early ... under the Abbasids ... a well developed, sophisticated administration, especially in fiscal matters such as tax collection.... However, it neither endorsed nor developed a policy of financing municipal services such as primary education, health or religious services, including mosques. This task was left in the hands of individuals" (2001, 60).

10 It also included "donations to the sanctuaries of Mecca and Medina—the Islamic equivalent of sending money to the Holy See" (Kuran 2001, 853). Governments also used the waqf system to woo chosen constituencies by the extension of patronage, while the donor could be driven by a desire to spread an ideology by funding a university, an ideological program, or appointing loyal teachers to their cause. Although the three main motives were piety, position (i.e., status), or politics, for some the main motive was to shelter wealth. Ironically, the Muslim waqf was a defense against greedy rulers who justified their confiscation by invoking the Islamic principle that all property belonged to God. Another motive was "asset laundering," where state officials who took over properties belonging to the government or to other individuals would transfer them into waqfs to legitimize their confiscations (854–55). All these diverse motives gave rise to a distinction between the *waqf khayri* (charitable waqf), which serviced the public good, and the *waqf ahli* (family waqf), which bestowed the main benefits on their own kin.

execute the wishes of the founder per the stipulations for the beneficiaries. The appointments and activities of the managers were overseen by a local judge (*qadi*). In principle, the waqf system had five actors: founders, managers, employees, beneficiaries, and judges (861). In practice, the state served as the critical sixth player if it had vested interests in the matter. However, depending on the Islamic schools of law, the administration and execution of the waqfs varied (871).[11]

Towards the second half of the nineteenth century, giant cities of the Middle East began to establish municipalities in lieu of waqfs to deliver urban services in a centralized and coordinated manner. Several factors led to this change. The need to follow the founder's stipulations to the letter made the system inflexible in keeping up with rapidly changing economic conditions (Kuran 2001, 842–43). For example, the stipulation of fixed amounts (instead of percentages) to be endowed became problematic when market conditions changed and the decline in revenue directly affected the payouts to the beneficiaries, creating a dilemma concerning the division of the actual amounts between them (Shatzmiller 2001, 63). Another problem was the endowment of property that the waqf could not rehabilitate for other purposes when it could no longer serve its original intended purpose. In these ways, rather than being the promoter of social and economic integration, the distresses tore into the social fabric and pitted members of the community against each other (67–68). As an unintended consequence, generations of waqf officials had to make changes in the rules through questionable legal means. This weakened the respect for law, made the managers look for loopholes in the system, fostered a culture of

---

11   Under the Maliki school (one of the interpretive traditions of Islam), previous owners were forced to sever links to their own property once it was endowed. In the Hanafi or Shafii schools, the practice was not to oppose or prevent the donor himself or a member of the endowing family from becoming de facto manager of the endowed properties (Shatzmiller 2001, 57). In eleventh-century Iran, the *qadi* (judge) had the power to intervene and make changes to the waqf, and the fact that he was in the government's service could be taken as a sign of the state's involvement in the operation of the waqf. But in the Islamic West, the *qadis* resisted acting on behalf of the state in any intervention of the waqf (61). In the East the Hanafi *qadis* and managers could also effect changes to the waqfs, while elsewhere they could not (69).

corruption, and ultimately legitimized lawbreaking (Kuran 2001, 844, 883–85). The most frequently encountered problem in waqfs was the free riders. There were three kinds of people: those who benefitted from the public good without contributing to its maintenance, those who took too large a share from the public-good benefits, and those who appropriated public-good property for their exclusive use. An example is teachers who used mosques as public domain, thus saving themselves the cost of private rentals (Shatzmiller 2001, 52–53).

Eventually, due to this situation, the modernizing Middle East states chose to nationalize vast properties belonging to waqfs. Only when economic Westernization began did the waqf system respond by adopting its own modern features, such as (1) establishing its right to be sued as a legal entity rather than having a *mutawalli* represent it before the courts as an individual plaintiff or defendant, and (2) providing oversight by a board of mutawallis endowed with powers similar to those of a corporate board (Kuran 2001, 843).

Some family waqfs neglected the public good and enticed envy in the local population, inducing Muslim governments to seize waqfs for public use (Kuran 2001, 887). The final blow came when the colonial powers arrived. Western interest in freeing vast sums of money tied up in waqfs provided an incentive to discredit the system, enact new laws usurping the waqfs, and reshape some of their form and function (Powers 1993, 29).[12] In the end, the inflexibility and static nature of the traditional system were the seeds of its downfall (Shatzmiller 2001, 45).

---

12 When the French colonized parts of Africa, their jurists concluded that property rights were a "grey area in Islamic law and that there was a basic contradiction between the inheritance system and *waqf* making which needed to be solved if lands were to be rescued from eternal immobilization" (Shatzmiller 2001, 49). This is because the French jurists "questioned whether Islamic law possessed property rights at all since ownership of the land was reported, in theory and in practice, to be in the hands of the state, and only the right to its cultivation and building on it, lay in the hands of the individuals" (ibid.). By this token, then, the colonial powers easily expropriated the same lands by exercising state power that later came under their control to rescue it from becoming waqf. Perhaps this outlook might explain why many Middle East Islamic governments (e.g., Egypt, Syria, Jordan, Iran) still view the socialist system as more amenable to the local economy and continue resisting Western capitalism.

At present waqfs are treated as juristic persons.[13] They may be formed by pooling the resources of thousands of small contributors, and their founders may be governments and firms. The assets that support their activities may consist partly or even entirely of movables such as cash and stocks. Their operations may be overseen by mutawalli boards rather than by mutawallis exercising responsibilities on their own as individuals. Mutawallis have broader powers than in the past to alter investment and spending. Because private property rights are much more secure than in the past, the "waqf system is no longer seen as the most reliable vehicle for sheltering wealth.... This system is no longer expected to be the primary supplier of public goods [as they] are being supplied mainly ... by government agencies" (Kuran 2001, 890).

ISLAMIC BANKING AND INTEREST-FREE FINANCING

Today there exist over 160 Islamic banks in the world (Sufian 2007, 174). Malaysia is often cited as the pioneering example of Islamic banking, though Pakistan, Iran, and Sudan actually established them first in the 1970s. Malaysia is, however, the pioneer in innovating instruments that arise from the subset of Islamic banking, such as *takaful* (Islamic insurance) and having a dual system of banking (Mokhtar et al. 2008, 29). It now attracts many Middle East Muslims to study Malaysia's experience. Historically Islamic banking was born of the private initiatives of Muslim revivalists in countries such as Egypt, Pakistan, and Sudan (Aggarwal and Yousef 2000, 94) who began experimenting in the 1960s, often meeting opposition from secularist regimes (Trofimov 2007). In the last fifteen years, though, Malaysia and Saudi Arabia have joined the ranks of these other countries. In the United States, the first Islamic bank appeared in Chicago in 2005 (Rodkin 2005). The banks reflect a Muslim sense that Western capitalism has failed to address economic issues affecting the ummah such as (1) the

---

13   In reference to waqfs in Egypt, Morocco, Iran, and Turkey (Kuran 2001, 890).

modern banking system's distrust of low-income earners' ability to possess sufficient credit or repay loans and (2) Islam's rejection of, and challenge to, the premise that *riba* (interest-bearing transactions) are the basis for profit and service.

The Islamic prohibition of interest, or riba,[14] which is any "predetermined or fixed return in financial transactions" (Aggarwal and Yousef 2000, 96), is found in the Qur'an in sura 3:130 ("O ye who believe! Devour not usury, doubled and multiplied") and sura 2:275 ("Allah permits trade and forbids riba"). Alhabshi (1994, 219) comments that the prohibition of riba, particularly the *riba an nasi'ah*, used to be practiced during the pre-Islamic days when a person who took a loan agreed to pay up within around three months. If the loan recipient paid up, there would be no charge on the loan. However, if the recipient failed to pay up at the end of the three months, he or she could negotiate to postpone payment at an agreed-upon rate of interest. This kind of loan is still considered riba.

In modern times, the Qur'anic injunction against interest in commercial transactions is significant for pious Muslims. Some have stayed renters, unable to own homes due to the herculean effort required to raise large amounts of cash to buy a home without using home-loan programs. Others use credit cards to secure hotel reservations and conduct other business but diligently pay off the balance each month, eliminating interest charges. However, in spite of sura 3:130, most Muslims use standard interest-bearing transactions (Rodkin 2005). One may classify three groups of Muslims who differ in how they approach economic decisions within Islam (Alhabshi 1994, 221): (1) Strict followers involved in lawful activities, particularly in consumption and production. They will avoid indulging in transactions that involve interest, gambling, and other unlawful activities. They number in the minority. (2) Those who do not adhere to Islam in their economic decisions except that they probably avoid consuming unlawful food. They also number in the minority, but are bigger than the previous

---

14   See also Yusuf Ali's comment on sura 30:39 on the definition of riba.

group. (3) Those who abide by most Islamic dictates as far as their consumption goes, but not entirely by the dictates concerning lawfully earned incomes (i.e., the restriction on income earned with interest). They may avoid being involved in directly producing unlawful items like liquor but still be involved in financing their production from interest-bearing sources of funds. They are the largest group.

   Despite the fact that it had plagued them in their daily lives, Muslim scholars only began examining the problem of interest-based financing about fifty years ago (Alhabshi 1994, 222). For most of Islamic history, the Qur'anic injunction again riba had gone unfulfilled. While the stricture against borrowing with interest goes back centuries (Aggarwal and Yousef 2000, 97), the desire among Muslims to avoid interest has developed "since the revolutions and religious resurgence of the 1970s.... The premise is that Western-style financing is not acceptable anymore" (Rodkin 2005). This dissatisfaction may include practical skepticism about the exploitative nature of the banking services they receive, personal reasons for viewing banks as unethical, or religious reasons that consider interest-based banking to be sinful. While the ban on interest has been ignored by many secular Muslims, some say this ban has in fact denied the benefits of modern banking to strict believers and contributed to the Muslim world's relative decline after interest-based bonds and loans powered the West's Industrial Revolution (Trofimov 2007).

   As the main alternative to interest-based financing, Islamic banking developed finance instruments based on profit-and-loss sharing (PLS) and the price markup (see table 3.2). The former is universally accepted in Islamic law and economics, as "the bank may earn a return on invested funds provided that the bank shares in the risk of the investment and bears a loss if the project fails," while the acceptability of the latter is disputed because it can "imply a fixed return on investment for the bank" (Aggarwal and Yousef 2000, 96). Legally, the "fear is that the markup financing may open a back door to interest" (97).

TABLE 3. 2

Islamic finance instruments

PROFIT-AND-LOSS SHARING (PLS) PRINCIPLE	PRICE MARKUP PRINCIPLE
Mudarabah (profit-sharing) financing: Bank provides capital and entrepreneur contributes effort and exercises complete control over the business venture. In case of loss, bank earns no or negative return on its investment. In case of gain, returns are split to a negotiated equity percentage. It is akin to a limited partnership.	*Murabaha* (cost-plus) financing: Bank purchases an asset on behalf of an entrepreneur and resells the asset to the entrepreneur at a predetermined price that covers the original cost and an added, negotiated profit margin. Payment is made in lump sum or in installments. Ownership resides with the bank until all payments are made.
Musharaka (profit-and-loss) financing: Entrepreneur and bank jointly supply capital and manage the project. Losses are borne according to the contributions of capital, while profit proportions are negotiated freely. Its close cousin is a traditional equity stake with rights or control.	*Ijara* (lease) financing: Bank purchases an asset and allows the entrepreneur to use it for a fixed charge. Ownership of asset either remains with bank or is gradually transferred to entrepreneur in rent-to-own contract. In the West, this is also known as leasing.

There are four types of alternatives to interest-financing: investment-based, sale-based, rent-based, and service-based (Sufian 2007, 175). Profit-sharing, leasing, and trading are all "permissible in Islam because they involve entrepreneurial work rather than simply money-lending" (Trofimov 2007).

The ethos of PLS is that the "relationship between borrower, lender and intermediary are rooted in financial trust and partnership" (Sufian 2007, 175). In terms of economic rationales for the superiority of PLS over the use of interest, Aggarwal and Yousef (2000, 97–98) cite five reasons: (1) The return on capital will depend on productivity, as the allocation of investable funds will be guided by the soundness of the project, thereby improving the efficiency of capital allocation. (2) The creation of money by expanding credit will be created only when there is a strong likelihood of a corresponding increase in the supply of goods and services. Thus, in the PLS, the supply of money is not allowed to overstep the supply of goods and services, eventually curbing inflationary pressures in the economy. (3) The shift to profit sharing may increase the volume of investments that translate into job creation, as the interest mechanism makes feasible only those projects whose expected profits are sufficiently high to cover the interest rate plus added income. (4) The new system will ensure more equitable distribution of wealth and will bring more wealth to its owners only when its use has actually resulted in the creation of additional wealth. (5) The abolition of interest will curtail speculation.[15] Aggarwal and Yousef (2000, 97) observe that while there is a formal equivalence between

> markup financing and debt … the equivalence is not based on the payment of interest … as the salient feature of debt is that it transfers control of an asset to the debtholder in cases of default …[,] while in markup contracts … the bank retains ownership of the asset and can seize it in cases of default.

In markup contracts, the bank acts as a trader and not a lender who would buy the asset to sell back to the customer (Prystay 2002). Such contracts may be called debt contracts, as they "have the critical feature [ascribed] to debt: default on a payment triggers a shift in control over the asset from the entrepreneur to the bank" (Aggarwal and Yousef 2000, 108).[16] Salman Ibrahim, an Islamic scholar who sits on the panel of the first Islamic interest-free home-buying program in the United States, notes the following: "From a financial standpoint there may not be much difference, but what matters is the way you

---

15   Interestingly, the authors later proceed to critique the arguments to show that many of its rationales are untenable, and that most Islamic banks rely more heavily on markup financing than on PLS financing in Islamic countries such as Egypt, Jordan, Iran, Pakistan, and Malaysia (Aggarwal and Yousef 2000, 98–106), since "the principal shortcoming of Islamic economics is that it does not properly account for the impact of economic incentives [in that] religious norms are unlikely to change human behavior when fundamental economic considerations such as wealth maximization are present" (118–19).

16   For a discussion of how Muslims see alternatives to Western accounting methods, see Shanmugam, Perumal, and Ridzwa 2005.

conduct the transactions.... The taste of a chicken does not change whether it is *zabiah* [slaughtered according to Islamic principles] or non-*zabiah;* what changes is the way you slaughter it" (Rodkin 2005). Lest Christians dismiss this, one could argue a familiar example: referring to Christmas presents as "presents" rather than "items"—the items are the same, but what matters is the way in which they were given.

However one decides the matter, Aggarwal and Yousef (2000, 97) note that one benefit of markup contracts relative to standard Western debt contracts is that, in cases of default, there is no ambiguity about control of assets. The bank retains title to the asset until all payments are made. In most Western countries, default triggers bankruptcy proceedings, during which the entrepreneur/manager continues to control the assets (e.g., Chapter 11 of US bankruptcy law). Because of the delay induced by formal bankruptcy proceedings in the shift in control over the assets, bargaining problems are introduced that can significantly decrease the efficiency of investment. In principle, these problems are avoided under Islamic markup contracts (ibid.).

While the calculation for how much an interest-bearing loan will cost in *x* years and the translation of that calculation into a markup keeps the Islamic purchase "clean," it creates three dilemmas for the buyer and the bank (Rodkin 2005): (1) If getting a home in a way that adheres to one's religious principles means shelling out a prohibitive additional sum, customers will feel that the cost is too high and keep renting. Thus an Islamic bank tries to ensure that this fee is minimal, just enough to cover the cost of processing two deeds (one for the sale to the bank, the second for the sale to the buyer) instead of just one. (2) Few people buy a house with a fifteen- or thirty-year loan and stick around for that whole term. With an interest-bearing loan, it is unproblematic. Sell the house, settle the debt still owed to the bank, and walk away with the remainder. But because a buyer using an Islamic purchase plan is not paying interest, how much debt is left if one sells before the term is up? (3) Every year at tax time, millions of American homeowners cash in on their most lucrative tax break, the deduction for mortgage interest they have paid. Because it amounts to thousands of dollars for most people, it is a major factor in what makes a home affordable. The essential problem for buyers in Islamic programs is that, to comply with mortgage regulations, the bank is required to report the amount buyers paid that would have been interest in a standard loan. Should the buyer take advantage of that deduction, then, or stand on principle and refuse the deduction because it is premised on paying interest?

Because of the great demand for Islamic banks to provide religiously acceptable services for Muslim customers, each of these dilemmas gets resolved with varying degrees of effectiveness.[17] As Muslim international ambitions have grown in the area of Islamic banking, Islamic states have set up a base in Malaysia to form an Islamic Financial Services Board to establish global standards for Islamic banking (Prystay 2002).

In addition to PLS and markup financing, Islamic banks are encouraged to make *Qard Hassan* loans—social or charitable loans to individuals and organizations that need funds or real assets (materials, supplies, etc.) (Aggarwal and Yousef 2000, 99). With respect to the simple savings account, the return on these accounts technically comes from a profit-sharing contract with the bank. To mitigate big fluctuations if a bank posts a loss of higher-than-expected profits, Malaysian banks, for example, use a "special profit reserve that allows them to keep these payouts relatively steady and similar to conventional interest rates" (Trofimov 2007).

The following are other important features in establishing an Islamic bank: (1) The formation of a shariah board that is usually made up of three to five Islamic authorities who vet the bank's documentation and certify that products comply with Islamic law (Pope 2005).[18]

---

17   For further discussion, see Rodkin 2005.

18   Each institution has its own shariah board. Thus shariah compliance is effectively privatized, and rather than being a matter of national law, each shariah board passes its own *fatwas* (religious rulings), which further extends choice in the marketplace for religious ideas (Wilson 2007). Because each Islamic bank keeps its own payroll of advisers on shariah law, some banks disagree as to the degree of shariah compliance each instrument adheres to, and they end up competing against one another for theological purity (Trofimov 2007). However, so accepted has the notion of Islamic financing been in the West that even the *Wall Street Journal* now retains at least five Islamic scholars to consult on its indexes of shariah-compliant companies (Slater 2007).

If the new contracts are incompatible with shariah principles, they are to pursue a dialogue with the lawyers concerning amendments and redrafts to make it more Islamic (Wilson 2007). (2) When the instruments are approved, this financial instrument or division is run in a way that mimics conventional banking systems but is actually Islamic (Mokhtar, Abdullah, and Alhabshi 2008, 31–32). (3) Ensuring some measure of sufficient startup capital and profitability for the sustainability of the concept (ibid.). (4) Avoiding principles and companies that conduct their business beyond fair and equitable dealings and that are deemed un-Islamic and socially unacceptable (such as businesses that deal with alcohol, gambling, high debt ratios,[19] pork, pornography, and tobacco).[20]

The increased success of Islamic banking has spurred other financial innovations, such as Islamic bonds (*sukuk*) and credit cards, Islamic insurance (*takaful*) and derivatives, banking by cell phone, zakat payments via ATM and credit card, and Islamic cross-currency swap agreements. Space does not permit their full details, but they are summarized below in table 3.3.

---

19 There are different rulings among Muslims on its degree. "High" typically means "one-third of either market capitalization or assets—and thus pays a significant amount of interest" (Slater 2007).

20 Most Muslim investments lie in oil, technology, or health stocks, in which the list of un-Islamic or socially unacceptable items does not apply. In practice, acceptable companies include Microsoft, ExxonMobil, and Pfizer (Pope 2005), though one wonders how Muslims square with Pfizer's chief role in manufacturing abortifacients, which evangelicals oppose. Alhabshi comments that Islam also prohibits "monopolistic hoarding of essential goods (*al ihtikar*), price control by the central authority in contravention with the natural forces of demand and supply, etc." (1994, 214). In light of current practices by many Islamic nations, it is difficult to see how many are conforming to these values.

TABLE 3. 3
Other financial instruments offered in the Islamic banking system

ISLAMIC FINANCIAL INSTRUMENT	NATURE OF THE FINANCIAL INSTRUMENT
Sukuk (Islamic bond)	•Adheres to the shariah's call for ethical and equitable financing and bans speculation (Lane 2006). •De-emphasizes financial speculation (e.g., selling what one does not own). •Unlike conventional bonds where "the lender recoups his investment through the interest paid on the bond, *sukuk* are essentially corporate securities which provide an investor with ownership in an underlying asset, usually based on the balance sheet of the issuing company" (Smith 2007, 43). •Similar to "asset-backed bonds, but instead of a fixed annual interest rate, payouts to investors over the life of the bond are derived from leases, profits or sales of tangible assets such as property, equipment or a joint-venture business" (Lane 2006, C1). •Leases, profits, or sales can be structured to deliver the equivalent of a fixed annual interest rate, yet they technically aren't the forbidden "interest" payment variety (Lane 2006, C1).
Islamic credit card[21]	•Operates like a combination debit/cash-advance card. •To avoid charging credit and also limit the sum that is available to the card owner, the bank may sell a piece of land to the customer at an agreed price or re-purchase the land from the customer at a lower price. •The price difference is the bank's maximum profit (determined in advance), unlike conventional credit cards where interest charged is undetermined and may further increase. •The bank then disburses cash proceeds of the second agreement into the customer's wadiah Bank Islam card account, created and maintained by the bank. •Subsequently, customers may use the card for retail purchases and cash withdrawals like a conventional credit card. However, each transaction is backed by the cash held in the wadiah account. •Annual fees are charged for holding a credit card as well as withdrawal or late fees. •*Qardhul Hassan* is a facility granted for emergencies. It allows cardholders to utilize higher than the available financing limit, subject to approval. This amount is levied with any charges, but the sum eventually has to be settled in full.

21   Example taken from Bank Islam of Malaysia.

ISLAMIC FINANCIAL INSTRUMENT	NATURE OF THE FINANCIAL INSTRUMENT
Takaful (Islamic insurance)	• An insurance system that does not hold conventional interest-yielding bonds where shareholder funds and premiums paid by policy holders cannot be co-mingled, which could result in the former exploiting the latter's misfortune.[28] • As an "alternative to conventional insurance companies, takaful does not deal with the fixed 'no claims bonus' system" but with one based on principles of voluntary contribution, joint protection, and profit-sharing (Haneef 2005, 90). • Akin to Lloyds in the U.K., where private "names" invested in the corporation form a reserve pool of funds ready to insure losses but also benefit from premiums on policies, though no insurance losses are claimed. • The earliest takaful was established c. 900, when Muslim sailors pooled their funds into a premium to support themselves in case of disasters at sea. This early form of marine insurance was later copied by the Spanish and other European traders (Alhabshi 1994, 205).
Islamic derivatives	• Similar to Western financial products but designed by Muslim investment banks to hedge the risk of Islamic debt. • Adherence to shariah prevents Islamic investors from using conventional hedging tools such as interest rate swaps, forwards, or options to offset fluctuations in interest rates and currencies (Lane 2006). • Helps Muslims to overcome obstacles in short-selling—the need to know ownership and control (e.g., if an investor borrowed shares in a company and the same company went bankrupt, who had voting rights?). • Creation of the *arboon* as the down payment that enabled short-sellers to take ownership of the share rather than just borrowing it (Slater 2007).

The breadth and offerings of Islamic financial instruments at present demonstrate that "for the Islamic market to exist in the proper manner, it must have all the relevant products that befit the financial market. For every single conventional product, [Muslims] want to have the equivalent Islamic product" (Lane 2006, C1). So successful has this been that all Islamic banks in Malaysia now offer products and services that range from "savings, current and investment deposit products to financing products such as property financing, working capital financing, project financing, plant and machinery financing, etc." (Sufian 2007, 177).

Generally most Western bankers "view Islamic finance as a curiosity, and perhaps even a business opportunity, but seldom as a threat comparable to that from Muslim extremism" (Wilson 2007). In fact, Islamic banking and finance can be regarded not only as a gentler aspect of Islam, and one that lends itself to dialogue between Westerners and Muslims (ibid.), but also as *financially* appealing to non-Muslims (Smith 2007, 44). Islamic banking has risen as the showcase of the Islamic modernization project and key to Muslim mission—contrasting with the inadequacy of other religions to offer alternatives to Western capitalism but also attracting non-Muslims into the Islamic orbit, a chief example being Malaysia's Islamic banking system.

As a measure of Malaysia's leading status in Islamic finance, PricewaterhouseCoopers, a major global finance auditing firm, has a Malaysian as the global head of its Islamic finance department. Much of what is now considered conventional in the financial industry was pioneered in Malaysia and "often against the objections of conservative clerics in places like Saudi Arabia[, but now] such innovations are … common-place in the Gulf [and] become an important revenue source for Western financial giants." Malaysia is so influential that the importation of such innovations to the Middle East marks a shift in the Muslim world's power balance (Trofimov 2007).

As the attraction of Islamic financing spreads, Muslims are opting to stress the competitiveness of their products compared to conventional banking, leaving their Islamic credentials in the background and targeting ad campaigns to other faiths. For example, Saudi Arabia's Al-Rajhi Bank (which states it is the world's largest Islamic financial institution), had 52 percent of non-Muslim customers in Malaysia in 2007 following a campaign appeal to them (Wright and Yuniar 2007). Malaysia itself is educating and spreading this form of Islamic banking worldwide[22] by sponsoring and inviting outside scholars for a program of shariah dialogue (Trofimov 2007) and by offering a

---

22   This is a part of Malaysia's vision of how Islam can coexist with modernity—
an Islam called "Islam *Hadhari*," or civilizational Islam, which stresses economic
development, scientific progress, and educational innovation as part of its values.
For further details on its foundations, see Badawi 2006.

university degree in Islamic economics at its International Islamic University. In addition, Malaysia funds centers to develop consultancy services, share financial expertise, and disseminate knowledge for the industry's development, especially to the non-Muslim business community (Alhabshi 1994, 224–25). All this is done to show that Islam is "not a hindrance to economic growth and development and that Islam could play a positive role and example of moderate and progressive Islam in a plural setting" (Haneef 2005, 95). By channeling its form of Islamic resurgence along a modernization path that does not focus on Islamic economics per se but on corporate culture and Muslim participation in the global economy, Malaysia has in some measure "de-radicalized the Islamic fervor which has gripped some parts of the Muslim world" (ibid.).

ISLAMIC BANKING AND ECONOMICS AS A MIRROR FOR CHRISTIAN MISSION

For Muslims, issues of money, finance, and economics located in a moral and ethical matrix with theological underpinnings in the Qur'an form a historical and contextual practice that constitutes a "spiritual economy" (Rudnyckyj 2010). Because of this, any witness of Christian mission that touches upon the material and economic aspects of Islam in such contexts must consider what Muslims conceive to be the normative good.

Modernity has not eliminated expressions of religion in society but rather has displaced them to the private sphere (Aupers and Houtman 2010). For the West, the ethos of individualism has combined with a privatizing impulse to produce a faith that is *personalized* and *customized*. In so doing, economic aspects of Christianity such as tithing, benevolence or aid, and funding for church projects have become relocated to the "private" sphere of the church, and church and Christian life have become separated from the public and secular world. However, if Islamic banking and economics can be used as a mirror in which to understand Christian mission and its relationship to the economic dimensions of life, it can open up new spaces to rediscover the practice of mission in more biblically faithful and holistic ways, in both Muslim *and Christian* settings.

Ramadan as a Mirror

The Christian parallel to Ramadan is Lent. Zakat and sadaqa can be compared to the tithe and the freewill offering respectively. In Christianity, Christians generally connect giving and ministering to the poor with Christmas.[23] However, theologically and historically the link between fasting and giving has been just as strong with Lent.

Lent is a forty-day fast that typically begins around February or March and culminates in Good Friday and Easter. Traditionally Lent has encouraged Christians to give up some aspect of their consumptuary life considered to be luxurious or ostentatious. In contemporary contexts, Lent may now involve fasting from media (e.g., TV, Internet) or from purchasing goods (e.g., withholding the buying of nonessentials). For the most part, Lent is only celebrated among churches that are liturgical in orientation or that retain strong historical roots that predate the twentieth century, such as the Anglicans, Lutherans, Methodists, and Presbyterians.

For the vast majority of evangelical Christians in the United States, fasting has been an infrequent practice of their shared ecclesial and community experience in modern times, much less an expression of solidarity and identification with the poor. Yet there are strong theological foundations for associating fasting with caring for the poor in Scripture:

> Is not this the kind of fasting I have chosen: to loose the chains of injustice and untie the cords of the yoke, to set the oppressed free and break every yoke? Is it not to share your food with the hungry and to provide the poor wanderer with shelter—when you see the naked, to clothe them, and not to turn away from your own flesh and blood? (Isa 58:6,7)

---

23 In America the Thanksgiving holiday has also had strong Christian elements that have connected giving and ministering to the poor.

Not many churches have combined Lent with an annual call for congregations to give to the poor. In this respect, churches could consider revisiting the biblical relationship between fasting and the call to care for the poor in ministry and connect this concern to social justice. Recalling these links would highlight the inequalities that exist between the poor and the rich and critically challenge the structures and systems that allow for poverty in the midst of wealth.

For ministry in Muslim contexts, a Christian link between fasting and giving to the poor can become a type of Christian *fitrah* with which Muslims will readily identify as a commendable form of witness. Such a witness testifies to a giving that is not merely individualistic but a communal act of the body, as well as a tangible and public form of love. If Christian ministries around the world such as churches and parachurch organizations serving in Muslim contexts actively practice Lent in solidarity with the poor, it can highlight a powerful point of commonality with Ramadan in a visible, symbolic manner.

An alternative would be to structure an annual giving to people outside the church at the end of the forty days, coinciding with Christ's resurrection, or Easter Sunday. A strong theological justification for this is found in Ephesians 4:8: "When he ascended on high he led a host of captives, and he gave gifts to men" (ESV). In this manner, Easter would become not merely a time of privatized celebration within the walls of the church (which accentuates the secular versus spiritual split in modern societies), but a public demonstration of Christ's gifts to all humanity.[24] While Christmas has enjoyed a strong social, cultural, and ecclesial tradition of giving to the poor, Easter has not shared in this tradition, even though the gift that Christ gives to all in his resurrection provides the most powerful biblical rationale for doing so. If Christians around the world were to give to the poor on Easter, they

---

24 Though not directly related to economic aspects of the faith, as a regular blood bank donor myself, I have wondered about the potential power that might be unleashed for churches around the world by organizing national blood drives on Good Friday. These might be centered on the theme of Christ's blood sacrifice as God's gift to humanity for eternal life, conceptualized and symbolized in terms of the thought, "He gave his blood so that we might have life, now we give ours to you so you may have life."

would share in the suffering of the poor on the most important day of the Christian calendar.

Zakat and Sadaqa as a Mirror

Church tithes primarily serve the functions of the church, which include the salaries of its ministers, building maintenance, and other pertinent ministry programs. However, when Christians become unemployed, they are often left to seek help from the government instead of the church. To their credit, churches connected to denominations and megachurches often have had strong compassion ministries that provide assistance to church members. In addition, churches with lesser capacities have ministered through soup kitchens or charitable donations in kind. However, rarer is the church that disburses funds to assist nonmembers, especially those of another faith. One should ask, if Muslims were historically able to use zakat to give to non-Muslims, what prevents the church from giving similarly today, particularly to Muslims in places where the specter of Christian-Muslim tensions is evident? There are many issues that must be considered in such discussions (e.g., wisdom and policies that would decide the proper amount of giving towards those in the immediate community of faith versus those who are not). But if such a self-examination is to begin, passages like Deuteronomy 14:29, in which the tithes of Israel are used to benefit not only God's people but also *strangers,* may speak anew today.

Waqfs and Islamic Banking as a Mirror

The principle of the waqf can be seen in the biblical illustration of the manager, or steward, of the master's property (Matt 24:45–51).[25] While Muslim waqfs play myriad roles in assisting the ummah, perhaps the modern Christian parallel is that of trusts and foundations. Interestingly, trusts are not always identified as Christian institutions, and are perhaps one of the least-known Christian sources of finan-

---

25   In any comparison between the Islamic system and Christianity, however, we should note that Islamic economics is intended to reveal the *will* of Allah, while biblical ethics and economics primarily reveal the *character* of God and how he works in the affairs of humanity.

cial support and financing. Historically they have played key roles in funding literacy programs, fighting diseases, and supporting scholars by giving grants to pastors or promising laity overseas. However, in comparison to the waqfs, which have funded financial assistance to converts to Islam, few Christian foundations have ventured deeply into financing Christian mission for evangelism, discipleship, and church planting.[26] There is great potential for Christian foundations and mission agencies to form strategic partnerships for the purpose of joint projects in missions, especially as mission agencies and missionaries are challenged in the coming decades to seek new sources of funding apart from the traditional paradigm of raising support.

Christian foundations, for example, may offer four potential benefits to mission workers. First, their position as actors independent of the daily vicissitudes and short-term vagaries of market forces or stockholders in a free-market capitalist system means that they can tackle long-term goals or strategic projects. This independence frees them from issuing the frequent emergency appeals that are the staple of mission agencies involved in rescue and relief operations especially. For the most part, mission agencies have tended to issue such appeals to individuals so that they will give more and to highlight pressing needs. But these tasks consume large amounts of time and entail contacting many individuals to raise money. The stability of Christian foundations would free up mission workers' time and allow them to engage more in direct ministry.

Second, Christian foundations have the ability to provide seed or startup money to stimulate joint giving with nationals, such as matching grants, or to provide an initial boost to projects requiring large capital expenditures above and beyond the means of nascent local church movements. Examples may include funding vernacular Bible colleges or seminaries, endowing faculty salaries and library resources, starting up printing presses, and building capacity for publishing and distribution. This funding would be important to local pastors who are commonly

---

26 If one includes funding printing presses and Bible translation and distribution as part of evangelism, then strong historical support is evident—but otherwise they have largely been absent.

underresourced and consumed by pressing church planting needs, and for whom there are few resources left over to prepare trained leadership when church movements mature and such needs arise.

Third, when there is a large social need, a variety of Christian foundations might tackle issues such as operating, grant making, business, or community foundations (Frumkin 2006, 221–23). As an example, in a community with endemic poverty that is lacking government resources or fighting rare/intractable local diseases that require outside expertise, mission workers might consider foundations that have specialized in health causes to fund part of their mission work.[27]

Fourth, foundations open up an alternative source of advice beyond the traditional faculty expertise from the seminary, as they often have a wider or deeper potential network of experts in business, administrative help, and research staff or assistants who can step in when seminary professors are too busy or inadequate to the task. If such synergies can occur between the foundation, the seminary, and mission agencies, then theoretical, biblical, and missiological insights could be synthesized in partnership with mission workers to craft better mission practices. Such practices can become more culturally sensitive, biblically faithful, and economically astute business and financial models that are contextually appropriate to support local economic structures that empower the poor and transform communities socioeconomically. In such discussions, any outside funding by foundations should also take into account the issues of dependency or community development that have typically challenged mission work, as Doug Wilson (chap. 6) and Mike Mtika (chap. 7) show in their respective chapters in this book.

---

27 One especially pressing need in ministering to Muslim converts to Christianity is assisting their financial or material needs when they have been ostracized from their former community or are now religiously discriminated against by Muslims due to their newfound faith. Meeting these needs in a transitional phase of their conversion can help those who are tempted to return to Islam by bribes or loss of privileges or education allowances. A service model paradigm can be used by foundations to step in to assist converts in this process. If foundations fulfilled this need, they could also partner with others to establish a self-sustaining structure, such as startup seed money for microcredit loans, to avoid long-term dependency issues (Anheier 2006, 18–19).

A key for mission workers partnering with foundations is to study and discern local economic systems in serious engagement with nationals, so that such a mission is not only holistic, promoting kingdom justice and love, but also takes into account the reality that all local economic practices have both sociocultural upsides and downsides.

Riba as a Mirror

In the Bible, the prohibition against interest is found in numerous passages, such as Exodus 22:25; Leviticus 25:36,37; Deuteronomy 23:19; Nehemiah 5:11; Psalm 15:15; and Ezekiel 18:8,13. While Israel was forbidden to charge interest amongst themselves, there was no such prohibition towards foreigners (Deut 23:20; though in principle the Israelites were to be as fair as possible to Gentiles—see Deut 24:10–15). Numerically, though there are more passages in the Bible that speak against usury than in the Qur'an, the avoidance of interest has been wholly missing from any contemporary Christian writing on economics.[28]

Historically the church had long opposed usury before the rise of global capitalism as the major economic system of the twentieth century. By the time of the Industrial Revolution, though, the church had abandoned this prohibition. Though many questions remain regarding its abandonment, a key factor may have been the church linking its mission to that of the colonial expansion of Western civilization. By doing so, many Christians accepted colonialism's underlying assumptions and practice of economics as valid for funding their own extension of the kingdom of God. Generally Protestant churches have become chaplains of *laissez-faire* capitalism rather than critical examiners or the conscience of the system (Budde and Brimlow 2002). The consensus is that "the high efficiency inherent to [capitalism] favours earthly life plans" but in so doing "removes the churches to a marginal position [so that] they restrict themselves to formulating some rather general

---

28 In Matthew 25:27 and Luke 19:23, Jesus seems to support a return on investment through the use of interest. Thus the biblical data on the use of interest is varied. There is need for deeper study of such biblical passages to comprehend the full range of understandings on this topic.

economic principles" (Miegel 1994, 239).[29] Consequently this opposition to usury no longer exists; not only are Christians impoverished in their understanding of the church's history in dealing with it, but few if any mission workers are aware of its implications for mission. This hinders their ability to understand Muslim opposition to riba in financial transactions or the ways in which such opposition might mirror notions of equality, holism, justice, and righteousness in the Christian community. The lack of a critical perspective on the matter also results in assumptions about business models that may seem good to mission workers but not to local Muslims. As Lederleitner shows in her chapter (chap. 2), if finance accounting standards are not morally neutral, the manner in which Christians do "business" when utilizing the tools of *laissez-faire* capitalism and modern / Western-style business practices in mission may prove unattractive to the very pious Muslims to whom Christians seek to witness with God's love, care, compassion, and justice.

Christians must begin to explore alternative means of financing that are more faithful to biblical and historical practices of the church that eschew interest. For businesses that require longer-term projects with large infusions of financing normally funded through usurious loans from banks, Christian foundations might be better equipped to explore, in serious conversation with mission workers, alternatives for financing that mirror the ways in which Islamic banking spreads the financial risks of default and minimizes or eliminates interest on business loans. The ability to provide jobs and businesses may be especially important in mission contexts where converts are ostracized or denied jobs due to discrimination by their former religious communities.

Finally, because all forms of business entail an element of risk and failure, everyone involved in such joint ventures should grapple with

---

29 For Catholics, however, Miegel observes that "for more than a hundred years the popes have been tackling questions of economic and social order" (1994, 237). He also explains why Protestants have generally not taken this stance compared to the Catholics (236–39). Reasons include Protestantism's position on "individualism, work and [the] material [that] are now transcendentally elevated in the course of the Reformation" and its acceptance of "the high efficiency inherent to these systems [that] favours earthly life plans" (235, 239).

passages such as Deuteronomy 15:1–18, which dictates the forgiveness of debts to debtors over a seven-year cycle. When defaulting on debt is a possibility, it should be sensitively discussed with all partners on the home and mission front and with the nationals. Together they should formulate biblically faithful and culturally appropriate responses to contextualize the handling of financial loss. Not all losses should be modeled on the US Chapter 11 bankruptcy proceedings, as these laws do not work as well in Muslim societies, where there are shame-honor codes. It is important to reexamine the law of Jubilee in Deuteronomy 15, which not only forgives debts but is concerned to preserve or restore relationships and ensure harmony within the community. In the Bible, the writing down of unpayable debts and its relational component to forgiveness is seen as part of the call of the community of God's people.

TOWARDS AN INTERDISCIPLINARY STUDY OF ECONOMICS AND MISSION

Laurence Iannaccone, an acknowledged economics expert, notes that studies of religion and economics can be separated into four areas: (1) religious behavior from an economic perspective; (2) the economic consequences of religion; (3) religious economics—writings that invoke theological principles, and sacred writings to promote or criticize economic policies; and (4) studying religious organizations from a practical business perspective (1998, 1466). Less studied have been the cultural and religious dimensions of economies and their systems. For many economists, economics as a discipline is assumed to be culturally neutral, and its principles are reckoned to be universally applicable regardless of local moral, ethical norms or religious codes.

This chapter has argued that due to the pervasive influence of economics in our life today, Christianity should not only concern itself with the economy of the spirit (as evident in books on Christian discipleship or spiritual formation) but also with the *spirit of the economies*, or "spiritual economies" (Rudnyckyj 2010). Doing so would open up seminaries and schools of theology to new interdisciplinary course offerings that would address areas such as the preparation of ministers-in-training in the spiritual-economic aspects of the church (e.g., job and financial counseling of their parishioners, raising building funds, the overseas financial impact of short-term missions that are supported by the church) or the equipping of missionaries-in-training on the economic considerations of support raising (locally or overseas), on sociocultural aspects of corruption, and on dependency in mission. If economics as a key area of study were included in ministry preparation, some courses that seminaries or Christian universities might offer would include a history of Christianity and economics in historical studies, a theology of economics and the church in systematic theology, the spiritual economy of God's people in the Bible and in biblical theology,[30] and aspects of ecclesial spiritual economy in pastoral theology.

With regard to mission, if an interdisciplinary approach to economics can be formulated, missiology could be best placed to lead in the following areas:

- business ethics and morality in mission
- the cross-cultural dimensions of local economies
- social enterprises and contextual models of socioeconomic innovations
- globalization, mission, and economics
- the role of NGOs, foundations, and nonprofits, and their interaction with major financial and economic actors (e.g., World Bank, governmental economic bodies, funding agencies, multinational corporations)

In such courses, pertinent questions that should be on any syllabus of an interdisciplinary study of mission and economics would include those below:

---

30 A recent book by Bruce W. Longenecker and Kelly D. Liebengood (2009) is a welcome introduction and will hopefully herald further discussion and biblical study.

- How can ministry be done in non-Western socioeconomic cultures?
- How oblivious are missionaries to the culturally conditioned practices of the economic models they bring with them when working with nationals?
- For nationals motivated to use Western-style economic systems and models, does utilizing Western, capitalistic instruments help in their contexts, or are other economic paradigms more applicable?[31]
- Under what circumstances, and to what degree, should Christian NGOs and mission agencies do the job themselves, and to what degree should they collaborate with government or supragovernmental organizations that have global reach and a vast pool of resources but operate using Western models of capitalism and accountability?
- How does the role of state economic policies, such as taxation, affect the mission of the church?[32]

CONCLUSION

A critical assessment of the cultural and religious dimensions of economics raises fresh questions on the nature of how missions can be biblically faithful with regard to these dynamics. Where the Islamic economy is concerned with the life of the Muslim as a person in community, the foundations and practice of its values assume the integration of the believer as part of the larger whole. In contrast, popular and contemporary Christianity is often full of financial self-help books on money, personal savings, and investments, but addresses little analysis of the systematic structures of Christian life, work, and

---

31 See, for instance, Maranz 2001.
32 For example, the tax deduction for American churches has long influenced them to take nonpartisan stances in politics (thus creating a separation of church and state) for fear of losing their tax status. However, in Germany, where churches are supported by state taxes, churches become a visible symbol of the power of the state in controlling religious affairs.

giving as part of the larger economic dimension of faith in the context of community, culture, religion, and modernity. For the most part, Christianity's relationship with modernity and the rise of the nation-state in history has meant that the church deliberately separated itself from the realm of macroeconomics. Thus major financial institutions such as the banking system and stock markets have engendered little biblical engagement among evangelicals.[33]

The study of Christianity's relationship to economics must also assess how modernity and the West have shaped Christian practices to better understand how to recover a more holistic gospel that is truly good news, not only to the individual poor but also to the community at large. By doing so, it can better recover Christian practices that witness prophetically and that engage with secular marketing strategies that "divide and conquer" a community into atomistic, autonomous individuals, making Christianity a "chaplain for capitalism" (Budde and Brimlow 2002). In this we must remember that people are more than "economic men" or mere consumers—at our core, we are all bearers of the *imago Dei*. Because of this, Christians cannot divorce financial doings from ethics, business from morality, or economics from human relationships.

---

33 Where it has occurred, its presence has been scattered; for example, with conscience- or ethics-driven mutual funds in the stock markets. These funds are a basket of stocks bundled into funds that are designed and managed by committed religious followers. The Timothy Plan and NOAH Fund, for instance, are administered by Christians, while the Amana Growth Fund is Muslim-run. The latter screens out companies involved with alcohol, tobacco, and gambling, while NOAH omits companies that produce or distribute pornography or abortion-type services or products. NOAH also donates 10 percent of its management fees to missions, discipleship, and the poor (Foster 1999).

REFERENCES

Aggarwal, Rajesh K., and Tarik Yousef. 2000. Islamic banks and investment financing. *Journal of Money, Credit and Banking* 32, no. 1: 93–120.

Alatas, Syed Farid. 2005. Islam and modernization. In *Islam in Southeast Asia: Political, social and strategic challenges for the 21st Century,* edited by K. S. Nathan and Mohammad Hashim Kamali, 209–30. Singapore: ISEAS.

Alhabshi, Syed Othman. 1994. The Influence of Islam on economics. In *The role and influence of religion in society,* edited by Syed Omar and Syed Othman Alhabshi, 201–27. Kuala Lumpur: Institute of Islamic Understanding Malaysia.

Ali, Abdullah Yusuf. 1999. *The meaning of the Holy Quran.* 10th ed. Beltsville, MD: Amana.

Anheier, Helmut K., and Diana Leat. 2006. *Creative philanthropy: Towards a new philanthropy for the twenty-first century.* New York: Routledge.

Aupers, Stef, and Dick Houtman, eds. 2010. *Religions of modernity: Relocating the sacred to the self and the digital.* Boston: E. J. Brill.

Badawi, Abdullah bin Haji Ahmad. 2006. *Islam Hadhari: A model approach for development and progress.* Petaling Jaya, Malaysia: MPH Publications.

Benthall, Jonathan. 1999. Financial worship: The Quranic injunction to almsgiving. *Journal of the Royal Anthropological Institute* 5, no. 1: 27–42.

Bonk, Jonathan J. 2007. *Missions and money: Affluence as a missionary problem . . . revisited.* Maryknoll, NY: Orbis.

Budde, Michael L., and Robert W. Brimlow. 2002. *Christianity incorporated: How big business is buying the church.* Grand Rapids: Brazos.

Foster, Malcolm. 1999. Money: Religious mutual funds flourish. *Christianity Today,* September 6. http://www.christianitytoday.com/ct/1999/september6/9ta028.html?start=2.

Frumkin, Peter. 2006. *Strategic giving: The art and science of philanthropy.* Chicago: University of Chicago Press.

Haneef, Mohamed Aslam. 2005. The development and impact of Islamic economic institutions: The Malaysian experience. In *Islam in Southeast Asia: Political, social and strategic challenges for the 21st century,* edited by K. S. Nathan and Mohammad Hashim Kamali, 82–99. Singapore: ISEAS.

Hauerwas, Stanley. 2000. *A better hope: Resources for a church confronting capitalism, democracy, and postmodernity.* Grand Rapids: Brazos.

Higgins, Andrew. 2006. Fund-raising target: Branded terrorist by U.S., Israel, microcredit czar keeps lending. *Wall Street Journal,* December 28, A1.

Johnson, C. Neal. 2009. *Business as mission: A comprehensive guide to theory and practice.* Downers Grove, IL: IVP Academic.

Iannaccone, Laurence. 1998. Introduction to the economics of religion. *Journal of Economic Literature* 36: 1465–96.

Khan, Shujaat A. 1998. Two pathways to development: Capitalist versus Islamic approach. *Hamdard Islamicus* 21, no. 2: 7–15.

Kuran, Timur. 1995. Islamic economics and the Islamic subeconomy. *Journal of Economic Perspectives* 9, no. 4: 155–73.

————. 2001. The provision of public goods under Islamic law: Origins, impact, and limitations of the waqf system. *Law and Society Review* 35, no. 4: 841–98.

Lane, Karen. 2006. Islamic-bond market becomes global by attracting non-Muslim borrowers. *Wall Street Journal,* November 16, C1 and C6.

Longenecker, Bruce W., and Kelly D. Liebengood, eds. 2009. *Engaging economics: New Testament scenarios and early Christian reception.* Grand Rapids: Eerdsman.

Maranz, David E. 2001. *African friends and money matters: Observations from Africa.* Dallas: SIL International and International Museum of Cultures.

Miegel, Meinhard. 1994. The influence of Christianity on economics. In *The role and influence of religion in society,* edited by Syed Omar and Syed Othman Alhabshi, 228–41. Kuala Lumpur: Institute of Islamic Understanding Malaysia.

Mokhtar, Hamim S. Ahmad, Naziruddin Abdullah, and Syed M. Alhabshi. 2008. Efficiency and competition of Islamic banking in Malaysia. *Humanomics* 24, no. 1: 28–48.

Moten, Abdul Rashid. 2005. Modernization and the process of globalization: The Muslim experience and responses. In *Islam in Southeast Asia,* edited by K. S. Nathan and Mohammad Hashim Kamali, 231–55. Singapore: ISEAS.

Muzaffar, Chandra. 1998. Globalisation and religion: Some reflections. In *Globalisation: The perspectives and experiences of the religious traditions of Asia Pacific,* edited by Joseph A. Camilleri and Chandra Muzaffar, 179–90. Kuala Lumpur: International Movement for a Just World.

Novak, Michael 1993. *The Catholic ethic and the spirit of capitalism.* New York: Free Press.

Pope, Hugh. 2005. Islamic banking grows with all sorts of rules. *Wall Street Journal,* May 3, C1.

Powers, David S. 1993. The Islamic inheritance system: A socio-historical approach. *Arab Law Quarterly* 8, no. 1: 13–29.

Prystay, Cris. 2002. Malaysians take Islamic banking to mainstream: Banks aim to carve niche in products complying with religious principles. *Wall Street Journal,* November 20, B5.

Riddell, Peter G., and Peter Cotterell. 2003. *Islam in context: Past, present and future.* Grand Rapids: Baker.

Rippin, Andrew. 2006. *Muslims: Their religious beliefs and practices.* New York: Routledge.

Rodkin, Dennis. 2005. Faith, finance: Two city banks offer devout Muslims a way to buy homes without violating usury beliefs. *Chicago Tribune,* February 6. http://articles.chicagotribune.com/2005-02-06/business/0502060481_1_sizable-markup-charge-interest-credit-sale.

Rudnyckyj, Daromir. 2010. *Spiritual economies: Islam, globalization, and the afterlife of development.* Ithaca, NY: Cornell University Press.

Rundle, Steven, and Tom Steffen. 2003. *Great commission companies: The emerging role of business in missions.* Downers Grove, IL: IVP Books.

Salleh, Awang Had. 1985. Modern concept of hajj management: The experience of Malaysia. In *Readings in Islam in Southeast Asia,* edited by Ahmad Ibrahim, Sharon Siddique, and Yasmin Hussain, 262–67. Singapore: Institute of Southeast Asian Studies.

Schwartz, Glenn. 2007. *When charity destroys dignity: Overcoming unhealthy dependency in the Christian movement.* Bloomington, IN: Authorhouse.

Shanmugam, Bala, Vignesen Perumal, and Alfieya Hanuum Ridzwa. 2005. *Issues in Islamic accounting.* Serdang, Malaysia: Universiti Putra Malaysia Press.

Shatzmiller, Maya. 2001. Islamic institutions and property rights: The case of the "public good" waqf. *Journal of the Economic and Social History of the Orient* 44, no. 1: 44–74.

Slater, Joanna. 2007. When hedge funds meet Islamic finance: U.S. firms hire scholars to help design products; the "rent-a-sheikh" issue. *Wall Street Journal,* August 9, A1.

Smith, Pamela Ann. 2007. Islamic capital markets set to soar. *Middle East,* October, 42–44.

Steffen, Tom, and Lois McKinney Douglas. 2008. *Encountering missionary life and work: Preparing for intercultural ministry.* Grand Rapids: Baker Academic.

Sufian, Fadzlan. 2007. The efficiency of Islamic banking industry in Malaysia: Foreign vs. domestic banks. *Humanomics* 23, no. 3: 174–92.

Trofimov, Yaroslav. 2007. Borrowed ideas: Malaysia transforms rules for finance under Islam; In a lesson to Arabs, Asian bankers mix religion, modernity. *Wall Street Journal,* April 4, A1.

Weber, Max. 1963. *The sociology of religion.* Boston: Beacon.

Wilson, Rodney. 2007. Islamic banking—opportunity or threat? Common Ground News Service, January 23. Accessed July 5, 2013. http://www.commongroundnews.org/article.php?id=20284&lan=en&sp=1.

Wright, Tom, and Yayu Yuniar. 2007. Islamic finance widens pitch: Banks aim to show shariah products can be competitive. *Wall Street Journal,* September 5, B3.

4

CHRISTIAN MISSION AMIDST THE CULTURAL AND SOCIOECONOMIC DYNAMICS OF BRIBERY AND EXTORTION PRACTICES IN THE PHILIPPINES

Jason Richard Tan

This chapter is a study of the socioeconomic dynamics behind the practice of bribery and extortion in the Philippines. I will argue that, contrary to popular belief, the practice of bribery and extortion is never a private matter involving two parties engaged in a discreet transaction. Rather it is a known and often public practice regulated by specific socioeconomic assumptions and cultural expectations among participants within the system. Though it is commonly thought that people living under the influences of bribery and extortion are victims of its effects, often they become willing participants through deliberate personal choices to take part in the system.

The aim of this chapter is to understand the system of bribery and extortion in order to better engage the nature of its socioeconomic practice, along with the cultural assumptions behind it, and to assist missionaries and other Christian workers in dealing with the situation. Thus the chapter will explore the nature of bribery and extortion, its domains and boundaries, historical and cultural notions of what bribery means, and how it exerts itself in uses of power and reciprocity. It will also compare bribery and extortion in relation to modern sociocultural assumptions of capitalism and patronage systems. Finally, there will be a section on how bribery is morally reasoned by participants within the system, followed by some suggestions for missions work.

THE NATURE OF BRIBERY AND EXTORTION

The words "bribe" and "extortion" are usually understood as deviant economic practices. However, we must also see that they are words loaded with social and moral values with which people make judgments.

Most if not all societies of the world identify certain illicit activities as bribery or extortion. However, what is considered a bribe or extortion differs in various contexts. What is considered a bribe or an extortion in Singapore or elsewhere may well be acceptable in the Philippines. In the latter, policemen in some provinces may take or receive a "love gift" or "donation" from a grateful patron after responding to a call or an emergency at night. These gifts are given as tokens of appreciation by patrons who know that many public servants have to pay for the fuel when responding to an emergency call.[1] So the act of giving gifts for services rendered by the police, which is not acceptable in many countries, is legitimate in this circumstance in the Philippines.

From the above example, we note that in order to better understand bribery and extortion practices, we must first see their fundamental cultural and socioeconomic roots. In his study of the dynamics of reciprocity and gift giving in Polynesian and other traditional societies, Marcel Mauss observed that "it is not individuals but collectivities that impose obligations of exchange and contract upon each other" (1990, 5). According to Mauss, certain societal discourses created by the group are imposed upon individual members of a village (or a social system) in order to coerce them to adhere to the values of the group. Thus bribery and extortion can be considered forms of "collectivist"

---

1   The fuel is often reimbursable, but only after a significant delay.

practice based on a sociocultural peer pressure that perpetuates the behavior through a kind of logic and shapes the nature of transactions.

In fact, the rules and even the prices of bribes can be quite standardized and can reflect the full structure of society. For instance, in the Philippines, a jeepney[2] driver caught beating a red light may bribe an apprehending policeman or traffic enforcer with P300 pesos (USD5) to let him off the hook. However, the amount of the bribe may change depending on the nature of the violation and/or the type of vehicle. A driver will find it hard to convince an apprehending officer to take a bribe over the same traffic infraction if he offers the same amount but is driving a Mercedes-Benz or a BMW. In the Filipino case, one could ask who decides the range of monetary exchanges—how did the jeepney driver or the policeman know that certain price ranges apply only to certain types of vehicles or violations?

In another example, when applying for or renewing a driver's license in the Philippines, a person is expected to add about P300 pesos (USD5) on top of all the legal fees in order to expedite the process. However, to expedite a paper is illegal (unless there is a clear procedure for it), since the money collected is not receipted. When one attempts to ask any of the clerks working in the same office concerning the same procedure, the cost will be the same with all of them. Every employee working in the same office will know the cost for certain procedures.

These two incidences reflect the fact that bribes and "grease money" are not byproducts of a spontaneous, spur-of-the-moment decision between two separate contracting parties, but are rather products of a gradual and carefully calibrated process that has evolved over a long period of time. In these situations, local policemen, traffic enforcers, drivers, and license bureau officers in Filipino society may be thought of as representatives of collectivities that regulate and impose laws

---

2   A kind of public utility vehicle that evolved from the military jeep US soldiers used in World War II.

of exchange within the system of bribery and extortion.[3] The "collectivities" are composed of all of the participants within the system, which includes government officials, clerks, fixers, security guards, and clients, along with other ordinary people. There is an informal and implicit "regulatory law" that such insiders understand that specifies how certain monetary exchanges are to be processed through the interaction and experiences of those offering and extorting bribes.

This domain of consensual knowledge, i.e., insider talk and understanding, has a dominating influence on participants within the system.[4] Some participants are effectively forced to observe and accept certain expected roles and behavior. People are under strong constraints to accept the consensual definition of the situation even when they are not happy about it. Like actors in the theater, people act not as they are nor as they would wish to be, but as if they have accepted the role assigned to them (Goffman 1959, 17; Gregor 1977, 10). While many are willing participants of the system, some are forced to perform according to the "script" purely by societal pressure. To refuse to participate is to violate the social norm within the system; it is interpreted by participants as a hostile act against the whole system and its associated culture.

---

3   In societies such as the Trobrianders in the South Pacific, the "collectivities" are people from different islands within a certain atoll who are participants of a system of distribution. In this sense, the whole community contributes to the collective knowledge they possess and create in order to regulate a certain system of distribution, such as the practice of *kula* exchanges (Malinowski 1984). A *kula* is an elaborate form of gift exchange between tribal groups involving red shell necklaces and white shell armbands. This exchange ritual sets the stage for political negotiations and economic trade between islands. Paul Hiebert explains, "The economic importance of the Kula ring did not lie in the gifts of armbands and necklaces. Rather, these highly ritualized exchanges led to friendly trade relationships between men whose tribes were often hostile to one another. When men on one island accumulated enough goods, they set sail for a neighboring island on a gift-giving expedition, to a tribe that might normally be their enemy" (1999, 304–5).

4   There is a similarity to parliamentary laws in that "regulatory laws" in the system of bribery and extortion are created by observing certain procedures, such as debates. These insider debates are usually held at the side or the back of a government agency. Instead of politicians and lawmakers, the debate is handled by fixers and clients who haggle for the best bribe price. These interactions form and create a domain of discourse that influences the rates of the bribe.

When we understand bribery in this way, we may find it easier to refrain from judging too quickly a person who participates in bribery and extortion. We must first realize that he or she may be enmeshed in a system of intersecting social linkages that forces participation due to sociocultural peer pressure. This is a dilemma for many well-meaning government workers in the Philippines. I have encountered testimonies of government workers who have become Christians; although they refuse to accept bribes for themselves, they will yet facilitate transactions for their boss or supervisor lest they create too much trouble for the system as a whole.

When this dynamic occurs, it creates a kind of social and economic subsystem within the larger culture. The jeepney drivers in the Philippines, for instance, share information with each other, while the policemen share information among themselves. Each group becomes an interlocutor to the debate, and together they form the discourses that regulate the praxis. The "rate of exchange" demanded by each group will depend on the "successful" experience of most of the participants within their respective networks. This means that while bribery and extortion practices are hidden to those who are nonparticipants, they are well known to those who take part in the system.

THE DOMAINS AND BOUNDARIES OF BRIBERY AND EXTORTION

Filipino police officers who extort motorists for cash tend to observe certain boundaries. For example, there are certain places where they know that illegal activities are seldom challenged and certain zones that belong to other police officers plying the trade. There are cases in the Philippines where even the security guards of a government institution are participants in the system. These guards control and regulate the gates of the system and are mandated to keep outsiders from penetrating it. Based on my personal observation, security guards regulate the domain where extortion or bribe practices thrive by policing the boundaries. The guards personally know the fixers and allow the latter to enter and exit those areas that are restricted to the public. Once such space has been created for them, the fixers are allowed to run their errands freely. The guards protect the system by creating a spatial and imaginary boundary that only vested participants are permitted to cross.

Bribery and extortion practices are deviant behaviors in modern Filipino society. Otherwise no one would go through elaborate means to conceal them. The system survives because it has acquired a certain domain or boundary that sets it apart from customary Filipino practices. This arrangement has made possible the proliferation of illegal activities within government bureaus, because they are carefully tucked away from plain sight. In Goffman's words, such activities are relegated to the "backstage" of a government institution (1959, 22).

In the Filipino value system, the word for "bribe," *suhol*, signifies a payment to someone to coerce or induce the person to violate a moral code or responsibility. It is never used in a positive sense as is, for instance, the word *regalo*, "gift." In fact, *suhol* is used in the strongest possible negative sense. For example, it is commonly used in connection with a judge who received a bribe to overturn a judgment in favor of the giver. Filipinos seldom use *suhol* to describe "grease money" paid to a government clerk in order to expedite paperwork. The proper Filipino term used in this case is *lagay*, literally meaning "to put something." When a Filipino uses the phrase *humihingi ng lagay* (literally, "asking for a bribe"), the context means that it is extortion money. It usually refers to police or government officials insinuating that a person under their custody can pay them for his or her release. Since *suhol* and *lagay* are negative deviant behaviors, Filipinos who are part of the system of bribery and extortion have developed insider lingo to conceal their practice. Here are some examples of it (see Ilagan 2008):

> "All-around" (ol-arawnd): It describes a fixer who can do any corrupt transaction for a fee.
>
> "All in" (ol-in): It means that the transaction includes bribe money or grease money.

"Anointed ones" (a-noyn-ed-wans): People who have the blessing of high government officials to do transactions on their behalf.

"Apprentice" (a-pren-tis): a new fixer being trained for the work.

"Araw" (a-raw): Literally, "the Sun." It refers to the highest official who is part of an illegal transaction.

"Chocolate boys" (tso-ko-leyt-boys): These are corrupt traffic policemen.

"Commissioner" (ko-mis-yon-er): These are people who collect part of the grease money as their commission.

"Connection" (ko-nek-syon): These are "go-in-between" people with connection to a high ranking official.

"Fixcal" (fiks-kal): A fiscal who fixes cases for a price.[5]

"Tagaloob" (ta-ga-lo-ob): A government employee involved in illegal transactions.

"Three little pigs" (thri-li-tel-pigs): It is equivalent to P1000, since there are three faces in the one-thousand-peso bill.

In order for a deviant practice to continue, it must be cultivated separately from the competing values of the larger social and ideological systems, such as religion or free-market capitalist ethics (which I shall further discuss later). Thus there is a need to maintain a separate domain with a protective boundary in order for the system of bribery to flourish.

People may vacillate between systems with opposing ethical or moral values. In Burkina Faso there are pastors who have no qualms about giving "bribes" to public officials in order to have their papers processed. Christians who do this have coined another term for grease

---

5   In the Philippines a "fiscal" is a public prosecutor or a procurator fiscal.

money, calling it "encouragement."[6] The dual system of vocabulary used by some Burkina Faso Christians reveals how membership in two social systems with opposing ethical and moral values is negotiated or maintained. When such dynamics exist, it is not inconceivable that government officials who take bribes may also be well-regarded individuals who are members of other social systems such as religious communities. Likewise, well-meaning pastors or missionaries may traverse social boundaries with competing moral values with no sense of culpability because of the varying roles they play within each system. I shall discuss the ministry implications of this further in my conclusion.

HISTORICAL AND CULTURAL NOTIONS OF BRIBERY AND RECIPROCITY

Noonan (1984) in his book *Bribes* states, "The core of the concept of a bribe is an inducement improperly influencing the performance of a public function meant to be gratuitously exercised" (xi). He admits that although this concept seems straightforward, what constitutes "an inducement," an "improperly influencing" action, a "public function," or the phrase "meant to be gratuitously exercised" is ambiguous since cultures may vary in their definition of the individual components (ibid.). This fact makes the practice of bribery and extortion a difficult and highly controversial subject, as it touches on the meanings assigned to it by locals in the cultural "imbeddedness" of such a practice (Philips 1984).

In cultures where systems of distribution involve reciprocity (a discussion that Meneses and Mtika elaborate elsewhere in this book; see chaps. 1 and 7), the line that delineates between a gift, a tip, a reward, an "encouragement," and a bribe is very thin. Reciprocity is in any society "a rule of life, and in some societies at least it is *the* rule of life." So, for example, Michael Philips states, "In some places transactions that many Americans would consider bribes are not only expected behavior but accepted practices as well" (1984, 621).

---

6   Interview with an anonymous Burkina Faso informant, October 27, 2008, Deerfield, IL.

Based on his study of ancient literatures of the Middle East, Noonan (1984) suggests that there was originally no specific word for "bribe" in antiquity. He states, "At the beginning there is no specific, unambiguous word for bribe, no common terms designating and denigrating the briber and the bribe, no noun summing up the action to be shunned and naming it bribery" (3). According to him, stories in antiquity such as "The Poor Man of Nippur" (Akkadian literature, ca. 1500 BC) or "The Protests of the Eloquent Peasant" (Egyptian literature, ca. 2000 BC) reveal that cultural constructions of these practices were about reciprocity rather than bribery (4–7).

Even the Old Testament does not have a word for "bribe," but instead uses the word *kopher*, which means "ransom," or *shachad*, translated as "gift" or "present." These two Hebrew words are not equivalent to the English word "bribe," but may be interpreted as such depending on the context. For instance, Proverbs 17:23 states, "A wicked man accepts a bribe in secret to pervert the course of justice." In this context *shachad* is rightly interpreted as a bribe, but in Proverbs 17:8 the same word should be interpreted as meaning a gift instead. If we were to translate the word as "bribe" there, the verse would read, "A bribe is a charm to the one who gives it; wherever he turns, he succeeds." Changing the word "bribe" to "gift" in this context removes the ambiguity in the passage. This means that although the word "bribe" is lacking in ancient literatures, the concept cannot be said to be absent. But it is viewed as a negative form of a positive concept, that of reciprocity.

Reciprocity, whether it is performed as a gift or as a bribe, is important, because the allocation of resources is a serious matter in all societies. Thus a system for distributing and redistributing valuable resources such as food or wealth is necessary in every society. In Meneses' chapter (chap. 1), we see how the free-market system is one system of allocation that competes with another; i.e., reciprocity. In Mtika's and Wilson's chapters (chaps. 7 and 6), we see how collectivist systems function on the ground level with reciprocal assumptions.

Reciprocity is a system in which resources are distributed to various members of society through patterns of exchange. One such pattern is called "balanced reciprocity," where goods and services of equal value are exchanged between contracting parties (Womack 2001, 109–10). Since it is risky to enter into an economic transaction with unknown groups, it is necessary that such activity be protected by a system that ensures the safety of exchanging parties. This system, according to Womack, "establishes an alliance of equality between individuals or groups, and participants in balanced reciprocity usually keep a formal or an informal record of what is exchanged" (110).[7]

Reciprocity is not the same as barter and trade, although goods and services of equal value are also exchanged in barter. The difference is in the relationship of the contracting parties. In balanced reciprocity, there is an ongoing social relationship between the two parties, while in barter and trade, as in the market system, the relationship ends as soon as the economic transaction ends (Womack 2001, 113). Thus bribery and extortion are actually wrong, because they abuse societal power in order to gain a purely economic end (Noonan 1984, xii).

POWER AND RECIPROCITY

When elements of power and coercion are added to the system of reciprocity, the rules of the playing field change. Based on his observation of archaic societies, Mauss (1990) states, "To refuse to give, to fail to invite, just as to refuse to accept, is tantamount to declaring war; it is to reject the bond of alliance and commonality" (13). This "power" to obligate the contracting parties to reciprocate is symbolized in the gift itself. Noonan explains,

> Relations with peaceful strangers are established by an exchange whose essential function is to oblige the offeree. The recipient is bound by receiving. If he does not accept what is offered he is hostile. If he does not respond after accepting he is hostile. The requirements of acceptance and reciprocation make exchange risky. *Offerings are, however, a necessary way of creating relationships beyond kinfolk and tribe.* (1984, 3; emphasis added)

---

7   See also Mauss 1990 and Malinowski 1984.

Mauss observes that gifts are symbolic representations of the giver and imply a relational transaction, just as burnt offerings or libations are gifts offered to a god or gods with the intention of obligating the gods to grant the petitioner's request. In archaic societies, a gift functions as an offering with an expectation of return. Gifts, according to Mauss, are in theory voluntary, but "in reality they are given and reciprocated obligatorily" (1990, 3).[8] According to Noonan (1984) and Philips (1984), a bribe must *coerce or induce the recipient to violate a moral responsibility.*[9] So this means that a gift given with the expectation of being reciprocated or with the intention to obligate the recipient to perform a certain expected task is not necessarily a bribe.

In the modern worldview, as well as in the assumptions of capitalism, the "duties" and "responsibilities" of people, especially those that are given power and authority, must be discharged objectively and separated from "favors" or the "subjective" use of power. But this idea of a non-personal economic transaction is unintelligible to many people groups who have not been exposed to the philosophical ideals of the Enlightenment nor socialized into Western cultural norms of capitalism. Disinterested transactions are offensive to Filipino sensibilities, because they reduce a person to an impersonal entity, a statistic, a number to be served.

In the case of reciprocity, the inducement of the gift is more than just an invitation to the other party to participate in a relationship of exchange. The gift is actually an invitation to deepen a relationship,

---

8   Sherry B. Ortner in her book *Sherpas through Their Rituals* observes how the Sherpa community in Nepal uses hospitality as a form of reciprocal exchange. Among the Sherpa, a person needing assistance from a neighbor will serve food and beer in an effort to convince and obligate the guest to come to his aid. Ortner discovered that such practices have correlations with the Tibetan "paradigmatic myth," where "the people learn how to make offerings to the gods, and the offering rituals take the form of parties" (1978, 85). In this sense, offerings and libations to the gods "serve the purpose of buying peace between them both" (Mauss 1990, 17).

9   John Danley defines a bribe as "offering or giving something of value with a corrupt intent to induce or influence an action of someone in a public or official capacity" (quoted in Philips 1984, 623n). Philips also distinguishes his position from that of Tom Carson, who describes a bribe as "a payment to someone 'in exchange for special consideration that is incompatible with the duties of his position'" (ibid.).

and in this sense a gift is not always immoral. Furthermore, Noonan states, "The exchange of favors with a powerholder is otherwise like other reciprocal transactions in the society" (1984, 3). Offerings and gifts given to "powerholders" (in this case the gods) are not new in traditional societies. But in modern civilizations there are powerholders who hold offices and other prestigious positions as part of a larger bureaucracy. Giving gifts to these powerholders may be seen as an attempt to circumvent the bureaucratic system.

The culture of free-market capitalism assumes that any form of gift or offering given to a powerholder, such as a government official, has the power to corrupt and distort judgment. This assumption is "not self evident," according to Noonan (1984, 3). Often powerholders in many underdeveloped countries are given gifts as gratuities for services rendered or services yet to be done. Gifts are not always given in order to compel a powerholder to take biased action but may be a means of ensuring fairness. In this case, the gift becomes leverage for the giver to acquire a degree of influence over the powerholder. The powerholder may or may not receive a gift, but if a powerholder denies it, he is sending a message that he does not want to get into a social contract with the giver.

CAPITALIST ECONOMICS, COMPENSATION, AND DIGNITY

According to Weber in his *Economy and Society* (1978) and *The Protestant Ethic and the Spirit of Capitalism* (1930), the bourgeois form of free-market capitalist economy depends on "impersonal decision makers" or "functionaries" who are supposedly "disinterested" neutral agents given a public trust to run the bureaucracy (Clarke 1983, x). Elements that corrupt and distort the judgment of such functionaries are perceived as attacks on the bureaucratic system. Proper compensation is supposed to encourage government officials, judges, and clerks to act and make decisions in accordance with their offices based purely on the *merits* of the case. This type of economic system eases the need to give gifts to powerholders as compensation for their services. Their "calling" as public servants, and the compensation they receive from the state in behalf of the public they serve, ideally nullifies any need for tips, rewards, or gifts. Gifts and tips to such officials are therefore inappropriate and threaten the system of justice and fairness.

The problem of corruption arises in countries such as the Philippines when government officials do not receive proper compensation and so engage in extortion and bribery to meet their own economic needs. The need for government bureaucracies to sufficiently compensate their employees is a basic element in addressing corruption and bribery practices. Mauss explains:

> We sense that we cannot make men work well unless they are sure of being fairly paid throughout their life for work they have fairly carried out, both for others and for themselves. The producer who carries on exchange feels once more—he has always felt it, but this time he does so acutely—that he is exchanging more than a product of hours of working time, his life. Thus he wishes to be rewarded, even if only moderately, for this gift. To refuse him this reward is to make him become idle or less productive. (1990, 77)

Thus in countries where customs officials or police officers are not properly compensated, there is a general permissiveness to look for compensation elsewhere. Jin-Li Hu et al. (2004) note that bribery "is sometimes part of a government employee's income and may 'lubricate' the inefficiencies caused by a fixed salary and hierarchy" (178).

Mauss (1990) believes that a wage is not enough to cover society's obligation to the worker. This is especially true when the daily living wage is not even enough to meet his or her own basic needs. There is another type of compensation that is needed, and that is the acknowledgment of a person's dignity or honor. People live not only on material things but on the significance awarded to them and their work. They must find meaning in what they do. Compensation is supposed to forge social bonds and to enhance a person's social identity and social status.

Human beings are social beings. We don't just work in order to put food on the table; often we use our resources in order to build social relationships. The money from wages may be used to build social relationships by sharing, giving, or lending wealth. In this way a person can build esteem and a good reputation. A person who is generous in Filipino society is seen as *mabait* (literally understood as both "kind" and "good"). *Mabait* is a social value many people strive to achieve. Filipinos would rather be known as *mabait* than *mayaman* (rich or affluent). Low wages in this sense limit a person's generosity and ability to share (although many still do share their limited resources) and thus keep them from achieving the status of a *mabait* person. A similar situation can be found among pastors in Mali, as described by Wilson in this volume (chap. 6).

In a way, corruption is an attempt to raise a person's social status and to improve his or her social identity. This is a void fallen human beings try to fill with power transactions of all types. Given this situation, it is possible that government officials who receive bribes or extort money from their clients believe that they are merely asking compensation for what, in the first place, they rightfully deserve. Mauss (1990) explains that this sense of honor and compensation is reflected in our "social insurance legislation":

> All our social insurance legislation, a piece of state socialism that has already been realized, is inspired by the following principle: the worker has given his life and his labour, on the one hand to the collectivity, and on the other hand, to his employers. Although the worker has to contribute to his insurance, those who have benefited from his services have not discharged their debt to him through the payment of wages. The state itself, representing the community, owes him as do his employers, together with some assistance from himself, a certain security in life, against unemployment, sickness, old age, and death. (67)

Mauss suggests, then, that beyond wages, society owes all of its workers the dignity of protection against unemployment, ill health, and death. In societies where such benefits are not guaranteed, government employees may resort to extortion or receive bribes to ensure themselves a dignified future.

Seen in this perspective, extortion and bribery are not always products of greed; they are just as much a byproduct of a certain sociocultural logic at work in a particular economic structure, and may even be motivated by a basic need to recover dignity in one's work. In some cases the inability to feed one's family after a long day of work is more dishonorable than to accept payments in order to expedite the processing of a paper. Although such an action constitutes violating the ethics of a free-market capitalist economy, it is easy to understand why some would violate their moral responsibility towards an impersonal bureaucracy in order to provide for their own family.

If the above argument is valid, this raises the question, would raising the compensation of government officials automatically address the practice of bribery and extortion? While this seems a logical solution, it does not always hold true. A city prosecutor in Manila was proud to show me his family, their modest house, a few square feet of farmland (where his son raised fighting cocks), and several cars, one of which was a red sports car. Intrigued by the car, I inquired whether it belonged to him or his son. He casually answered, "This car is being used by my son, but I got it from a client whose case I was prosecuting." I asked what the case was about and he said it involved drugs. The client had been caught in possession of an illegal drug, and the prosecutor was required to indict him. However, the father of the accused offered to give the prosecutor the car if he would drop the case.

Since this prosecutor was a neighbor, I could visit and observe his family life more closely. He seemed to be well respected by his family and was very generous to his relatives and friends. Anyone needing financial help could always depend on him. On special occasions, truckloads of his relatives would travel for eighteen hours in order to celebrate with him. One may ask, how can a perfectly respectable person in the community also be a "corrupt" official? Noonan (1984) observes that "there is a fallacy of the perfectly corrupt man—the belief that vices are linked and that unless a man is thoroughly corrupt in every aspect he can be no bribe-taker or bribe-giver" (xiii). As a result, people may maintain their moral approval of someone they perceive as honorable even when bribes have clearly been taken. This brings us to another sociocultural element in the system of bribery and extortion, the patronage system.

PATRONAGE AND BRIBERY

The patronage system operates as a legitimate form of economic exchange in many societies. This system is based on principles of reciprocity. Here the "patron has needs which he relies on the client to fulfill, and when necessary the client can *initiate* services to his patron, obligating the latter to respond. This gives the client political leverage" (Goodell 1985, 253).

In real life, the process and nature of economic distributions are often highly embedded within political, kinship, and social systems. Political candidates in the Philippines, for example, are known to throw lavish parties for their supporters and colleagues in an effort to strengthen political alliances. This is similar to the practice of the *potlatch*. *Potlatch* is a Chinook word that means "gift" (Womack 2001, 112). Marvin Harris (quoted in ibid.) explains:

> The object of the potlatch was to give away or destroy more wealth than one's rival. If the potlatch giver was a powerful chief, he might attempt to shame his rivals and gain everlasting admiration from his followers by destroying food, clothing, and money. Sometimes he might even seek prestige by burning down his own house.[10]

In the Philippines, incumbent government officials are known to host lavish feasts and give extravagant gifts to their constituents and supporters during Christmas season in an attempt to maintain prestige and control of resources as the "big man" in the community.

---

10 For further discussion of ceremonial feasting in archaic societies, see Mauss 1990; Rambo 1995; Harris 1994.

In some groups, control over allocation of resources provides leaders with the means to command the labor of others, amass great stores of personal wealth, or wage war. In other societies, systems of distribution are organized so that access to resources is more or less uniform throughout the group, preventing some individuals from accumulating wealth or gaining control over others, thus effectively reinforcing egalitarian relationships. (Womack 2001, 108)

Karl Rambo (1995) explains that at ceremonies among the Simbu people, the host clan presents ostentatious gifts to the trading partners, who are expected to reciprocate it sometime later. The inability to reciprocate is a sign of a failure to achieve one's rightful place in society. So the wealth that is gifted and consumed during the ceremony is actually transformed into a higher value that connotes honor, prestige, power, and authority.

In modern society, philanthropy may be compared to the potlatch, as it too is a means of converting economic resources into social prestige. Mauss states,

Thus one section of humanity, comparatively rich, hard-working, and creating considerable surpluses, has known how to, and still does know how to exchange things of great value, under different forms and for reasons different from those with which we are familiar. (1990, 33)

Mauss (1990) and Rambo (1995) have also observed that the practice of the potlatch (among certain North American Indians and the Simbu people) involves the redistribution of valuable products, such as meat, to the whole community. Some scholars therefore argue that the practice of bribery and extortion may serve the same function (i.e., the redistribution of wealth to people who do not have access to it), since bribe money ends up in the local economy rather than in government institutions, where only a few have access to it (see Caiden and Caiden 1977; Bayley 1966; Banfield 1975; Nye 1967).

BRIBERY AND MORAL REASONING[+]

Robert Priest in his article "Missionary Elenctics" argues that moral conscience is culturally conditioned. All human beings have a moral conscience, but what triggers it varies from culture to culture. Priest states, "American missionaries internalize deeply held moral ideas about punctuality, egalitarianism, individual rights, privacy, cleanliness, etc., which derive much more clearly from their culture than from the Scripture" (1994, 300).

A mission worker may argue that a Christian should never pay a "bribe" under any condition in order to get a visa. However, he may also argue that mission workers may enter a restricted country using a student visa or a nonresident missionary visa (Falkiner 1999, 24). This attitude demonstrates that people are often selective in applying moral laws to themselves versus to others in other cultures.

> Paying what Westerners term as "bribe" in order to expedite the processing of a legal document is no different than paying the post office more money to expedite the delivery of a package. However, for many the written law is the ultimate arbiter of justice. As Falkiner argues, "Therefore, even if it were considered to be a cultural norm, and even if everyone else is doing it, the Christian is called to obey the law that prohibits it" (1999, 24). The problem with written law is that it is sometimes unrealistic and unreasonable in a given context. Ultimately, a Christian should abide by the standards of God's word and not simply by a written law. American Christians might drive over the speed limit, a clear violation of a written law, yet feel little or no guilt, but often react with great indignation to the expectation of a gift for services they feel they are owed. On the other hand, a Christian who hires the services of a prostitute in Amsterdam acts within the freedoms of the written law but violates God's moral law. (Tan 2011, 280–81)

+   This section is largely based on an earlier article of mine; see Tan 2011.

This shows that human beings make their own individual choices about moral values and motivations, and that they do so based on their different cultural backgrounds.

The practice of bribery and extortion is not always motivated by greed but may sometimes be motivated by a higher ethical value. For instance, when Adoniram Judson was imprisoned, Ann Judson tried to preserve his life by bribing prison officials to allow her to bring food to him and his fellow prisoners (Robert 1996, 46). Was Ann Judson guilty of committing bribery? Clearly the example of bribing a prison official for humanitarian purposes changes the dynamics and definition of what is considered a deviant behavior. It shows that there can be a higher ethical motivation for committing such an act. A man receiving bribes may do so for the sake of his starving family or relatives who expect him to take on the role of a clan patriarch and provide for the needs of the clan. Some, therefore, participate in the system of bribery and extortion in order to maintain their social role and status among their relatives and community as well as to provide for them.

While Christians may claim a higher ethical or moral purpose for refusing to participate in a "corrupt" system, in the eyes of their own internal sociocultural and economic logic and norms, bribe givers and takers may claim a higher purpose for what they do than outsiders might imagine. Thus it is critical for mission workers to know why people are involved in bribes and extortion, just as it is critical for mission workers to know why some women go into prostitution or some men become gamblers. Knowing why helps create a better approach to solving the problem. If the reason is merely greed, then it is important to simply tell people that greed is evil. If the reason is the inability to provide for the basic needs of the family, then in some cases raising the salary would address the issue of corruption. However, if the reason is social significance (and I argue that this is what many have been striving for), then the good news of salvation becomes indispensable in the war against corrupt practices, because it provides another avenue for meeting this need.

CONCLUSION

The failure to properly understand the complex social dynamics involved in activities such as bribery and extortion has limited the ways in which Christians have engaged the problem. For example, many Christian writings and Western missionary discourses on bribery and extortion have been shallow and simplistic in their treatment of the subject because they lack deep sociocultural engagement (see Falkiner 1999; Samuel 1995; Langston 1994; Wilson 1974; Ouko 1975; Ngun 1997). Bribery and extortion practices have been dismissed as a mere byproduct of greedy and sinful human beings. This examination argues that corrupt practices do not always result from greed. Rather they sometimes emerge out of a deeper need for dignity and honor, one that is universal in human beings.

Those whom Christians view as "corrupt officials" may actually be well-meaning people who participate in the system because they cannot achieve the honor expected of them by the patronage system if they must make a living under free-market capitalism. There are societies in which the free-market capitalist economy is still an incompatible system with regard to traditional social expectations (or where it functions haphazardly, as in the Philippines). Even though governments may attempt to modernize their economies, market capitalism may merely be overlaid on top of a society that has a reciprocity- or patronage-based system underneath. Here the old system may continue to work away from the public view, even as the new system seems to be in place.

What then are some of the ways to address bribery and extortion practices in Majority World countries?

1. Honor public servants. Local churches may create activities that recognize and honor public servants who are faithful in dispensing their duties. This may not alleviate the small salary they are receiving, but it may alleviate the burden of work, since they are valued and their sacrifices are recognized.

2. Create support systems for Christians in government. Often many of these Christians struggle against the culture of corruption in their workplaces. Churches may try and identify Christians working in government settings and provide a support group for them. Churches may also serve as a venue for Christians in government to create networks of support among themselves.

3. Conduct moral recovery programs. For many years the Philippine government has allowed churches to conduct what are popularly known as "moral recovery programs" to people in various government institutions, such as the police, military, and the bureau of internal revenues. These programs are designed to educate people on moral and ethical values.

How then should mission workers discern between what is a legitimate and what is an illegitimate transaction? If a worker is being extorted, what should they do? The following are some suggestions that mission workers should keep in mind.

1. Distinguish between extortion and bribery. A bribe, by definition, is any gift given or promised by a client to a certain power holder in order to coerce him or her to violate a duty or moral obligation in dealing with the client. On the other hand, "extortion" refers to the power holder's intention of obtaining any pecuniary gift from a client as a condition to dispense duty or services (Noonan 1984; Philips 1984). Distinguishing the terms will assist in producing sensitivity to the context and to the moral responsibility of the parties involved.

Depending on the situation, in some cases it might be "safer" to pay rather than insisting on one's right, since you may report the incident later if necessary. A desperate policeman will go out of his way to make money. This is an example of extortion, and the one paying is not the one violating a moral law. The person using his power to extort is the one at fault (see Tan 2011). On the other hand, if the documents of the traveler are not in order and the traveler offers an inducement to the immigration officer to overlook the discrepancy, then it becomes a bribe. In this situation the person paying the money is actually violating a moral law.

2. Consult with the local people to understand what they would consider acceptable versus unacceptable financial transactions. In the Philippines, for instance, Christians have been very vocal on the subject of bribery and extortion. There are strong admonitions among Filipino Christians not to pay "bribes" and "extortion money." Thus expatriate mission workers should not do so either. However, in places where local Christians have not yet properly confronted the issue head-on nor considered it deviant or wrong, it may be helpful for workers to consider that corruption should be fought, but by carefully identifying the true source of the problem. It is possible to waste all your time struggling with the victims of the system and have no time to address the real villains—the structure of the system and those who enforce it at a high level (Adeney 1995, 145).

To be sure, even when culture has been considered, there may be situations in which a worker may endanger his or her life and/or that of the family by refusing to pay "bribes." In such cases, workers should pay and accept that they have become a "victim of petty extortion [but] not a criminal" (Adeney 1995, 145). For instance, a close missionary friend admitted to me at one time that he was forced to pay a bribe when he and his family accidentally crossed a border in Niger at night. Fearing for their safety, he ended up paying a hefty amount to an officer to let them go. We should not be too quick to condemn such actions, but in all cases seek God's wisdom in dealing with such situations. A person under duress should not be blamed for breaking under pressure.

3. Be aware of the conflict of values that may arise between our own understandings of "bribery" and local perceptions. In some places "bribery is an accepted mechanism for legal transactions ... [and] Westerners should be cautious of immediately imposing their views or legal norms on a context in which small-scale bribery has almost the status of customary law" (Adeney 1995, 145). As we have seen, the practice of bribery and extortion may be motivated by a higher human value unseen by outsiders—the need for self-respect, dignity, and honor, and the need to protect and care for one's own family. Most people have a noble ambition in life; however, the means of attaining it varies.

Deviant behaviors such as bribery and extortion are symptoms of a person's deeper need for meaning in life. Perhaps Christianity in this context should present Christ not merely as one who saves us from our sins but also as one who came to give meaning to our very existence and restore the dignity that we lost as human beings when Adam fell into sin. Christ came to die for us because we are worth dying for, and so that by believing in him we might regain our self-worth.

REFERENCES

Adeney, Bernard T. 1995. *Strange virtues: Ethics in a multicultural world.* Downers Grove, IL: InterVarsity Press.

Alam, M. Shahid. 1989. Anatomy of corruption: An approach to the political economy of underdevelopment. *American Journal of Economics and Sociology* 48, no. 4: 441–56.

Ashforth, Adam. 2005. *Witchcraft, violence, and democracy in South Africa.* Chicago: University of Chicago Press.

Azfar, Omar, Young Lee, and Anand Swamy. 2001. The causes and consequences of corruption. *Annals of the American Academy of Political and Social Sciences* 573: 42–56.

Banfield, Edward C. 1975. Corruption as a feature of governmental organization. *Journal of Law and Economics* 18: 587–605.

Bayley, David H. 1966. The effects of corruption in a developing nation. *Western Political Quarterly* 19, no. 4: 719–32.

Bardhan, Pranab. 1997. Corruption and development: A review of issues. *Journal of Economic Literature 35*, no. 3: 1320–46.

Bruce, Willa. 1994. Ethical people are productive people. *Public Productivity and Management Review* 17, no. 3: 241–52.

Caiden, Gerald E., and Naomi J. Caiden. 1977. Administrative corruption. *Public Administration Review* 37, no. 3: 301–9.

Carson, Thomas L. Bribery, extortion, and "the Foreign Corrupt Practices Act." *Philosophy and Public Affairs* 14, no. 1: 66–90.

Choi, Jay Pil, and Marcel Thum. 2004. The economics of repeated extortion. *RAND Journal of Economics* 35, no. 2: 203–23.

Clarke, Michael, ed. 1983. *Corruption: Causes, consequences and control*. New York: Martin.

Danley, John R. 1983. Toward a theory of bribery. *Business and Professional Ethics Journal* 2, no. 3: 19–39.

Elmer, Duane. 1993. *Cross-cultural conflict: Building relationships for effective ministry*. Downers Grove, IL: InterVarsity Press.

Falkiner, Steven. 1999. Bribery: Where are the lines? *Evangelical Missions Quarterly* 35, no. 1: 22–29.

Foster, George M. 1972. The anatomy of envy: A study in symbolic behavior. *Current Anthropology* 13, no. 2: 165–202.

Gluckman, Max. 1963. Gossip and scandal. *Current Anthropology* 4, no. 3: 307–16.

Goffman, Erving. 1959. *The presentation of self in everyday life*. Harmondsworth, UK: Penguin.

Goodell, Grace E. 1985. Paternalism, patronage, and potlatch: The dynamics of giving and being given to. [With responses and author's reply.] *Current Anthropology* 26, no. 2: 247–66.

Gregor, Thomas. 1977. *Mehinaku: The drama of daily life in a Brazilian Indian village*. Chicago: University of Chicago Press.

Grodeland, Ase B., Tatyana Y. Koshechkina, and William L. Miller. 1998. Foolish to give and yet more foolish not to take: In-depth interviews with post-Communist citizens on their everyday use of bribes and contacts. *Europe-Asia Studies* 50, no. 4: 651–77.

Harris, Marvin. 1989. *Cows, pigs, wars, and witches: The riddles of culture*. New York: Vintage.

———. 1994. Life without chiefs. In *Annual editions: Anthropology 94/95*, 17th ed., edited by Elvio Angeloni, 81–85. Guilford, CT: Dushkin.

Hiebert, Paul G. 1999. *Cultural anthropology*. 2nd ed. Grand Rapids: Baker.

Hu, Jin-Li, Chung-Huang Huang, and Wei-Kai Chu. 2004. Bribery, hierarchical government, and incomplete environmental enforcement. *Environmental Economics and Policy Studies* 6: 177–96.

Ilagan, Bonifacio P., ed. 2008. *Corruptionary: Natatanging diksyonaryo ng mga salitang korapsyon*. Quezon City, Philippines: University of the Philippines Centennial Publication.

Kohlberg, Lawrence. 1973. The claim to moral adequacy of a highest stage of moral judgment. *Journal of Philosophy* 70, no. 18: 630–46.

Langston, Richard L. 1989. A biblical perspective on bribery and extortion and its implications in the Philippine context from a missionary viewpoint. DMiss diss., Trinity Evangelical Divinity School.

———. 1994. Alternatives to bribery: Philippines. *Evangelical Review of Theology* 18, no. 3: 248–60.

Lutwak, Nita, Jacqueline B. Panish, Joseph R. Ferrari, and Brian E. Razzino. 2001. Shame and guilt and their relationship to positive expectations and anger expressiveness. *Adolescence* 36, no. 144: 641–53.

Malinowski, Bronislaw. 1984 [1922]. *Argonauts of the Western Pacific: An account of native enterprise and adventure in the archipelagoes of Melanesian New Guinea.* Prospect Heights, IL: Waveland.

Mauss, Marcel. 1990 [1925]. *The gift: Forms and functions of exchange in archaic societies.* London: Routledge and Kegan Paul.

Mayer, Marvin K. 1976. *A look at Latin American lifestyles.* Dallas: SIL Museum of Anthropology.

Miranda-Feliciano, Evelyn. 1990. *Filipino values and our Christian faith.* Manila: OMF Literature.

Ngun, Yuhard R. 1997. *A biblical perspective on bribery with application to the Indonesian context* [microform]. ThM thesis, Dallas Theological Seminary.

Nichols, Gregory. 1999. A case for bribery: Giving versus taking. *Evangelical Missions Quarterly* 35, no. 1: 30–33.

Noonan, John T. 1984. *Bribes: The intellectual history of a moral idea.* Berkeley: University of California Press.

Ortner, Sherry B. 1978. *Sherpas through their rituals.* London: Cambridge University Press.

Ouko, Joseph J. 1975. *Bribery: It kills you and your nation.* Kisuma, Kenya: Evangel.

Parhizgar, Suzan S., and Kamal Dean Parhizgar. 2008. *Multicultural biomedical ethics and global biosophical moral logic.* Lanham, MD: University Press of America.

Philips, Michael. 1984. Bribery. *Ethics* 94, no. 4: 621–36.

Priest, Robert J. 1994. Missionary elenctics: Conscience and culture. *Missiology: An International Review* 22, no. 3: 291–315.

Rambo, Karl F. 1995. From shells to money: Ceremonial exchange among the Simbu of Papua New Guinea. In *Annual editions: Anthropology 95/96*, 18th ed., edited by Elvio Angeloni, 99–104. Guilford, CT: Dushkin.

Reisman, W. Michael. 1979. *Folded lies: Bribery, crusades, and reforms*. New York: Free Press.

Robert, Dana L. 1996. *American women in mission: The modern mission era 1792–1992*. Macon, GA: Mercer University Press.

Samuel, Vinay. 1995. Business and corruption. *Transformation* 12, no. 1: 23–27.

Seidman, Robert B. 1978. Why do people obey the law? The case of corruption in developing countries. *British Journal of Law and Society* 5, no. 1: 45–68.

Sherry, John F., Jr. 1983. Gift giving in anthropological perspective. *Journal of Consumer Research* 10, no. 2: 157–68.

Shleifer, Andrei, and Robert W. Vishny. 1993. Corruption. *Quarterly Journal of Economics* 108, no. 3: 599–617.

Smart, Alan. 1993. Gifts, bribes and guanxi: A reconsideration of Bourdieu's social capital. *Cultural Anthropology* 8, no. 3: 388–408.

Tan, Jason Richard. 2011. Missionary ethics and the practice of bribery. *Evangelical Missions Quarterly* 47, no. 3: 278–82.

Weber, Max. 1930. *The Protestant ethic and the spirit of capitalism*. London: George Unwin.

———. 1978. *Economy and society*. Edited by Guenther Roth and Claus Wittich. Berkeley: University of California Press.

Wilson, Marvin R. 1974. Prophets and green palms: Bribery in biblical perspective. *Christianity Today*, January 18, 13–19.

Womack, Mari. 2001. Being human: An introduction to cultural anthropology. 2nd ed. New York: Prentice Hall.

5

SYMBOLS OF THE WEAK, SYMBOLS OF THE GOSPEL: THE UPSIDE-DOWN GOSPEL IN RELATION TO PATRONAGE SYSTEMS IN WEST JAVA, INDONESIA

Lindy Backues

I initially moved to Indonesia in 1989 in order to participate in development work. I did just that for the next eighteen years in the province of West Java—for the first eight years in the capital city of Bandung and thereafter for ten years in the smaller city of Tasikmalaya, located about three hours southeast of Bandung. Alongside my involvement in grassroots development work, I was also briefly attached to the Indonesian Institute of Sciences, researching proper strategies for development practice. In the process, I discovered a grassroots-level mechanism that interested me a great deal, one that I will describe below. Upon sharing it with my research advisors, they asked if I had read Yale political scientist and anthropologist James Scott. I confessed that I had not. As I began reading Scott's work, I found that my discovery was strangely similar to what he had unearthed in Malaysia some fifteen years before. In both *Weapons of the Weak* (1985) and *Domination and the Arts of Resistance* (1990), Scott argues that "everyday forms of peasant resistance" tend not to be frontal nor overtly contentious, but mostly covert, off-the-record, Janus-faced, and thus pursued incognito behind the backs of persons in power. Such clandestine varieties of defiance seem intentionally open to multiple public interpretations, providing poor residents opportunities to nimbly deny the resistance nature of their actions when they find it expedient to do so. In many places Scott dubs such responses "foot dragging."

Another practice I discovered was that members of marginalized communities seemed to play with the words, symbols, and religious and cultural imagery that were directed their way by way of patronage relationships managed by the local elite in their community. At the root of many poor persons' coping mechanisms is a very pliable semiotic horizon, one that they themselves manipulate, reinterpret, and utilize for their own defense and psychic well-being. This upending of the symbolic arrangement seemed aimed at defying and contesting local as well as state-centered rhetoric about development. In short, there appeared to be a setting on its head of the semiotic domain of the state patronage system by persons disempowered in local communities. This seemed especially acute when historic patronage alliances became twisted and distorted by changes in government policy that were biased toward centralized nation-state purposes.

As an open, practicing Christian, I asked myself what I thought of institutions of patronage in the first place. I wondered if these alliances were not far too power soaked, far too hierarchical, and thus too susceptible to abuse and domination to be useful. If so, I continued, were they out-of-bounds for serious Christians seeking to offer hope through authentic development work in poor communities? In a word, were not patron-client relationships diametrically opposed to the model of Jesus?[1]

Something led me back to the "upside-down" nature of the gospel—something that predisposes followers of Jesus to challenge empires, oppose oppression, and, in the words of the old Quaker saying, "speak truth to power." Are we not called to stand alongside persons

---

1   This question arises most pointedly to the degree that one agrees with persons like Anabaptist ethicist John Howard Yoder (1972), especially when he states that Christians are only admonished to imitate Christ "at the point of the concrete social meaning of the cross in its relation to enmity and power" (134).

trapped in hierarchical power structures and help them resist, and at the same time learn how they might account for reality in light of a new interpretive field—one hopefully mirroring the kingdom of God? Surely we as Christians are called to "[move] into the neighborhood" (John 1:14 MSG) as Jesus did and take upon ourselves the symbolic oppositions and contests that the poor and marginalized face.[2]

I will explore these considerations below and examine the history of the traditional patronage systems in Indonesia. I will also probe the way patronage seems to have changed into something more costly to the poor than it previously was. In the process, I hope to show how certain marginalized persons have coped with the increasing pressure being put on them *by way of* their "everyday forms of peasant resistance," by way of their "weapons of the weak"—through their own deft recasting of local images and cultural artifacts, cleverly utilizing their time-honored positions as clients of those in power.

I will end by briefly examining patron-client relationships in light of the Bible and the pattern of Jesus, who seemed not to jettison them but instead upended their meaning, inverting them, subverting and reinterpreting them in a way reminiscent of marginalized persons worldwide. This should provide a distinct (if not unique) Christian approach to partnering with persons on the margins by illustrating a stance aligned with the biblical posture of Jesus as well as one that is often adopted by marginalized persons in tradition-based communities globally.

THE SYMBOLIC TERRAIN IN WEST JAVA

Historically at the village level in West Java, *kampung*[3] patrons either occupied local governmental/quasi-governmental positions (the formal leadership structure) or were members of the local village elite

---

2   For more insight into this, see Backues 2009.

3   *Kampung* is generally translated "hamlet" or "village" in English (the former if constituting a borough on the fringe of an urban center, the latter if based as a community in a rural context). I am responsible for all translation of Indonesian sources in this essay.

(making up the informal leadership structure). These persons controlled strategic linkages with power sources outside the village, making them channels of outside resources for local, poor kampung residents. Local leadership held almost all village power. But poorer kampung residents could at least count on resources and protection from the leadership. Though disempowered, it was still true that poorer village folks knew the size, shape, and fashion of their place in the sun.

Leadership arrangements like these reflected traditional notions of personal authority and power in West Java. In sharp contrast to Western views of power as "an abstraction, a formula for certain observed patterns of social interaction," Javanese and Sundanese persons[4] cast power as a tangible, finite, and indivisible force requiring little in the way of moral reflection (Anderson 1990, 21). Table 5.1 below summarizes this difference.

TABLE 5.1
Contrasting images of power

POWER	MODERN WESTERN CONCEPT OF POWER	TRADITIONAL JAVANESE (SUNDANESE) CONCEPT OF POWER
TYPE	*Abstract* Strictly speaking, power does not exist. The term "power" is commonly used to describe relationships or observed patterns of social interaction.	*Concrete* Power exists, independent of its possible users. It is not a theoretical postulate but an existential reality.
SOURCE(S)	*Heterogeneous* Different types of power are treated as separate variables (e.g., political power, economic power, etc.), influencing behavior.	*Homogeneous* All power is of the same type, having the same source.

4   For a discussion on distinguishing the Sundanese from other ethnic groups in Indonesia, see Rosidi (1984, 130).

	No Inherent Limits	Limited
ACCUMULATION	Power is theoretically unlimited since it is conceptualized as abstract and hinges upon social interaction.	Since power simply exists, its amount is cosmically constant. Concentration of power in one place requires a proportional diminution elsewhere.
MORAL LEGITIMACY	*Ambiguous* Since power is heterogeneous in type and abstract in nature (with actual reference to relationships), it follows that not all power is legitimate—ethical deliberation is incumbent upon those seeking access to power	*Does Not Raise Questions of Legitimacy* Since all power derives from a single homogeneous source, power itself antecedes questions of good and evil.

(Source: Anderson 1990, 21–23)

This difference has had enormous bearing upon how leadership and authority have functioned in West Javan cultural settings.

A leader in West Java was traditionally framed as a *wadah* (container) for power. As such, the leader's ability to fortify his hold over devotees served to validate his power, legitimizing his right to it. Moreover, these power relationships enjoyed a transcendental, metaphysical, and even quasi-religious flavor,[5] experienced in patron-client alliances. Personal authority was primarily ascriptive in nature, sharing

---

5   "Power" in the Javanese/Sundanese sense seems to have latent within it a deified, independent quality. Cf. Anderson's comments: "The old usage of the word *power*, which survives in such phrases as 'The Great Power' or 'Power had gone out of him' (Gospel according to St. Mark, 5:30) approximates the Javanese idea, but by no means coincides with it" (1990, 20n8); likewise, "the well-known mystical formula *Tuhan adalah Aku* (God is I) expresses the concreteness of the Javanese idea of power. The divine power is the essence of 'I'" (22n11).

important similarities with Weber's classic concept of "charisma"[6] and with the leader functioning as mediator between power sources.[7]

The shape of these traditional patron-client structures might be depicted below in figure 5.1.

FIGURE 5.1

Traditional *kampung* patronage

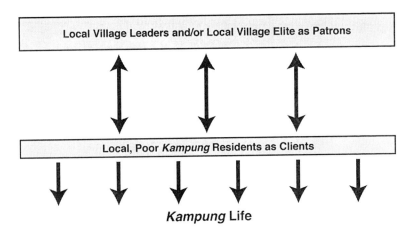

In light of the role played by these images of leadership, it is not surprising that a variation of these was chosen by the Indonesian government to represent itself at the local level, especially beginning in the middle part of the 1960s and extending until the end of the 1990s. During that time, former Indonesian president Soeharto boldly positioned himself as national benefactor–father figure, self-typified by his title

---

6   Cf. Anderson (1990, chaps. 1–2).
7   For a concisely detailed look at patron-client relationships, see Eisenstadt and Roniger (1981, 284) and Eisenstadt and Roniger 1984.

of choice: "Father of Development" (*Bapak Pembangunan*).[8] Studying this arrangement and the language surrounding "development" under Soeharto offers us a window into the configuration of governmental power at the time.

The Indonesian term glossed "development" (*pembangunan*) seems to be relatively new in the language, not appearing in any of the area's ancient manuscripts or even in the rise and fall of local kingdoms in the region's history. The word appears to have gained currency post–World War II, most prominently at the beginning of Soeharto's New Order administration in 1966. Heryanto claims that it served as a key word for the regime, representing and giving shape to its style (1988, 8). Most interesting, the New Order government chose this word to render the English term "development" in opposition to an equally appropriate term, *perkembangan*, derived from *kembang* (usually glossed "flower" in English). *Pembangunan* comes from the word *bangun*, a term that for the last couple of generations[9] has carried connotations of "building" or "construction." That choice strikingly underscored the government's rejection of natural, indigenous growth processes (perkembangan) in favor of an engineered process, concocted by formal regulators external to the context (pembangunan) (Heryanto 1988, 15–16).[10]

Development in Indonesia was intimately tied to Soeharto's person as the "Father of Development." To validate his hold on the presidency,

---

8   Something interesting to note about the semantic domain of this term, *bapak,* is that in the Indonesian language it can just as easily mean "Mr." as it can "father" (unlike how it is used in neighboring Malaysia, where it only means "father"). But as we shall see shortly, in light of the ubiquitous custodial image nationally promoted, the former notion clearly was *not* the meaning that Soeharto intended.

9   Heryanto points out that the term *bangun* actually designates two overarching categories of meaning: (1) to build, and (2) to arouse (a sleeping person) (1988, 9–10). During the period of Indonesian political and ideological foment in the 1930s, when the focus was upon rousing the masses in order to throw off the bonds of colonialization, the latter tended to be the connotation. However, in today's climate the former is the preferred connotation.

10   For a discussion on the two divergent styles in development planning ("blueprint" and "learning process" approaches) that is similar to the contrast being made here, see Korten 1980.

Soeharto needed to live up to his designation—the failure of which finally led to his downfall in 1998. Up until the midnineties, the success of his system further established the president as the fulcrum of the national patronage system. As the "Father of Development," Soeharto portrayed his grab for power in 1965–66 and his three-decade-plus struggle to maintain that power as events that were sacrally fated, rendering the result less a power grab and more a divinely consecrated, salvific confirmation of his patriarchal position.

This "consecration"—tied to nation building and economic recovery following the administration of the first president, Soekarno—supported a state image intimately tied to development schemes that Soeharto lionized as badges of legitimacy. Beginning with Soeharto's New Order government in the late 1960s, talk about development in Indonesia was fashioned from a range of symbolic elements injected from the outside, yet which also blended with the traditional patron-client relationships just described.

The first outside element (already briefly mentioned above) centered upon the term *pembangunan*. Eminently important, it was situated at the heart of all New Order national campaigns and government crusades. Beneath the pembangunan umbrella Soeharto slowly constructed his own unique nation-state paradigm, one that included strong "family" or "filial" undertones.

The second element revolved around the interplay of two additional state political clichés: *gotong royong* and *Pancasila*—each tied to pembangunan rhetoric in different ways. Gotong royong seemed aimed at restraining and domesticating poor kampung residents. Pancasila, on the other hand, was designed to unite, co-opt, and corral elite kampung as well as urban dwellers (Sullivan 1987, 207). It will assist our understanding of the situation to look briefly at each of these arrangements in turn.

Pancasila is a term of Sanskrit derivation probably best translated as "the Five Principles." These principles are more or less as follows: (1) belief in one supreme being, (2) a just and civilized humanitarianism, (3) national unity, (4) wise government based upon consultation and consensus, and (5) social justice for all. The concept of Pancasila has served as Indonesia's state creed since the country came into being in 1945. Nevertheless, many theorists have noted that one of Pancasila's most alarming characteristics during Soeharto's rule was its lack of discernibly consistent content. While initially seeming to say much (in Geertz' words, being "short, ambiguous, and impeccably high-minded" [1973, 225]), in the end it often seemed hollow, sounded vague, and consequently was rendered highly amorphous. Under Soeharto it carried no semantic center, making it especially susceptible to manipulation. In the New Order's interpretation, the focus was more on what was disallowed than what was permitted or encouraged (Mackie and MacIntyre 1994, 26), a fact that rendered the concept decidedly negative in connotation.

In like fashion, *gotong royong* ("mutual cooperation" or "mutual assistance") has been "an expression covering a familiar set of principles and practices and an elaborate inspirational discourse on neighbourliness" (Sullivan 1987, 71).[11] Contrary to a good deal of present-day Indonesian nation-state rhetoric that frames the idea as a time-honored concept bequeathed to the nation by its forebears, the phrase "appears to have emerged since the 1940s as an ideology of community earnestly promoted by the state" (4).[12] It seems that the reason for this fabrication was a need for passive communities that would not impede government programs *and* a desire for voluntary labor for village-level

---

11   Cf. Guinness, who defines it as "forms of balanced and generalised reciprocity among Javanese villagers" (1994, 279).

12   First president Soekarno seems to have played an instrumental part in introducing this term to the Indonesian political stage. "In his 1945 speech, after describing the five principles (*pancasila*) he thought it would constitute the *Weltanschauung* of the nation [and] be condensed into three (*tri sila*): social nationalism, social democracy, and belief in one God. He then proposed that this three could be compacted into one. 'If I compress what was five into three, and what was three into one, then I have a genuine Indonesian term, *gotong rojong*, mutual cooperation. The state of Indonesia which we are to establish must be a *gotong rojong* state. Is that not something marvelous: a *Gotong Rojong* state!'" (Sullivan 1987, 173). For an abridged version of this speech, see Sukarno 1969.

government projects organized from the top down and needing only to be implemented.[13]

Setia Permana and Dadi J. Iskandar (1994, 4) claim that, under Soeharto, alongside a "gotong royong"-ization of kampung life there was an accompanying "liturgization" of public political processes. The authors assert that

> political "liturgical ceremonies" arise and serve merely to maintain an air of ceremonial ritualism—clearly these are occasions not conducive as preconditions to empirical democracy. Consequently, the trappings of public elections frequently degenerate into "religious" ceremonies or programs; events impossible to evaluate critically and as a result left engineered epistemologically in order that they might be legitimized in the name of the people. Those attending are required not only to offer due respect but also passive acquiescence to "advice" and political banter. The general populace become quite good listeners—since at times like these, it is not considered good form to "hold up the hand" in disagreement (protest), responding negatively to the contents of the political talk (rhetoric).

Steeped in sacralized language and imagery, politics in Indonesia under Soeharto exhibited metaphysical and quasi-religious expression and control.[14]

---

13 "'Mutual help' (*gotong royong*) programmes are organized top-down, and it is those who suffer most who are expected to contribute their 'free' labour which they first of all need to struggle for their living, there being nothing 'democratic' in the condition of most villages" (Mulder 1987, 98). In relation to top-down development models extant in West Java, see Hardjono 1983.

14 Scott claims that "nothing conveys the public transcript more as the dominant would like it to seem than the formal ceremonies they organize to celebrate and dramatize their rule" (1987, 58). During Soeharto's reign, the New Order government often used the phrase "democratic party" (*pesta demokrasi*) to describe presidential elections whose results were actually controlled, predetermined, and thus anything but party-like.

Sullivan (1987, 134–60) describes the function of the Pancasila and gotong royong constructs by identifying the two social strata in which they were situated. He employs the label "invented community" to describe the lower level, centered on gotong royong, which has a top-down, fabricated image of local neighborhood communities held together by an elaborate village control mechanism known as the RT/RW system. RT is short for *Rukun Tetangga*, woodenly translated "Neighborhood Conviviality Unit," while RW stands for *Rukun Warga*, "Citizenship Conviviality Unit." Together these two administrative structures served as the lowest tiers in the Indonesian government,[15] ones Sullivan claims were for domesticating poor kampung dwellers (135). For Soeharto's New Order administration, the village and its RT/RW system served as the locality where gotong royong—the "invented construct" par excellence—flowed most effectively (212). The goal seemed to be to keep local kampung life ticking along, not derailing wider, more grandiose (and more elite-inspiring and intoxicating) images of the pembangunan formula.

The upper level is centered upon Pancasila as the key symbol for the New Order's "imagined community" rhetoric (Sullivan 1987, 208; cf. Heryanto 1988, 11, 21–22).[16] At this level the state served as the medium through which elite players in the public arena of the nation-state could be co-opted. The goal seemed to be to keep Indonesia's elite "imagining" (and craving) the same things, staking their claims on access to ever greater slices of what the New Order had to offer. This placed elite citizens in direct competition with each other on the national stage.

We now return to our earlier diagram depicting traditional kampung patronage. We clearly must redraw it in order to more accurately reflect how patronage ended up reconfigured to the detriment of poor residents—a process further described below.

---

15 Though they were actually more quasi-governmental in nature. Administrative heads for these units were not officially on the government payroll.
16 Sullivan leans heavily on Anderson 1991.

FIGURE 5.2
Reconfigured *kampung* patronage

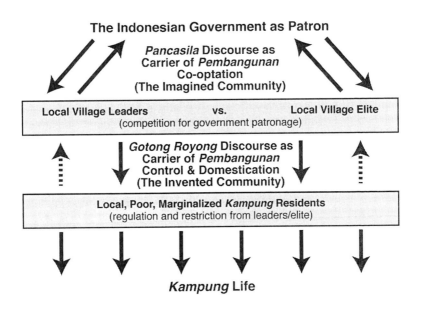

Here the elite (formerly patrons of poor kampung residents) were fashioned by the New Order government into new-sprung collections of clients competing over access to central state resources. The state assumed the position of patron, with Soeharto perched atop its peak as its symbolic, quasi-sacred benefactor. Similar to traditional patronage, co-optation in this scheme clustered all rival factions under one umbrella. While the umbrella of pembangunan, or "development," was offered as a unified project, the elite experienced competition, conflict, and fragmentation. In this way, potential threats to the New Order government were divided and, in the end, neutralized.

As an outgrowth of this formula, poor kampung dwellers were differentiated from local village leaders and elite by way of refashioned gotong royong communities (fig. 5.2)—the former no longer actually tethered to village leadership as before (Antlöv 1994, 92). Through this altered structure, Pancasila and gotong royong served as carriers of their respective pembangunan goals and purposes: (1) Pancasila aimed at competition, with the New Order co-opting the patronage of the elite; (2) gotong royong aimed at control and domestication, with New Order village-level regulation and restriction of kampung residents accomplished by way of the RT/RW system. Consequently there arose "competition among the elite scrambling for scarce positional and material rewards," resulting in a wide-scale "political marginalization of society" (Jemadu 1997, 5). Local village elite had little time, interest, or motivation to look after the needs of poor kampung dwellers as in days gone by. Thus, in the diagram, bold arrows of control (as opposed to requited patronage relationships) issue from kampung elite downward toward the marginalized, but only broken arrows of limited feedback flow up the other way. There was very little reciprocity between leaders and residents in the repositioned kampung. The village poor were left to fend for themselves from a position semidetached outside the pembangunan orbit.

The upshot of all of this was that Soeharto's pembangunan umbrella allowed no political space for poor kampung residents in the "great development family" (*keluarga pembangunan besar*), presided over by the nation's fatherly patron (*bapak*). On the contrary, outside, hierarchical control was established with a view toward domestication of the populace (Sullivan 1987, 207)—an undertaking of "national security and conflict management" (206) at the village level.[17] If co-optation of the elite client class was the primary goal under pembangunan-inspired images of Pancasila, then something needed to be done with the resulting discarded underclass. This was the role of Pancasila's sister pembangunan mantra: gotong royong—the tool of choice for "underwrit[ing] intervention into village life" (John Bowen, quoted in ibid., 178).

Domineered and domesticated, villagers found themselves collared as virtual "beasts of burden," employed without explanation to do grunt work at the local village level, nation-building chores concocted

---

17 For an especially probing comment on this, see Sullivan (1987, 207).

by those in power—work now labeled and made mandatory as "development" (pembangunan). Furthermore, if found less than forthcoming as gauged by the new rules in force, poor kampung residents could be categorized as obstructive to pembangunan, depicted as less than religious, labeled subversives, or, the worst scenario, branded pro-Communist.[18] Consequently these persons found themselves stigmatized, short of jobs and opportunities, lacking traditional leadership structures as safeguards, and shy of physical resources. As we will see below, they were shoved to the margins of kampung society as a byproduct of the New Order's pembangunan / Pancasila / gotong royong troika.

COUNTERVAILING SYMBOLIC RESISTANCE
AMONG KEMBANG ASRI CLIENTS

> In some countries, the populations pretend to comply but, behind the scenes, there takes place a sort of subversion of the logic accompanying the imported object or institution. Etienne Le Roy aptly speaks of "phagocytism," a term used in chemistry whereby one cell "absorbs and destroys" another, and indeed one sometimes wonders who has actually absorbed whom.
>
> Thierry Verhelst (1988, 42)

Poor kampung residents in West Java found themselves victims of a virtual assault of historically distorted symbols. They felt the full impact of the reconfigured kampung patronage system. No longer were they valued citizens in the kampung; instead they were left scrambling "patronless" while village elite were transformed into clients of the state.

---

18 The climate prevailing in Indonesia empowered the Soeharto government to demonize anything remotely related to communism and, thereafter, receive Western support for doing so. In the midsixties before Soekarno's fall, Indonesia boasted, after the Soviet Union and PR China, the third largest national Communist party in the world. Government warnings related to *komunisme laten* (latent communism) could easily be found throughout the country until at least the end of the 1990s—long after the fall of the Soviet Union near the beginning of that same decade.

My own involvement in kampung life was centered in a corner of the West Java city of Tasikmalaya; the locale I focused upon was known as Kembang Asri.[19] My participation began when I met a group of peasant/poor laboring residents in order to discuss village life with them: I will call them Pak Ujang (a rice farmer), Pak Cece (a cigarette peddler), Pak Tampan (my research assistant, who was at the time unemployed), and Pak Agus (a local handyman who happened to serve as the *Ketua RT*, "RT Head," in his portion of the region). These gentlemen and their families came from an area I am calling the Middle Region, as it was geographically squeezed between two opposing areas described below. All of them had gathered for several years prior in order to listen to Indonesian language broadcasts of foreign radio programs. The broadcasts were received via shortwave. Since they didn't trust the government-influenced news programs, these men listened to shortwave radio in order to "know what is really happening." I initially came along simply to listen and learn. But my invitation to participate soon developed into full-scale discussion sessions. It is those discussions that provided me with a full understanding of their situation, as described below.

Around 1992, the city government leased a very popular and historic recreation site in the area to a wealthy local businessman (the head of the municipal Chamber of Commerce), who thereafter proceeded to cosmetically manicure the surrounding lawn as well as refurbish and alter the grounds. Even the shape and location of the main entrance of the site was altered—the old entrance was shunted off to the side, such that it now leads nowhere but to a dead end blocked by a gate, enclosing a sizeable private residence. This by itself seemed to signal a shift in focus, since there were guards stationed at the entrance and people were charged admission. Poor kampung residents no longer could enter the site as they once could. This was especially ironic in

---

19 Analysis of the Kembang Asri region (a pseudonym), with conclusions quite similar to my description here, has been published elsewhere (e.g., Samandawai 2001). Similarities in perspective and analysis between what I present here and Samandawai's study are largely because the latter was influenced by my own fieldwork, which was already existent.

light of the site's significance as the location of a notable battle in the country's struggle for independence in the late 1940s, a significance that Middle Region ancestors helped to establish.[20] These changes to the structure clearly indicated an altered power arrangement.[21]

One could ask how pembangunan was actually guarded in Kembang Asri, and by whom. First, simple geography offers an answer to these questions—since 1989 the area has been divided into three distinct RWs. These divisions formally compartmentalized poor kampung residents into a squeezed geographical middle, framing them as scapegoats and buffers at the same time. Those who guarded the reconfigured pembangunan image were in reality residents living on both sides of the Middle Region folk. A bridge traversing a local stream conspicuously dividing one of the regions from the Middle Region area was a fairly strict boundary. Anyone from the Middle Region caught wandering into the area after dusk often received a sound beating from youth living there. The message was, *Remember where you come from and resist confusing the categories.*

At a more subtle level, there were at least two ways in which Middle Region residents were controlled by way of the rules and strictures related to language. First, the national Indonesian language was circumscribed with a host of rules from the center (in keeping with pembangunan dictum), prescribing to those at the periphery the "right and proper use" of the national language. An example of this can be found in the following statement, one of the countless times Soeharto publicly pronounced the Indonesian language, as a key symbol of the country's advancement, as constituting

---

20 Most interesting for our purposes, it was conceded by all I met in the area that those securing the victory on that fateful day were the ancestors—the grandfathers, the fathers, the uncles, the older brothers—of the very persons now associated with the Middle Region area. This is an irony not lost on those now living in that sector.

21 In actual fact, the area where the recreation spot is found is the only place ever to officially bear the name Kembang Asri. Nevertheless, popular references throughout the city of Tasikmalaya point to the whole stretch depicted as rightfully deserving this designation.

one of the components ... that forged us together as a nation.... We are proud that the Indonesian language has shown such a good deal of growth and development. It is now not just a language for socializing but it has also grown to become a language of formality, even a language of science. (*Pikiran Rakyat,* May 21, 1995)

Such a strong and deferential focus on the national language split development discourse in Kembang Asri into two types: (1) a discourse carried out in the national language of Indonesian (*bahasa Indonesia*), and (2) a discourse carried out in the regional language of Sundanese (*basa Sunda*). Since virtually all state-sanctioned pembangunan exchange was carried out in Indonesian, poor village residents much more fluent in the Sundanese language felt increasingly alienated from discussions and conversation related to the process. Given Indonesia's ethnic complexity and the consequent variety of regional languages, the fact that pronouncements and materials issued by the government were circulated in the national language was understandable; however, the type of speech generally used for this communication ranged from the jargonized to the technical to Indonesianized loanwords, all extremely difficult for poorer kampung dwellers to understand. Many loanwords were borrowed almost directly from English, such as *inovasi, partisipasi, orientasi, ekonomi,* and many others besides. As the patron of the country, the government became the principal steward of meaning—with pembangunan discussion cast as a center-oriented, scientific process only truly understood by experts. The concept of pembangunan represented an idea central to all community and national life, something strongly championed by the government but foreign to the average poor Sundanese-speaking kampung dweller in Kembang Asri. Such an arrangement put local people at a distinct disadvantage—since the national language was pitched as the proper vehicle for formality and science, the average person was left with significant embarrassment admitting that he or she was less than comfortable with it. After all, what sort of an Indonesian gladly confesses difficulty with the emblematic and official language of his or her own country? Nevertheless, one of my friends, Pak Cece, made just such a confession to me once: "I can speak the Indonesian language, that's not the problem," he said. "It's just that when I do, it's like being on a road that has not yet been paved." The result was that kampung dwellers often simply chose to stay off the "unpaved road," which helped local elite keep them in their place, labeling them as persons not to be trusted. Middle Region folk described their marked status with the phrase *ditulis tonggong,* "written on our backs"; we might say "branded" or "stigmatized."

The second way in which the pembangunan reconstruction was locally guarded in Kembang Asri was by way of religious language and terminology wielded against Middle Region residents, usually on the part of those living to each side of them. This religious language was intimately attached to the two primary national Islamic organizations that had a presence in the region—*Nahdlatul Ulama* (NU) and *Persatuan Islam* (Persis).[22] While these two organizations held significantly different doctrinal positions when compared to each other, they remained united in seeing themselves as more religious, more pious, and spiritually superior to residents hailing from the Middle Region. Fundamentally, such a perspective arose from both groups strongly resisting the religious innovation historically embraced by persons from the Middle Region's far more syncretistically steeped worldview; i.e., a more sufistically oriented, folk Islamic *hakikat*,[23] or core. It should be no surprise that people from the NU and Persis areas were generally in charge of gotong royong projects and events.

In the process, overt religious observance became ostensibly and formally linked to secular gotong royong activities. Thus Middle Region kampung residents were often kept in check by way of a religious yardstick. NU and Persis residents glossed fulfillment of gotong royong responsibilities as at least including faithful attendance at weekly community *pangajian* (Sundanese Qur'anic recitation events) gatherings at the local mosque. To these more powerful local persons,

---

22   For a deeper look at the history of NU, see Wahid 1987; for a historical survey covering both NU and Persis, see Jackson 1980.

23   Deriving from Arabic, *hakikat* is usually rendered "essence" in English.

those not in attendance were seen as insufficiently community minded. Since the men coming from the Middle Region did not particularly care for the power disparity palpable at such events, they told me they simply could not stomach going. Pak Agus even observed that, in relation to these community religious spectacles, gotong royong rhetoric regularly was discarded altogether—though community participation and control features buttressed by religious obligation remained. "Used to be 'gotong royong,' now it's 'for Allah.' It's all the same," Pak Agus observed.[24] But in any case, poor kampung residents remained branded, with many elite openly using the Communist label to keep Middle Region persons in their place: "Ah, basically they're all PKI [Indonesia Communist Party]," one authoritarian, local non–Middle Region person once told me.

We might ask how Middle Region residents coped in such a situation. What forms of subversion were they capable of—individuals so beaten down, so controlled, so domesticated?

The first thing that might be said is that, regardless of power disparities, these folk would survive.[25] As Verhelst says in the epigraph above, there often exists "a sort of subversion of the logic accompanying the imported object or institution" in the development context. It is this easily overlooked subversion that we must look at now. We will notice that persons like Pak Ujang, Pak Cece, Pak Tampan, and Pak Agus generally work toward rearrangements designed not to overwhelmingly disturb the prevailing power alignment but to somewhat reorder it by way of small yet meaningful protests, ones that can signal a deeper reality, sometimes to others but most importantly to themselves.

---

24 For a detailed discussion on this sort of politicized religious power in West Java, see Glicken 1987.

25 Obviously I am speaking of these folk here as a class of people—in other words, they will not be exterminated. In fact, considering the manner in which power is arranged in Kembang Asri (and in other poor villages in West Java), the wealthy need the poor, if for no other reason than to implement their preconceived pembangunan projects. However, it would be overly simplistic to suggest that Pak Cece, Pak Ujang, and Pak Agus were not vulnerable to the force of this power discrepancy. That would be simply untrue.

The first instance of pembangunan subversion can best be seen in the activity that drew me to the house in the first place: their regular practice of clandestinely listening to the BBC World Service on shortwave radio. When I first arrived, these men had been doing this for years. They explained, "We do it for our consumption only. When people tell us about an incident reported on TVRI,[26] we simply smile. We already know the true details—we don't need to let anyone know *how* we know." They saw this as their own private rebellion—something others actually need not know they did. Additional participants were not invited in randomly or carelessly. As I witnessed these gatherings, they would keep the radio volume low and the front door closed, growing especially quiet if someone was approaching. But continue to listen they did.

The second means of subverting pembangunan logic in the Kembang Asri related to their manipulation of the belittling and marginalizing speech directed their way. True subversion of the symbolic terrain seemed to take place via a "turning upside-down" of the meaning and import of words. An example can be found in the Sunda term *mikung*. At face value, *mikung* refers to a particular genus of grasshopper-like insect (the wider, more all-inclusive category for grasshopper is *jangkrik* or *kasir*). Distinctive characteristics of a mikung are that (1) it cannot fly, since it has no wings, and (2) it does not make noise, as other jangkrik or kasir do. Mikung are, by definition, mute. Young boys in West Java frequently enjoy digging in rice fields in search of jangkrik, placing them in jars for the noise they make or tying strings around them in order to let them fly, as veritable lead-tethered kites. The trouble is, mikung nests look almost identical to jangkrik nests, except for the fact that mikung nests are often bigger and more deeply burrowed into the ground, making them especially difficult to reach. Digging for a jangkrik yet winding up with a mikung is a disappointing experience for a child, yet it happens often since the two creatures and their nests are so similar on the surface. Thus, when the more scripturally aligned

---

26 The national Indonesian television station, which served as a mouthpiece for the national government in the Soeharto era.

residents of Kembang Asri label the Middle Region residents mikung, they emphasize that, while the latter appear Islamic, they are in fact not true Muslims. They are implying that, like mikung, Middle Region residents cannot fly (i.e., they do not understand or enjoy the blessings of being truly Muslim), nor should they have voice in the community (they should remain unheard, since they are impostors).[27]

In the face of this, Middle Region residents countered by embracing the term but contorting it with their own linguistic defenses, employing the very same symbolic imagery while turning it on its head. They pointed out (more often to themselves than to others) that mikung grasshoppers tunnel deeper than do jangkrik (a zoological fact clear to everyone). That being so, Middle Region residents took great pride in the fact that they were "deeper—we need not prattle on." They held to an almost covert understanding, a reorientation pointing to the true nature of religious allegiance—a "grasp of reality" completely overlooked by NU and Persis folk. Middle Region residents defined spirituality more in terms of service rendered to the community than in terms of attendance at ritually adorned public performances (mandated or not).

Another way Middle Region people upended the symbolic terrain was through their covert understanding of the concept of gotong royong.[28] They rejected the way the notion was normally glossed,

27 Even Sundanese dictionaries list both zoological as well as metaphorical definitions of mikung: "1. not yet adult, not yet having wings (grasshoppers, etc.); 2. false or deviating from genuine teaching" (Tamsyah 1996, 170).

28 This reinterpretation of gotong royong is reminiscent of something described by Scott related to indigenous Filipino reinterpretations of the passion narrative in the face of Spanish overlords: "A cultural form that might have been taken to represent the submission of the Filipinos to the religion of their colonial masters and resignation before a cruel fate was infused with quite divergent meaning. In its many variants performed throughout Tagalog society during Holy Week, the vernacular pasyon managed to negate much of the cultural orthodoxy of the Spanish and their local, Hispanicized illustrado allies....The vehicle ... was, of course, a church ritual authorized from above—a fact that made it a more sheltered social site for subversive meanings. This is not at all to claim a premeditated and cynical manipulation of the passion play; rather it was simply that the religious experience of ordinary Filipinos gradually infused this folk ritual which came to represent their sensibilities—within the limits of what might be ventured in comparative safety" (1987, 159).

emphasizing instead that its true nature could be found in sincere, un-discriminating assistance offered to bereaved families who had just lost a loved one. This last aspect almost always included the washing of the deceased's body, the digging of the grave, as well as assisting the family in other necessary preparations. They felt that all of this needed to be proffered without fanfare or request for payment. Middle Region residents were cognizant that other Kembang Asri residents generally did not help with these necessary, loathsome tasks, meaning that bereaved family members were often left to fend for themselves. Even in the rare case where NU or Persis residents did assist in such a way, it was almost always in support of those within their own region.

Thus Middle Region men took great pride in formulating their own unique, esoteric understanding of local language and symbolism. The term *mikung* as well as many other phrases, activities, and religious obligations connoted something entirely different to them—a fact that made them especially (if still privately) proud. Inwardly it set them apart from others and consequently served as a source of increased self-esteem. This is because "each and every regional language possess-es great potential for creating strangers out of persons located outside their communal-ethnic confines.... These are conduits of precise com-munication demanding the highest level of interpretation" (Abdullah 1996, 351–52).

Underground resistance on the part of Kembang Asri Middle Region folk, while admittedly meager, demonstrates one overarching point: these residents felt no obligation to succumb to the labels thrust upon them by the elite. They continually reminded themselves that there were other ways of defining these labels and of viewing them-selves in a more positive light. As Scott says,

It may seem that the heavy disguise [maintained by marginalized and silenced communities] must all but eliminate the pleasure it gives. While it is surely less satisfying than an open declaration of the hidden transcript it nevertheless achieves something the backstage can never match. It carves out a public, if provisional, space for the autonomous cultural expression of dissent. If it is disguised, it is at least not hidden; it is spoken to power. This is no small achievement of voice under domination. (1987, 166)

THE SYMBOLIC TERRAIN OF WEST JAVA COMPARED WITH THE CHRISTIAN SYMBOLIC TERRAIN

We have seen how, in coping with their situation at the bottom of a hierarchical constellation of power, Middle Region residents upended the symbolic terrain, manipulating it and turning it on its head. If Christians find themselves in a similar situation, how should they act? Do biblical themes speak to the sorts of arrangements we see at work here?

To answer this question, let us focus primarily upon patron-client relationships—whether traditional or those reconfigured as in Indonesia. How should a Christian posture herself or himself in the face of such linkages? Some might take it that Jesus—as the emptied one, the consummate servant who was no "respecter of persons"—came to do away with such oppressive, authoritarian arrangements in order to flatten society and democratize our involvement with each other. What we will find is that the image of the descending Christ does indeed reconfigure these relationships, but in ways more subtle and shrewd, and perhaps even more slowly, than we might expect.

Firstly, we must realize that relationships between parties regulating the exchange or flow of resources between social actors in Indonesia differ markedly from those one generally encounters in Western societies. This fact has been discussed in Meneses' chapter on exchange and reciprocity (chap. 1). In Indonesia, the exact nature of patronage relationships seems to be a consequence of the transitional quality of a society undergoing a significant shift; they are caught between a history heavily influenced by ancestral conceptions of power and an increasingly adopted quest to build a "modern" (read: Western, industrialized) society. Cultures like those in Indonesia shift and change rapidly, and the sorts of configurations of patronage we have been looking at seem to be a byproduct of that change.[29]

---

29 See Jackson (1978, 350).

Consequently, due to their transitional nature, patron-client relations generally arise as informal, voluntary, diffuse, and hierarchical, yet generally lifelong and mutual. As a result, it is not uncommon for a client to "shop around" for a patron to whom she or he gives this type of allegiance. There does appear to be some sort of choice and control available to clients, even if these persons remain in the "down side" of the relationship.

Yet it remains true that to sensibilities fashioned from within industrialized societies (including "Christian" sensibilities), patron-client affiliations often seem highly susceptible to exploitation and abuse. The primary reason for this is their implicit hierarchical distribution of power and resources—of the type we have just seen in Kembang Asri. In this they differ from our "universalist societies," where we

> expect to have access on an equal basis to goods and services ... based on universal criteria, e.g., being a citizen and taxpayer or a member of a certain age group. Thus, these goods and services are regarded as a right, not a favor provided by the state. To emphasize this point many states have passed laws to ensure that these rights are not made dependent upon race, gender, or religion.... For many, "patronage" is a bad word. (Moxnes 1991, 243)

Many social theorists, however, have noted that in patron-client societies it is not easy to determine who has the greater ability to satisfy her or his wishes in such a linkage, the patron or the client.[30] There is a reciprocity to the relationship that is often overlooked by the casual, non-tradition-based observer. Consequently the imbalance of real power might not be as skewed as one thinks. This is an important point for us to bear in mind as we probe more deeply into the nature of these structures below.

We are still left wondering about the hierarchical nature of the arrangement. For instance, is it not true that a *sine qua non* of the Christian faith is equal status of all persons before God? How then

---

30 See, for example, Pye (1985, 118).

can such relations be justified by Christians? Do they not ontologically elevate some persons above others, rendering them more powerful and important than persons and communities for whom God cares equally?

Moxnes (1991) has helpfully analyzed this issue via the corpus of Luke-Acts, exploring the type of exchange most commonplace during the New Testament period. After identifying the New Testament norm as patron-client in form, he goes on to explore the way in which the biblical text judges the pattern. He claims that Luke-Acts material does not take patronage to be an *a priori* evil construct. On the contrary, the

> central theme of [Luke's] Gospel is that God acts as a benefactor-patron through Jesus. Jesus is not a patron in his own right, distributing his own resources, but a broker who gives access to the benefactions of God. He mediates between the people of Israel and God.... And so his conflict with the old leadership of Israel becomes understandable, for it is a conflict over the right and the power to give access to God. (Moxnes 1991, 258)

In this light, Jesus does not simply jettison the prevailing relational structures of his day. Instead he radically redefines them. At that time (as in present-day Indonesia), the patron was customarily associated with the center of society, the actor most aligned with the wealthy or the gentry. The client's status was more properly located at the periphery of society, associated with persons poor and lowly. But this is the first place where the elements are rearranged by Jesus:

> Jesus as mediator clearly identifies with the periphery.... It is to them that he gives direct access to God. The controversial point, however, is that in doing this, Jesus is not a mediator along the center-periphery axis. He does not have access to the traditional channels to God, via temple and Torah, which are localized in Jerusalem, the center. Instead, he comes from Galilee, from the periphery. The conflict with Jewish leaders presented in Jesus' travels through Galilee and Judea intensifies when he enters

Jerusalem. Thus, he does not conform to the model "media-tion" or brokerage imposed from the center upon the periphery. Therefore, Jesus as broker has a problem within Israel in that he does not represent the center. As a mediator from the outside he is rejected by the elites and the establishment. (Moxnes 1991, 258)

Related to this structural realignment and reinterpretation of the pa-tronage system, Jesus also reinterprets the function of the benefactor. Hence

> a new form of leadership is necessary. And this leadership is not based on extraction from people, such as the temple economy, but on "serving," the simple and life-giving activity of the house-hold, associated with women and servants. There is a strange transformation of the very concept of patronage. The institution is preserved, but the greatness traditionally associated with the role of the patron is now intimately linked with the act of serv-ing. This transformation of roles is not confined to Jesus; it also becomes visible in Luke's description of the disciples of Jesus. (Moxnes 1991, 260)

Finally, Jesus not only transforms both the power structure of patron-age and the function of the patron, he also recasts the nature of the exchange as he

> urges a break with the system of reciprocities in which a gift is always repaid by the recipient.... [This] represents an important transformation of the very basis for patronage. First, one is urged to give to the poor who cannot repay in kind. The second and main point is that one shall not expect any return from them, not even in terms of gratitude or glorification. "Giving" shall no longer be used to create clients, and thus the very basis for patronage is taken away. (Moxnes 1991, 264)

Therefore,

> if one is to act as a patron but without any expectations of reci-
> procity in terms of gratitude and loyalty from one's client, the
> power aspect is removed from the relationship. Then social rela-
> tions are supposed to *function on the basis of an equal status as fictive
> kin in God's household*, differences in resources notwithstanding.
> It is a radical departure from a situation in which wealth, status,
> and power determine social relations. (Moxnes 1991, 264; em-
> phasis added)

In Moxnes' analysis, we see biblical patronage focused upon the poor
of society, leadership validated as acts of service as opposed to being
served, and the reciprocity element and its accompanying means for
control being virtually eliminated. This is a reversal of fortunes—an
upside-down flipping of the entire patronage relationship. The only
patronage aspect left is the God-ordained fictive kin alliances, which
cause the participants to relate to each other based upon their status
as brothers and sisters in Christ. Interestingly enough, some social
scientists see this last characteristic, the family-like quality, as the most
distinctive aspect of community-based patronage systems, especially
in contrast to the state-reconfigured varieties we saw above. For us as
Christians, reinterpreted filial relationships are also a truly important
characteristic of the kingdom of God.

Realizing the mechanics of patronage and working from within
these in order to reconstruct and reinterpret them seems to be a wise
move—even a Christian move, since this is what we see God in Christ
has done. But a fully Christian approach to this process will cast the
entire relationship into a different form, one similar to the way Jesus is
shown doing in first-century Israel. The essence of that recasting will
align with the way Jesus took up the posture of adopting a prophetic,
critical stance in defiance of those subjugating the disenfranchised of
his day. We must, alongside poor clients and in line with their own resistance, speak against prejudicial arrangements, resist unfair laws, and
seek release for the downtrodden from biased interpretations, edicts,

and pronouncements. Old Testament theologian Walter Brueggemann reminds us that this was at the heart of Jesus' ministry:

> The law had become in [Jesus'] day a way for the managers of society, religious even more than civil, to effectively control not only morality but the political-economic valuing that lay behind the morality. Thus his criticism of the "law" is not to be dismissed as an attack on "legalism" in any moralistic sense.... Rather, his critique concerns the fundamental social valuing of his society. In practice Jesus has seen ... that the law can be a social convention to protect the current distribution of economic and political power. (2001, 87)

We must focus our attention and our empowerment efforts unmistakably upon those lying (sometimes literally) at the edges of any society. However, we must realize that opposition will come if this sort of an emphasis is championed. Those at the center, like residents in the NU and Persis regions, will feel their power base threatened.[31] Such a perceived threat will not go unanswered. Anabaptist sociologist Donald Kraybill asks,

> Why did Jesus become a threat? His very life and message menaced political and religious authorities. Designating himself a waiter, he criticized the scribes' pursuit of prestige. He condemned the rich for dominating the poor. By challenging the oral law and purging the temple, he assaulted the citadel of religious power. His appeal to servanthood offered an alternate model

---

31 Neyrey claims this was a standard confrontation faced by early Christians. "Many Jews ... perceived Jesus, Stephen, Paul, and other Christians as subverting the Jewish 'world.' They were accused of attacking the major institution of the day, the temple, by rejecting the major symbol of Israel's faith[,] as dismissing the prerogatives of Israel as a chosen collective[, as] abrogat[ing] the principles by which the faith of this chosen people was structured ... and the rituals which symbolize that faith.... They were perceived as rejecting 'God' and even upsetting the system of nature by 'turning the world upside down.' In the eyes of some, then, the Christians appeared to urge a revolution against traditional values and structures of Israelite faith" (1991, 272).

of power. He hardly was a politician, but the kingdom he announced had political implications. It was a political movement that promised to reorder social and religious life. (2011, 235)

Speaking specifically about the theology of the Gospel of Luke, missiologist David Bosch echoes this theme:

[Jesus] championed "God's preferential option for the poor." He announced the Jubilee, which would inaugurate a reversal of the dismal fate of the dispossessed, the oppressed, and the sick, by calling on the wealthy and healthy to share with those who are victims of exploitation and tragic circumstances. He did this in the teeth of the ideological defense mechanisms of the privileged, who only too frequently convince themselves that Jesus was more interested in the "correct attitude" toward wealth than in its possession and use. These mechanisms then allow free range to the privileged's unsatiable urge to move upward, socially and economically, and to pursue a hedonistic lifestyle devoid of an ethic that exalts values like self-sacrifice, restraint, and solidarity. But where self-centered sentiments reign supreme, the rich cannot claim to be involved in mission and cannot be in continuity with the Lukan Jesus and church. (1991, 118)

Bosch goes on to say more generally that

[Jesus] is ... the one who today sides with those who suffer in the favelas of Brazil and with the discarded people in South Africa's resettlement areas. In this model, one is not interested in a Christ who offers only eternal salvation, but in a Christ who agonizes and sweats and bleeds with the victims of oppression. One criticizes the bourgeois church of the West, which leans toward docetism and for which Jesus' humanness is only a veil hiding his divinity. This bourgeois church has an idealist understanding of itself, refuses to take sides, and believes that it offers a home for masters as well as slaves, rich and poor, oppressor and oppressed. Because it refuses to practice "solidarity with victims" ... such a church has lost its relevance. Having peeled off the social and political dimensions of the gospel, it has denatured completely. (1991, 513)

So Brueggemann, Kraybill, Bosch, and many others now challenge the church to take up this missiology of Jesus. This is the challenge, they say, that Jesus placed before the church in mission.

But the claim I am making here is that such a holistic and "upside-down" challenge is sometimes best accomplished from *within* the system; embedded within the symbolic terrain, it can partner with those at the margins, allowing for a reconfiguration and reinterpretation of meanings springing from local contexts, playing with the moral horizon and morphing it so as to better serve the marginalized. Perhaps such a move is available to us via patronage linkages since

the patron stands *with* his clients vis-à-vis the outside: sometimes he processes flows downward as well, but once this becomes his main job he has shifted his stance, now essentially being set off against them.... [There is] a fraternal quality of patronage which always belongs to some *pays reel* [real country] which is ambivalently conscious of not being the *pays legal* [legal country]. (Goodell 1985, 253)

The task before us seems not to rid local communities of all vestiges of patronage, but to partner with locals in their quest to prophetically yet deftly refashion these structures—to alter them in ways similar to what we have seen Middle Region folk and Jesus do above.[32] Korten comments,

---

32 James Scott has examined patron-client relationships in Southeast Asia, suggesting that a better understanding of these will assist outsiders in comprehending local political machinations. See Scott 1972.

The sort of "work-from-within" I am advocating here is quite similar to the type seemingly favored as well by H. Richard Niebuhr—what he describes as the "Christ the Transformer of Culture" position—in his famous book *Christ and Culture* (2001 [1951]). Niebuhr contrasts this preferred image with four alternate types he outlines earlier in the book: (1) Christ against culture, (2) the Christ of culture, (3) Christ above culture, and (4) Christ and culture in paradox.

> More realistic than seeking to eliminate power holders … are efforts to increase the likelihood that power will be used in ways that take responsible account of the interests of the weak. This is partly a function of structures that establish checks and balances among power holders and increase their accountability to the people on whose lives they are in a position to influence. It is partly a function of the political consciousness of the otherwise disempowered. It is also, however, a function of the values of the power holder. (1990, 168)

However, in order to effect such change, we need to cultivate nimble abilities and acumen similar to that possessed by Middle Region residents. Both the skill with which they manipulated their semiotic horizons, internally redefining themselves and withstanding very serious and subjugating pressures, as well as the way they continued to serve others from the margins, offer us key insights. Though they would never describe themselves as Christian, many characteristics these persons displayed mirror precisely what Moxnes underscored by way of Luke's picture of Jesus as he stood patronage on its head.

Those of us trained in the West are often ill-equipped for such a task. Anthropologist Clifford Geertz (1973) long ago lamented that most social scientists lack a hermeneutical approach to cultural contexts, approaches that might allow us to read more deeply into the local context and decipher what truly goes on there. We are often surprised and unprepared when local residents in tradition-based societies are more up to the task of redefining structures and implementing real change than we are. As such, we need to learn from those already living in such places.[33]

Christians who worship a God who physically entered our world and semiotically upended its value system should recognize the task before us. We need to pattern our actions and approaches after Christ, even when it means learning about nuanced constructs such as patronage, so as to better understand how to work from within them and through

---

33 See also Geertz (1983, 19–35) for more on this.

them. Once we realize this and take it up, we will arrive at a process of true "development"—a natural, organic *perkembangan* (flowering) variety that produces from within the local context in incarnational partnership with resident populations. From there, we will be better equipped to read the signs, subvert the arrangements, and serve the poor, learning alongside those who have long been in the struggle well before we arrived. This will no doubt help "turn the world upside-down." That is what Jesus did—that is what we should do.

REFERENCES

Abdullah, Taufik. 1996. Situasi kebahasaan masa kini: Kepungan eksternal dalam perkembangan bahasa dan wacana. In *Bahasa dan kekuasaan: Politik wacana di panggung orde baru,* edited by Yudi Latif and Idi Subandy Ibrahim, 345–62. Bandung, Indonesia: Penerbit Mizan.

Anderson, Benedict R. O'G. 1990. *Language and power: Exploring political cultures in Indonesia.* Ithaca, NY: Cornell University Press.

———. 1991. *Imagined communities: Reflections on the origin and spread of nationalism.* Revised and extended edition. New York: Verso.

Antlöv, Hans. 1994. Village leaders and the new order. In *Leadership on Java: Gentle hints, authoritarian rule,* edited by Hans Antlöv and Sven Cederroth, 73–96. Richmond, UK: Curzon.

Backues, Lindy. 2009. The Incarnation as motif for development practice. In *World mission in a Wesleyan spirit,* edited by Darrell L. Whiteman and Gerald H. Anderson, 310–23. Nashville: Providence.

Bosch, David J. 1991. *Transforming mission: Paradigm shifts in theology of mission.* Maryknoll, NY: Orbis.

Brueggemann, Walter. 2001. *The prophetic imagination.* 2nd ed. Philadelphia: Fortress.

Eisenstadt, S. N., and Luis Roniger. 1981. The study of patron-client relations and recent developments in sociological theory. In *Political clientelism, patronage, and development,* edited by S. N. Eisenstadt and Rene Lemarchand, 271–97. London: Sage.

———. 1984. *Patrons, clients and friends: Interpersonal relations and the structure of trust in society.* New York: Cambridge University Press.

Geertz, Clifford. 1973. *The interpretation of cultures.* New York: Basic.

———. 1983. *Local knowledge: Further essays in interpretive anthropology.* New York: Basic.

Glicken, Jessica. 1987. Sundanese Islam and the value of *hormat*: Control, obedience, and social location in West Java. In *Indonesian religions in transition,* edited by Rita Smith Kipp and Susan Rodgers, 238–52, 273–74. Tucson: University of Arizona Press.

Goodell, Grace E. 1985. Paternalism, patronage, and potlatch: The dynamics of giving and being given to. *Current Anthropology* 26, no. 2: 247–66.

Guinness, Patrick. 1994. Local society and culture. In *Indonesia's new order: The dynamics of socio-economic transformation,* edited by Hal Hill, 267–304. St. Leonards, Australia: Allen & Unwin.

Hardjono, Joan. 1983. Rural development in Indonesia: The "top-down" approach. In *Rural development and the state: Contradictions and dilemmas in developing countries,* edited by David A. M. Lea and D. P. Chaudhri, 38–65. London: Methuen.

Heryanto, Ariel. 1988. The development of "development." Trans. Nancy Lutz. *Indonesia* 46: 1–24.

Jackson, Karl D. 1978. Urbanization and the rise of patron-client relations: The changing quality of interpersonal communications in the neighborhoods of Bandung and the villages of West Java. In *Political power and communications in Indonesia,* edited by Karl D. Jackson and Lucian W. Pye, 343–92. Berkeley: University of California Press.

———. 1980. *Traditional authority, Islam, and rebellion: A study of Indonesian political behavior.* Berkeley: University of California Press.

Jemadu, Aleksius. 1997. Indonesia's nation-building process at a crossroad. *Jakarta Post,* March 3, 5.

Korten, David C. 1980. Community organization and rural development: A learning process approach. *Public Administration Review* 40, no 5: 480–511.

———. 1990. *Getting to the 21st century: Voluntary action and the global agenda.* West Hartford, CT: Kumarian.

Kraybill, Donald B. 2011. *The upside-down kingdom.* 5th ed. Harrisonburg, VA: Herald Press.

Mackie, Jamie, and Andrew MacIntyre. 1994. Politics. In *Indonesia's new order: The dynamics of socio-economic transformation*, edited by Hal Hill, 1–53. St. Leonards, Australia: Allen & Unwin.

Moxnes, Halvor. 1991. Patron-client relations and the new community in Luke-Acts. In *The social world of Luke-Acts*, edited by Jerome H. Neyrey, 241–68. Peabody, MA: Hendrickson.

Mulder, Niels. 1987. *Individual and society in Java: A cultural analysis*. Yogyakarta, Indonesia: Gadjah Mada University Press.

Neyrey, Jerome H. 1991. The symbolic universe of Luke-Acts: "They turn the world upside down." In *The social world of Luke-Acts*, edited by Jerome H. Neyrey, 271–304. Peabody, MA: Hendrickson.

Niebuhr, H. Richard. [1951] 2001. *Christ and culture*. Reprint, New York: Harper & Row.

Permana, Setia, and Dadi J. Iskandar. 1994. Ritualisme politik dan praktik demokrasi. *Pikiran Rakyat*, May 26.

Pikiran Rakyat. 1995. Tegakkan disiplin nasional. May 21.

Pye, Lucian W. 1985. *Asian power and politics: The cultural dimensions of authority*. Cambridge, MA: Belknap.

Rosidi, Ajip. 1984. *Ciri-ciri manusia dan kebudayaan Sunda*. In *Masyarakat Sunda dan kebudayaannya*, edited by Edi S. Ekadjati, 125–61. Jakarta: PT Girimukti Pasaka.

Samandawai, Sofwan. 2001. *Mikung: Bertahan dalam himpitan; Kajian masyarakat marjinal di Tasikmalaya*. Bandung, Indonesia: Yayasan Akatiga.

Scott, James C. 1972. Patron-client politics and political change in Southeast Asia. *American Political Science Review* 66, no. 1: 91–113.

———. 1985. *Weapons of the weak: Everyday forms of peasant resistance*. New Haven, CT: Yale University Press.

———. 1990. *Domination and the arts of resistance: Hidden transcripts*. New Haven, CT: Yale University Press.

———. 1998. *Seeing like a state: How certain schemes to improve the human condition have failed*. New Haven, CT: Yale University Press.

Sukarno. 1969. The birth of *Pantja Sila*. In *Man, state and society in contemporary Southeast Asia*, edited by Robert O. Tilman, 270–76. Westport, CT: Praeger.

Sullivan, John. 1987. *Local government and community in Java: An urban case-study.* New York: Oxford University Press.

Tamsyah, Budi Rahayu. 1996. *Kamus lengkap Sunda-Indonesia Indonesia-Sunda Sunda-Sunda.* Bandung, Indonesia: Pustaka Setia.

Verhelst, Thierry G. 1988. *No life without roots: Culture and development.* Trans. Bob Cumming. London: Zed.

Wahid, Abdurrahman. 1987. The *Nahdlatul Ulama* and Islam in present day Indonesia. In *Islam and society in Southeast Asia,* edited by Taufik Abdullah and Sharon Siddique, 175–86. Singapore: Institute of Southeast Asia Studies.

Yoder, John Howard. 1972. *The politics of Jesus.* Grand Rapids: Eerdmans.

6

WESTERN MISSION–ESTABLISHED CHURCHES AND MINISTRY IN MALI'S COLLECTIVIST ECONOMY

Douglas Wilson

The majority of Christians in the world today are living in the context of poverty, political powerlessness, and religious pluralism (Bediako 1995, 128). The church in the economically prosperous West is in decline, while it is growing rapidly in the Majority World. There is also an increasing economic gap between the richer nations of the North and the poorer nations of the South (Schaeffer 1997, 26). Full-time Christian workers living in the non-Western world face many challenges, and for those living in the context of poor communities, one of the greatest challenges is their own economic circumstance.

The West and Africa have developed different economic systems out of distinct historical contexts. Both systems have been successful in their respective contexts. Maranz notes,

Contrary to what Westerners think, the African economic system works well indeed in doing what it was designed to do. And the Western system has worked extremely well for what it is designed to do. Yet, if African people attempted rigorously to follow Western financial principles, their societies would collapse economically. By the same token, if Westerners attempted to follow

African financial principles, their economies could not achieve what they are primarily designed to accomplish. (2001, 1)

How do these two economic systems differ? The fundamental economic consideration in Western society is the accumulation of capital and wealth. The fundamental economic consideration in African society is "the distribution of economic resources so that all persons may have their minimum needs met, or at least that they may survive" (Maranz 2001, 4). This is accomplished through family and kin sharing available resources. Thus church workers in Africa face distinct challenges around managing their own economic resources.

THE AFRICAN ECONOMIC SYSTEM AND COLLECTIVISM

Researchers have discovered that the "vast majority of the world lives in societies in which the interests of the group prevail over the interests of the individual" (Hofstede 1991, 50). These are called collectivistic societies as opposed to individualistic societies. Hofstede explains what significance this has in terms of the sharing of resources:

> The loyalty to the group which is an essential element of the collectivistic family also means that resources are shared. If one member of an extended family of 20 persons has a paid job and the others have not, the earning member is supposed to share his or her income in order to help feed the entire family. On the basis of this principle a family may collectively cover the expenses for sending one member to get a higher education, expecting that when this member achieves a well-paid job the income will also be shared. (59)

African cultures heavily stress collectivism. Whatever one person has is shared. If we are both members of the same extended family, then what's mine is yours and what's yours is mine. This distribution of resources is the African social security system. For the Westerner "there is perhaps no aspect of African life more important to understand" (Richmond and Gestrin 2009, 2). The collectivistic focus of African cultures has in turn shaped the African economic system. Concerning economic systems and collectivism, Hofstede notes,

> Economics as a discipline was founded in Great Britain in the eighteenth century; among the founding fathers Adam Smith (1723–1790) stands out. Smith assumed that the pursuit of self-interest by individuals through an "invisible hand" would lead to the maximal wealth of nations. This is a highly individualist idea from a country which even today ranks near the top on individualism. Economics has remained an individualist science and most of its leading contributors have come from strongly individualistic countries like the UK and the USA. However, because of the individualist assumptions on which they are based, economic theories as developed in the West are unlikely to apply in societies in which not individual interest, but group interests prevail. Unfortunately there are few alternative economic theories yet to deal with collectivistic economies. (1991, 71–72)

In this chapter I shall examine the dynamics of how Christian work functions in the context of collectivist societies and economies to which Western economic theories do not apply but which adversely affect the economic realities of mission-established churches and Protestant, urban pastoral ministry in the Republic of Mali, West Africa.

CHRISTIAN MISSION IN MALI'S ECONOMIC CONTEXT

During the past several centuries Western missions have established new churches in thousands of different cultures around the world. In many of these cultures the mission-established churches are very similar in form to churches found in the West. They have a choir, church building, similar order of worship, and a pastor who is supported financially by the congregation. However, many of these churches exist in economic systems different than those of the West, and are themselves poor. The question is, how effectively are Western mission–established churches operating in such contexts?

Economic Realities of the Republic of Mali

Africa is home to many poor countries, and the Republic of Mali is considered one of the poorest, with an annual per capita income of just $1,100 (IndexMundi 2013).[1] Mali is approximately 95 percent Muslim, 2 percent animist, 2 percent Catholic, and 1 percent Protestant Christian. It has a predominantly agrarian economy, with about 80 percent of the labor force engaged in farming and fishing and 10 percent practicing a nomadic pastoral lifestyle (CIA 2013). Economic development has been hampered by the country's deficient infrastructure, administrative inefficiency, corruption, and poor social conditions, including a low literacy rate and high population growth rate. Mali remains heavily dependent on foreign aid. It does have a fledgling market economy, but economic performance is fragile. It is vulnerable to climatic conditions and fluctuating terms of trade. Since it is a landlocked country, it is dependent on ports in neighboring countries. Mali's economy suffers from high levels of poverty and unemployment. Almost half of the population survives below the international poverty line (Economy Watch 2010). In sum, Christians in Mali, along with other parts of West Africa, live in poverty, powerlessness, and religious pluralism. To understand the economic realities of Malian pastors and how they negotiate life and ministry in this context, we must first compare this to the situation of pastors in the West.

Economics and the Pastorate

Few Christians who are going into ministry do so for its financial rewards. Most of the research done on finances and the pastorate has been done in the West. A study done in the US showed that most pastors

---

1   Economic historians have noted a trend of divergence during the past two centuries in which the richest countries are pulling ahead of the rest of the world and becoming proportionately even richer (Milanovic 2005, 70).

(65 percent) felt they were fairly paid. However, some (16 percent) felt they were barely surviving financially. Almost half (49 percent) of respondents said that at least once a year they considered leaving the ministry to find a better-paying job. Still, spouses tended to be more concerned with finances than are pastors themselves (LaRue 1998).

A more recent study found that clergy salaries correspond more to church size than years of experience or education of the pastor (McMillan and Price 2003, 7). Generally, connectional churches[2] pay their ministers better than congregational churches.[3] The study also found that, regardless of polity, only a small percentage of pastors earned a salary equivalent to others with a similar level of education and training (13). Prospective pastors generally realize that they are trading off a sense of calling and purpose against lower financial rewards (16). The bottom-line conclusion was that, in the US, "pastors are poorly paid" (26). This report highlighted the fact that the financial burden of ministry makes it difficult to be true to one's calling. In examining how mission-established churches operate in an African economic system, we will see similar beliefs about pastoral compensation operating.

Research Problem

Africa is home to many Protestant churches. Many were established by Western mission agencies. Others are what are called African Independent Churches (AIC). These churches emerged and exist with no involvement with Western churches or mission agencies. There are AIC churches in Mali, but not as many as there are in East Africa. Most of the Protestant churches in French-speaking Mali were established by Western mission agencies after Mali's independence in 1962. In 2005–6 I conducted a study focused on the Western mission–

---

2   Connectional churches are those in which there is a centralized decision-making process to determine clergy salaries. These would include the Methodist, Lutheran, Presbyterian, and Episcopalian churches.

3   Congregational churches take a decentralized, or "free market," approach to clergy salaries. These would include Baptist, Pentecostal, and United Church of Christ churches.

established churches that was designed to reveal the economic realities in which Malian urban pastors live and serve. At the time of the study, almost nothing was known about how Western mission–established churches operated economically in urban environments. The goal of this study was to help the church in Mali better understand the challenges confronting urban pastors with regard to meeting the needs of their families, and to help Western Christians appreciate the realities in which their Majority World coworkers in Christ serve.

Research Methodology

In my study I examined pastors from the six principle Malian church denominations working in the two largest urban centers of Mali. These churches were established by the Assemblies of God, Avant Ministries, the Christian and Missionary Alliance, Evangelical Baptist, Evangelical Free, and Southern Baptist missions. Mali has a rudimentary postal system and few phone books. However, there is a network of friendships among the Protestant pastors, and I was able to use my friendship with a number of pastors to access the cell phone numbers of all of the denominational leaders and church district presidents serving in urban centers. I was then able to call and arrange interviews. After the personal interviews, church leaders arranged for me to conduct focus-group interviews with their pastors. Because the Protestant clergy is not a large population, I interviewed every pastor who agreed to be a part of the study. This is called a convenience sample approach, since subjects are selected because of their convenient availability (Vijver and Leung 1997, 27). All of the pastors were men. I know of no women pastors in the country.

A Malian Christian trained in qualitative and quantitative research methods was hired to work as a research associate. He assisted me in translating research material into French and with conducting the focus-group interviews. The research was conducted in two stages. The qualitative interviews during the first round of research were used to inform the construction of the questionnaire used in the second round of research. A question about retirement was added to the interview guide during the second round of interviews, since it emerged as an issue of great importance to urban pastors. A total of 33 urban pastors were interviewed for the study. Eight personal interviews were conducted with church presidents and district leaders. Six focus-group interviews were then conducted with 25 pastors. During the interviews pastors were also asked to fill out a worksheet on monthly expenses. A 98-item questionnaire in French was also distributed, and 30 were completed. I transcribed the interviews into English and coded them using Ethnograph software. I analyzed the data generated by the questionnaire using SPSS software.

THE URBAN PASTORATE OF MALI

When assessing how mission-established churches operate in Mali's economic system, one becomes aware of fundamental differences between urban and rural experiences. While several pastors noted that a rural pastorate can be difficult if there is a shortage of rain, most urban pastors believe that in the city it is much more difficult to provide for one's family. Over 80 percent of the pastors surveyed agreed at some level with the statement that it is more difficult in the city than in a village to provide for one's family.

I chose to focus this study on urban pastors for several reasons. Generally, rural pastors are expected to farm, and if there is adequate rain they are able to provide for the basic needs of their families. Urban pastors, however, live in a cash economy, and everything they need must be bought. Unlike rural pastors, a majority of urban pastors report that they believe that members of their churches may disapprove if they are involved in income-generating activities to provide for the needs of their families. Finally, food, transportation, education, clothing, and health care all cost more in the city, so the need for an income in the city is greater.

Pastors' Families

The study indicated that 90 percent of the pastors surveyed were married and had an average of about 4 children. Pastors and their wives also had members of their extended family living with them. The average number of relatives living with the pastor and his wife was roughly 4 people. Almost all pastors also had nonrelatives living with them. The average number of nonrelatives was 3 people. Thus the average urban pastor's household had a total of at least 12 persons for whom the pastor was financially responsible.

Average Monthly Expenses

During the first focus group, pastors were given a blank sheet of paper and asked to record all of their expenses during the previous month. Using the categories created by these pastors, a standardized worksheet of monthly expenses was established and used with all subsequent focus groups. Urban pastors reported spending an average of $113 (USD) per month for food, $32 for clothes, $25 for education of their children, $24 for health care, and $38 for transportation. Other average monthly expenses included $33 for rent, $16 for utilities, $11 for cooking fuel, $20 for tithes given to the church, $20 for telephone services, and some miscellaneous expenses. In all, their total average expenses were $337.71 per month.

Pastoral Income

Pastors indicated on the expenses worksheet the monthly salary they received from their church. The average salary of a pastor in an urban center was $111.64, with a low of $60 and a high of $182. Thus pastors receive an average of only 35 percent of what their families need in terms of financial support. As in the West, clergy salaries corresponded more to church size than years of experience or education of the pastor. Pastors in larger churches were generally paid more. Almost 80 percent of the pastors reported that they had never asked for a raise. One pastor stated that he had been a pastor for twenty years, and during this time he had never asked for a raise until the previous month. He said that one needed to be very careful to present oneself as not being in the ministry for money.

Pastors' Standard of Living

Pastors working in urban centers are generally required to speak French (the official language) and have a fairly high level of education. Pastors were asked to respond to the following question: "What do you estimate is the monthly income of other members of your community who have the same level of education as you do?" Eighty-three percent responded that they believed other members in the community earned more than they did. A number of pastors reported working in a variety of vocations prior to entering the ministry—as teachers, nurses, government officials, masons, and electricians. Thus they were aware of what people in these professions earn. When asked during interviews to give an estimate of the standard of living of urban pastors compared to that of other colleagues of the same age and education, the estimates ranged from 20 percent to 50 percent. Concerning pastors' standard of living, one church leader stated, "I think that the standard of living of urban pastors is a little bit deplorable. If we compare this with their friends or their colleagues at the same level it is the pastor who is the most unfortunate." Another pastor made this comment: "You see that materially and financially the pastors of Bamako suffer, especially if their wives make comparisons and if their children make comparisons." One church leader, who left a well-paying government job after sensing the Lord's call to become a pastor, had this to say about the lower standard of living he experienced after becoming a pastor:

When you live on the threshold of poverty, you do not have control of the house. The wife does not have much respect for you. Children do not respect you because you cannot respond to their needs. And you are a pastor. But your testimony about your own household is nothing because you have nothing in order to support them.

INCREASED FINANCIAL OBLIGATIONS AND
DEMANDS OF THE PASTORAL VOCATION

This study found that Malian men who respond to the Lord's call to give themselves to serve as pastors in an urban context will generally have an income that is inadequate to provide for their families' needs. It also suggests that because of the collectivistic nature of the Malian economic system, urban pastors experience an increase in the financial obligations and demands placed upon them by their pastoral vocation.

Visitors

One major reason for increased demand on pastors' financial resources is that they must host visitors. Every pastor interviewed mentioned people coming to stay with them. An elderly pastor explained:

> They [pastors] are the host of everyone. All the Christians in the countryside who become sick or who come for some business in town, who don't have relatives where they can go, find their way to the pastor's house. So the pastor and the members of his family are not the only ones, how can I say this, to benefit from their salary or eat from their salary, but other persons come and are added to them.

There are a number of reasons why an urban pastor receives so many visitors. One is that cities are the center of government, business, education, and health care, thus attracting people from all over the country. As one pastor noted, "Here in the city it is different than in a village or the country because it is the center of business. Everyone comes to the city." Another commented, "Everyone comes, even pastors who come from the country as well. They stay with the pastor. So we are responsible for them." Still another said, "There are visitors who come unannounced. We are obligated to manage this. That is a distinct feature of the ministry, of the ministry in town."

A second major reason why visitors end up at pastors' homes is that they want to stay with someone from their own religious community, even if it is somebody they don't know. This is not surprising, as Protestant Christians comprise only about 1 percent of the population. As one pastor observed, "When someone leaves the village, they are advised to go to a pastor's house." Protestant urban pastors have become part of the extended network of relationships of virtually every Protestant Christian living in the country, and even Protestant Christians living in neighboring countries. For an urban pastor this means an unending stream of visitors passing through his house. The better known a pastor is in the Christian community, the more visitors he will have. Even a new pastor will receive many visitors if he happens to live in the center of town, near a hospital, or in an otherwise desirable part of town.

In addition to visitors, pastors must host relatives and students. In my survey, 83 percent of pastors indicated that there were relatives living with them at the moment. Of these, 60 percent of the pastors had three or more relatives, and 27 percent had eight or more relatives living with them. As for nonrelatives, 67 percent of the pastors indicated that there were non-family members living with them. Of these, 40 percent had three or more nonrelatives living with them, and 13 percent had eight or more. One pastor said this about people staying with pastors: "When you are in town, most of the high schools are in town, and so cousins and brothers and their daughters and their sons will come for school. The pastor has to accept it, and they will not pay anything to the pastor."

Sharing resources among relatives is part of the social capital of Africa. Hospitality is a core value of Malian culture and is at the heart of its economic system. It is a primary way of ensuring that all people have their minimum needs met. However, the obligation to host visitors, relatives, and students places a serious financial burden on urban pastors. One pastor articulated the predicament in which most urban pastors find themselves:

You can't really limit these kinds of visitors who come, you see. It is obligatory. You cannot force them away, because the African character is such that you cannot eliminate them from our daily life. It is a serious problem, and we do not know what to do to escape this.

Requests for Help

Another area in which pastors experience increased demand on their limited resources is in the requests for help that they receive from others. One pastor explained, "Believers who have nothing fall back on the pastor. In the case of sickness or a lack of food, all the problems fall back on the pastor." This phenomenon of appealing to the pastor when one is in need is explained by the fact that the pastor is viewed as the center of the faith community. One pastor stated,

> The pastor has more obligations, more responsibilities than his colleague of the same age and same conditions living in town. When we have health problems, we see the pastor. When we have problems with the government, we see the pastor. So, the pastor is at the center of the life of the faithful [Christians]. With all of your problems, it is the pastor that you must consult. So this means that the pastor has more responsibilities.

Dr. Isaac Laudarji, a church leader from Nigeria, reflected on why so many people come to the pastor for help in Africa.[4] He observed that when the first missionaries came and new churches were started, missionaries became the center of the nascent church community. They had money and resources, and they were disposed to help those who requested it. The desire to help others and to be the center of activity in the church may or may not have been paternalistic, but the result was a link in people's minds between church leadership, access to resources, and help with the problems they face. The missionaries left and were replaced by African pastors as the center of the church

---

4   Personal conversation with Dr. Laudarji on April 23, 2006.

community. Thus people now come to pastors for help, despite the fact that they do not have the same access to outside resources that missionaries had. One pastor remarked that there were still people in his church who believed that Europeans were paying Malian pastors, while others thought that Western mission agencies funded them.

BURDENS OF MINISTRY

Mission-established churches are able to operate in urban centers in Mali, but not without considerable hardships for the pastors and their families. The collectivistic nature of the African economic system adds a number of significant financial obligations to those serving as urban pastors. Their vocation requires sacrifices that have an effect not only on their families but on how they are perceived by others.

Marriage

Malian urban pastors experience the adverse effects of their suboptimal living conditions on their marriages—84 percent of pastors indicated that their financial situation was a significant concern for their wives. One church leader had this to say about how their living conditions affected the wives of pastors: "The pastors' wives of Bamako do not live; they suffer. Really, they suffer. Often, when you see certain ones [pastors' wives], their eyes are red. The wife says straight out, 'I regret being married to a pastor.'"

Children

The economic condition of pastors and their wives also has an effect on their children. In Mali one regularly encounters rural pastors whose fathers were also rural ministers. Pastors were asked whether they knew of any sons of pastors in the city who had also become pastors. These are some of the typical responses: "Eh, (laughs) the son of a pastor who became a pastor in the city. In rural areas there are lots. But as we are in the city, in reality, I have not yet met one." Still another pastor remarked, "The children of a pastor, an urban pastor, becoming also a pastor in place of their papa or following the vocation of their papa—for the moment I do not know of one." Another pastor stated bluntly, "Pastors' children have been traumatized by their lives as children of pastors." When asked the reason for this phenomenon, one pastor explained,

> They saw how their papa was mistreated, how he suffers. And today I think that is what discourages the children of a pastor to become one. There are some daughters of pastors who refuse even to marry a young pastor because they were eyewitnesses of the suffering of their parents. I think that today this is a challenge … how we should treat the servants of God in order that we can really give hope to these children to go into the ministry.

During the research, one pastor was located who was the son of an urban pastor. His comments were very insightful and based on personal experience:

> Being a pastor is a source of pride for me, but in reality it is difficult for many reasons. The children of pastors in town are not able to attain the standard of living of the children of believers in the same church. You will find that with the pastor's son's wardrobe there is no comparison with that of the children of others in the church. He is going to think that either his father is doing nothing or that his father is so spiritual that he looks for nothing for his son. And the child grew up with this. He sees the suffering of his parents. He wants to have the luxuries that his father never had, such as those of the members in the church. He goes to someone else's house and the living conditions are good and at his house they aren't. At Christmas it is difficult to have clothes, and we the pastors get new clothes for our children at Christmas and Easter. I grew up in this situation. I got new clothes at Christmas and at Easter and nothing else. If you got some at Christmas, that could last the whole year (laughs). In these conditions it is often difficult, and I find that the fundamental reason [why a child of a pastor does not go into ministry] is the conditions and the diffi-

culties which their parents passed through. Really, they [children of pastors] are trying to hide themselves as an escape. We are fleeing. Even if God calls we flee.

Nutrition

The economic condition of urban pastors affects their own and their family's nutrition. When asked to respond to the statement "My family always has enough to eat," 32 percent disagreed at some level. Even if many pastors indicated that they had enough to eat, there is still a distinction between food quantity and food quality. One pastor observed,

> In the area of nutrition, lots of pastors are dressed like the others [in the community], but we strictly manage what we can eat. Many times we eat only enough [to satisfy] our hunger. The quantity is there but the quality is not there. Many times we eat some rice and *to*, which is made from millet. When we look at others [in the church and community], they have a diet which is much more acceptable. The pastor needs some vegetables, some meat, and many other things which are necessary for one's health in view of working hard in the ministry.

Another pastor shared the effects that poor quality of food had on his children:

> To say something about nutrition, often we are embarrassed in how to respond to our children, who ask, "When are we going to prepare a certain meal, papa?" such as macaroni or potatoes. We see others prepare these things frequently. But with us, we eat only to not die. We eat, but not quality food, and the children desire that. They want their papa and mama to prepare the same thing. So it is often a frustration. Often we try to calm the children and say, "When God provides for our needs. We are going to think about that."

Church Members' Perceptions

The economic realities in which Malian urban pastors live and serve also have an effect on how others in the community perceive the pastorate. Pastors were asked to respond to the statement "There are young women in my church who would be hesitant to marry a pastor or a man who wants to become a pastor because of financial concerns," and 87 percent agreed at some level. One pastor shared the story of a young Bible school graduate coming to his church in order to propose to a young woman in his congregation. In response to his proposal she told the man, "Sir, I'm sorry, but I cannot marry a pastor. When you look at the living conditions of a pastor, really, I do not have the nerve to try to be able to live as the wife of a pastor. I cannot do it."

Pastors were asked to respond to the statement "There are young men in my church who are gifted for the ministry but are hesitant to consider becoming a pastor because of financial concerns," and 97 percent agreed at some level. One pastor explained why he thought young men were not interested in going into the ministry:

> I have met children of pastors [who] said that even if the Lord calls them, they don't want to go into the Lord's service because of the conditions of their papas who are retired. If the pastoral life is like this, if it is going to end like this, it does not encourage them to go to Bible school.

Humiliation

Some reported experiencing humiliation as a result of serving as pastors. While it is not entirely clear why this is so, it may be a result of pastors' meager incomes or having to be dependent on others. One pastor said, "So, we are conscious that we serve God. That is why we accept being humiliated, because we know that we serve the God who is kind, who sees us as we are, who accepts us as we are in spite of the difficulties. Sometimes it is too much." Another pastor was more explicit in describing his humiliation:

Another thing which is humiliating according to our culture is that often it is the parents-in-law, that is to say the parents of our wives, who come to help the pastor because they see their daughter suffering and they are obligated to make a sacrifice. According to our culture, this is a humiliation for the husband. Yes. To marry a woman and to be taken care of by this woman and her parents—if it was not for the sake of the ministry, according to our culture, it is better to die than that. But the pastor is obligated to accept this in order to be able to serve God.

Financial Future and Retirement

Another area in which pastors suffer economically is in the lack of a secure financial future and retirement. Pastors were also asked to respond to the statement "I will be well-prepared financially when I reach the age of retirement." Of the respondents, 89 percent disagreed at some level. Of those who agreed, 7 percent mildly agreed and 4 percent agreed. No one strongly agreed with the statement. A second statement, "My church provides for the needs of pastors who retire," drew 73 percent disagreement at some level, while 19 percent mildly agreed and 7 percent agreed. Again, no one strongly agreed with this statement.

In interviews pastors had much to say about retirement. The Malian government requires all government employees to be enrolled at the *Institut National de Prévoyance Sociale* (INPS), which is their equivalent of the United States' Social Security. An employee at INPS informed me that the laws concerning retirement have been in place since the 1950s. When I asked a national church president if people in the community who work in the private sector are also enrolled at INPS, he said,

Yes ... even if you are working in the private sector the government will say that you need to have INPS so most people will have it. Churches are aware that it is normal for individuals working in the public or private sector to have some kind of retirement plan.

Yet when church leaders were asked if there was a retirement plan for their pastors, one former church president answered, "No. Truthfully, the retirement of pastors is a serious problem."

When pastors themselves were asked what their churches were doing for their retirement, there was an outpouring of response. One pastor stated, "Nothing. The answer is nothing. Nothing has been undertaken. We have not undertaken anything concrete." Another pastor said, "Nothing (shaking head in disgust). The church does nothing." One church leader declared, "I think that the retirement scheme is awful for pastors." Still another lamented, "We have … put nothing in place. We have created nothing which can, at the moment of retirement, satisfy the needs of these people, even the minimum conditions. And that is very serious."

Based on the amount of discussion generated, it is apparent that the issues of financial security and retirement caused widespread concerns. One pastor described the alarm experienced by those who have not made their own preparations for retirement: "When you reach retirement, if it happens that you have done nothing, your eyes begin to get big because you are afraid." A church president said retirement can be a scary prospect: "This is really sad. They have nothing, and often when the pastor thinks about the future it gives him lots of worry in his heart."

PASTORAL COPING STRATEGIES

How well, then, do mission-established urban churches work in a Malian economic system that is based on collectivism? The answer is that they do function, but not without significant hardship for the pastors and their families. The question one must ask is, given the increased financial demands, the low level of their salaries (roughly $112 per month), and their monthly expenses (roughly $338 per month), how do urban pastors actually make a living? This study revealed that in order to survive, urban pastors employ a variety of coping strategies to bridge the gap between their income and expenses.

Income-generating Activities

The first of these strategies is income-generating activities. In focus groups and individual interviews, pastors were asked what they did in order to help provide for their families. Their responses indicated different philosophies as to whether a pastor should be involved in income-generating activities. One pastor remarked that there were "certain pastors who did not even want their wives to sell pastries next to their house because ... the pastor must not work and his wife must not work." Yet, another pastor stated, "It is very important that the pastor have an activity which earns some money in order to complete what the church is able to give him." The former director of a Bible school that trained urban pastors confided that he believed that every urban pastor needed to be involved in income-generating activities unless it required so much time that he would not be able to fulfill his responsibilities as a pastor. He also acknowledged that Malian urban pastors did not agree on whether they should be involved in incoming-generating activities. One church leader summarized this disagreement when he observed,

> So I find that there are two categories of pastors. There are pastors who understand that they should be like the Apostle Paul, that they should be tentmakers. They should work and earn money, and along with the little that the church gives, [they] are able to survive and take care of their families. But there are other pastors who have been taught and believe that if they work with their hands they are wasting the time that the Lord has given to them to witness, to do evangelism, to preach and so on. So this is a problem I think.

Vocational and Nonvocational Activities

Some pastors possess certain vocational skills and training. Some have worked as teachers, usually in private schools. One pastor stated, "Since I am a teacher by training, this year I began to teach several hours of classes in a school. This is going to help me a little bit to make ends meet at the end of the month." Other pastors have been trained as carpenters, masons, or tailors, and they work part time in these vocations. Mali has a predominantly subsistence agricultural economy, and many pastors know how to farm.

For those who have access to a field and the means to undertake it, farming is a preferred activity. However, acquiring a field is extremely difficult, and the profitability of this activity often depends on the distance between the field and the pastor's residence. Another activity frequently mentioned is animal husbandry. A number of pastors raise pigs, chickens, and other small animals. A president of a national church stated, "Because the salary of the church is too little, the salary is not able to support all of my needs. It is better that I take some time to do something else to make ends meet. For example, I raise animals." Gardening is another activity. A president of a church district in Bamako knows a pastor who has a garden in his courtyard and lives for months on the squash from his garden.

Besides these activities, pastors at times resort to manual labor: "Certain pastors are obligated to do manual labor. That is to say work day by day as a laborer." Pastors also pursue a variety of small business activities. Some repair televisions and radios; others acquire a refrigerator or freezer and sell ice and cold water, especially during the hot season. Some make a local drink called *dabileni* or process milk and sell it in the market. Others acquire a donkey cart and use it to generate income by charging to haul loads in town. Others rent their donkey cart out to others so that it does not take up too much of their time. Some pastors even undertake door-to-door sales.

Pastors' Wives

One of the most important coping strategies for pastors in urban contexts is their wives being involved in income-generating activities. Of the pastors surveyed, 70 percent reported that their wives worked; of these women, 68 percent earned less than $30 per month in income, 9 percent earned between $30 and $60, 9 percent earned between $91 and $120, and 4 percent earned over $150. Pastors' wives are involved in a variety of nonvocational income-generating activities such as selling charcoal, ice, pastries, juice, peanuts, and other items. Some have learned to sew. Sometimes other family members are also working to contribute to the family's monthly income. Pastors were asked in my research if other family members contributed to the monthly needs. Responses indicated that 78 percent of the pastors had another family member contributing less than $30 per month, 13 percent had someone contributing between $31 and $60, 4 percent had someone contributing between $91 and $120, and 4 percent had someone contributing between $120 and $150.

Problems Associated with Income-generating Activities

Pastors who engage in income-generating activities do so with potential risks. One pastor articulated one of the greatest dangers—not having enough time for his pastoral responsibilities. "No matter what the activity of the pastor, there is often some risk of being too attracted to it so that he will not have enough time for the church." Another pastor observed that "by undertaking to provide for 80 percent of your needed revenue, you risk not being able to serve the church in the way that is required." In my study, 33 percent of the pastors reported having to spend too much of their time pursuing other income-generating activities in order to provide for the needs of their families, and 65 percent of pastors reported that there were certain activities they would like to pursue in terms of ministry but were not able to because they needed to work in order to provide for the needs of their families.

Another risk is the danger of having one's reputation damaged among church members because of the pastor's income-generating activities. Commenting on the dilemma of having to pursue income-generating activities in order to make ends meet, one pastor worries that his church members will say that "he is there for personal gain and not for the church." In the questionnaire, pastors were asked to respond to the statement "Members of my church disapprove if I have to spend some of my time doing other activities so that I can provide for the needs of my family." Of those who responded, 65 percent indicated some level of agreement with this statement (23 percent strongly agreed, 19 percent agreed, 23 percent mildly agreed), while 35 percent indicated some level of disagreement (15 percent mildly disagreed, 8 percent disagreed, 12 percent strongly disagreed).

Borrowing

A second major coping strategy for Malian urban pastors is borrowing. One of the primary ways many pastors deal with emergencies or unexpected expenses is to seek an advance on their monthly salary from the church. For some pastors, this is the first coping strategy when there is an emergency. As one pastor said, "First it is the IOU's that we use. We borrow from next month's salary." Another pastor remarked that, in the face of a crisis, "if God does not intervene we go and get an advance." The problem with this is that these IOU's must be repaid: "We can take advances, but there is always a hole [shortage of funds].... Once the salary has been given, they remove immediately what we had been advanced, and the gap is always there."

Assistance from Others

A third major coping strategy of urban pastors is receiving assistance from others. Since the fundamental economic consideration in Mali's culture is the distribution of resources so that all persons may have their minimum needs met, this is one of the key strategies used by urban pastors to meet financial difficulties—they access their bonding social capital[5] and ask for help from family, relatives, and friends. Reflecting on the different ways he and his wife had met the many financial hardships during almost thirty years in pastoral ministry, an older pastor remarked, "We prayed and we spoke to certain specific people, not to everyone, and certain ones helped us. Others saw our situation without our having to say anything and gave us some money." When a need arises, a pastor will often speak to a close friend or relative, but a favorable response to the request is not always guaranteed.

---

5   "Bonding social capital" describes social ties that link people to others who are primarily like themselves along some key dimension.

Friends and family members are not the only sources of assistance. The local church can also be an important source. One pastor stated, "When things are serious we can go to the church, to the community to which you belong." When an urban pastor approaches a friend, a family member, or his church, it is considered an appropriate use of the pastor's bonding social capital. However, frequent requests for assistance can be perceived as something else: "If the pastor has to spend time going door to door asking for help, this won't work. You become like a beggar with respect to the society and even with the church members that you teach."

Friendships between Malian urban pastors and others outside of the immediate church community are becoming more common because of the increasing frequency of international travel and short-term mission teams. Many of these teams come to assist with a church-related project such as constructing a church building. Then friendships are established between the short-term team members and the local pastor. When asked how many friends they had who were not Malian and lived outside of the country, 32 percent indicated that they had none, 21 percent indicated that they had one to two, 21 percent indicated that they had three to four, and 21 percent indicated that they had nine or more. Friendships with affluent Westerners function as a form of linking social capital.[6] For those living in a context of poverty, access to linking social capital is especially important. Urban pastors can facilitate connections between the poor in their communities and external development assistance, so pastors can be an important source of linking social capital for the church community.

Still another source of financial assistance is nongovernmental organizations (NGOs) and parachurch ministries working in the country. It is difficult to determine how frequently pastors contact these organizations in order to request financial aid. When asked concerning what pastors did to make ends meet, one church leader responded, "Well, the very obvious thing is that they will go from NGO to NGO, Christian NGOs, to ask for money. That's very, very common."

---

6   "Linking social capital" describes social ties to those with power, providing one with the capacity to gain access to resources from beyond the community.

BLESSINGS OF MINISTRY

While urban pastors in Mali face many challenges and difficulties, pastors generally reported being satisfied with being a pastor. When asked to respond to the statement "I am proud of being a pastor," all pastors agreed at some level. When asked to respond to the statement "If offered a well-paying job, I would consider leaving the ministry," all pastors indicated disagreement at some level. When asked to respond to the statement "In the past I have been tempted to quit the ministry in order to look for another job in order to better provide for the needs of my family," almost 80 percent disagreed. While there is the possibility that pastors were embarrassed to respond honestly or that they responded according to how they thought I wanted them to respond, during the interviews I encountered no pastor who seemed bitter or resentful of being a pastor. Malian pastors are proud of being pastors and of serving their churches in this capacity.

ABILITY OF CHURCHES TO SUPPORT THEIR PASTORS

During the interview process I began wondering whether pastors believed that their churches had the financial means to support them adequately. Even though this question was not directly addressed in the interviews, I did ask a certain number of pastors and church leaders what they thought. All the pastors I asked stated that they believed their churches had sufficient means to fully support or at least to greatly improve the pastor's financial situation. One pastor stated that if members gave a full tithe, there would be enough to support the pastor. Another stated, "Frankly speaking, the church is not as poor as we think, in seeing what the believers do individually." Still another stated, "I think if the Christians were doing their best they could help their pastors very much." Another church leader stated,

> It may be difficult with new churches when there are maybe five, ten believers, but with big churches with fifty or a hundred

people or more, I believe that it's a matter of their understanding the importance of giving and supporting their pastors and even sending missionaries. I believe that it is a matter of motivation, a matter of awakening their responsibility to fulfill their duty and their role in the church.

STANDARD OF LIVING OF OTHER CHRISTIAN WORKERS

Pastors are not the only full-time Christian workers serving in urban environments. A number of Western parachurch organizations working in the country have recruited Malian Christians to serve as staff. These workers are now required to raise their support from churches and individuals within the Malian church community. The national director of a large Western parachurch organization reported that the level of support for Malian nationals serving with his organization was set at $520 per month. A church leader informed me that the level of support for national workers of still another large Western parachurch organization was set at a minimum of $500 per month. These workers are generally able to raise their support in urban centers because they can solicit support from individuals and churches of different denominations. Because they serve with nondenominational organizations, they have "the freedom to go everywhere, but the pastor does not have this freedom."

CONCLUSIONS

The churches that Western mission agencies established in Africa and many other areas of the world are similar to the churches in the West, in that they generally rely on having a paid, full-time professional pastor. In Africa and in many other regions of the world, these mission-established churches operate in cultures and economic systems that are based on collectivism. Many of these churches also exist in poverty. Urban pastors in Mali, like pastors everywhere, must provide for the needs of their families. What is apparent from this study is that when a Malian responds to the Lord's call to serve as a leader in an urban church, this choice will almost invariably limit his earnings as the head of a household to anywhere from one-quarter to one-half of what other heads of household make who are of the same age and level of education. Because of the way Mali's collectivist culture and economy functions, the pastor also becomes part of the social networks of everyone in the church community. This increases the financial obligations and demands placed on his reduced financial resources. The data also indicates that many urban pastors carry on in less than adequate living conditions, and that this has an effect not only on them and their families but also on how others in the church and community perceive the pastorate. While this study was limited to Malian urban pastors, conversations with church leaders and missionaries from Nigeria, Ghana, Burkina Faso, Zimbabwe, and the Democratic Republic of Congo indicate that this phenomenon occurs elsewhere in Africa and may in fact be widespread.

Practical Implications

My study suggests that the Western mission agencies that established churches in urban contexts in Mali did not realize the effect that ministry in a collectivistic economy would have on the pastors of these churches. The Apostle Paul admonishes believers to provide adequately for their families, not only out of love and concern but as a witness to the community in which they live (1 Tim 5:8). Given the increased financial obligations and demands placed on urban pastors, the key issue that needs to be addressed is how to increase their income so that they can better provide for their families.

The Apostle Paul was a tentmaker (Acts 18:3), and many of the churches he established existed in conditions of "extreme poverty" (2 Cor 8:2). Where church tithes are insufficient to support local pastors, such as in Mali, one solution would be for churches to approve bivocationalism as an accepted practice for clergy. Churches could establish guidelines in terms of how many hours could be spent in income-generating activities each week. Businessmen and entrepreneurs in the church could also give guidance and advice in terms of what kinds of activities are the most profitable and require the least amount of work in hours. If pastors need to pursue other income-generating activities, then they should do so with the knowledge and approbation of their church. Pastors should not have to hide the fact that they are working outside the church, nor should they feel guilty about working to support their families.

The fact that urban churches are not supporting their pastors according to the means that they have available suggests that these churches were established in a way that left the congregants believing that the responsibility for taking care of their pastor ultimately resides with the mission. Dr. Nzuzi Mukawa, a church leader from the Democratic Republic of Congo, has remarked that most mission-founded churches seem to lack initiative when it comes to supporting their churches and ministries.[7] In contrast, the African Independent Churches, which lack connection to the Western church, have tremendous initiative:

> They don't have any connection with … the outside world, and they were born out of Africans' initiatives. These churches, they do wonderful things. They are building churches and even sending missionaries. But those churches who receive, who used to receive money from outside, it seems like they don't have any initiative.

This suggests that Western mission agencies need to reexamine the way in which they go about planting new churches. How can Western agencies plant churches in which new believers take responsibility for their own church? There has already been much discussion in mission circles of paternalism and dependency. The challenge for missions is to start new churches that are owned functionally and psychologically by their own members. Perhaps it is time to reconsider the methods of the Apostle Paul. Not only was he a tentmaker, but it was his practice

---

7   Personal interview on August 19, 2003.

to never stay long in any one place, thereby avoiding any kind of economic or psychological dependency. As Roland Allen asserts,

> Paradoxical as it may seem, I think that it is quite possible that the shortness of his stay may have contributed in no small measure to St. Paul's success. There is something in the presence of the great teacher that sometimes tends to prevent smaller men from realizing themselves. They more readily feel their responsibility; they more easily and successfully exert their powers, when they see that, unless they come forward, nothing will be done. By leaving them quickly St. Paul gave the local leaders opportunity to take their proper place, and forced the church to realize that it could not depend upon him, but must depend upon its own resources. (1962, 93)

A final factor that may contribute to the economic plight of urban pastors is the level of spiritual maturity in their churches. The Protestant church in Mali for the most part is driven by evangelism rather than church planting. The focus is on bringing people to Christ rather than on making disciples and establishing churches where members have been adequately taught, trained, and equipped for service. Many urban pastors admit that their members have not been taught as well as they need to be. Even the evangelism itself lacks material for doing follow-up. Thus churches may be suffering from "spiritual malnutrition." The implication for pastors is a need to spend more time teaching in their churches, even if it means less time on evangelism. This may help church members to better understand their responsibility to help their pastors provide for their families.

Final Suggestions

The following are some suggestions for improving the financial circumstances of pastors in Mali.

　　1. Pastors have confessed that they are reticent to teach about tithing because they don't want to give the impression that they are

only interested in money. A solution would be to have a mature and respected lay person preach or teach this subject.

2. Church members could be encouraged to give nonfinancial tithes (e.g., food, clothes, household effects).

3. Many pastors acknowledged that they are uncomfortable talking about money with their churches. Implementing an annual review of the pastor's salary and financial state would give pastors a regular opportunity to discuss their financial situation with their churches.

4. Since pastoral compensation strongly correlates to congregation size, implementing a central fund that pools all church tithes and offerings in a church district would allow pastors of large and small churches to receive more equitable compensation.

5. Churches should shield the pastor from excessive demands. They could intervene and limit the number of people who can stay with their pastor and perhaps set a fee schedule for those who do stay so as to help with the cost of food. Church members can also offer to host visitors, since this is a valid need. Families in the church could be encouraged to develop a ministry of hospitality and could rotate the responsibility among themselves.

6. Churches need to confront realistically the issue of their pastors' retirement. Pastors who are close to retirement are often at a loss for what they will do when they retire. This anxiety is discouraging to them, to young pastors, and to others in the church who may feel called to ministry. The church should be a source of hope, not despair, for those who are called to pastoral ministry.

In conclusion, many pastors in the Majority World are faithfully serving the Lord in situations that require great sacrifice and suffering, yet their voices are rarely heard in the West. In this chapter I have used numerous quotes from Malian pastors so that some of these voices might be heard. My hope is that it will promote greater understanding and empathy with our coworkers in Christ, whose faith, dedication, and perseverance is an inspiration and encouragement to us all.

REFERENCES

Allen, Roland. 1962. *Missionary methods: St. Paul's or ours?* Grand Rapids: Eerdmans.

Bediako, Kwame. 1995. *Christianity in Africa: The renewal of a non-Western religion,* Maryknoll, NY: Orbis.

CIA. 2013. *The world factbook.* Accessed March 29, 2013. https://www.cia.gov/library/publications/the-world-factbook/geos/ml.html.

Economy Watch. 2010. Mali economy. Accessed March 29, 2013. http://www.economywatch.com/world_economy/mali/.

Hofstede, Geert. 1991. *Cultures and organizations: Software of the mind.* New York: McGraw-Hill.

Index Mundi. 2013. Mali GDP–per capita (PPP). Accessed March 29, 2013. http://www.indexmundi.com/mali/gdp_per_capita_(ppp).html.

LaRue, John C., Jr. 1998. Pastors and salary satisfaction. *Your Church* 44, no. 3: 88.

Maranz, David. 2001. *African friends and money matters: Observations from Africa.* Dallas, TX: SIL International and International Museum of Cultures.

McMillan, Becky R., and Matthew Price. 2003. How much should we pay the pastor? A fresh look at clergy salaries in the 21st century. Pulpit and Pew Research Reports. Durham, NC: Duke Divinity School.

Milanovic, Branko. 2005. *Worlds apart: Measuring international and global inequality.* Princeton, NJ: Princeton University Press.

Richmond, Yale, and Phyllis Gestrin. 2009. *Into Africa: A guide to sub-Saharan culture and diversity.* 2nd ed. Boston: Intercultural Press.

Schaeffer, Robert K. 1997. *Understanding globalization: The social consequences of political, economic, and environmental change.* New York: Rowman & Littlefield.

Vijver, Fons J. R. van de, and Kwok Leung. 1997. *Methods and data analysis for cross-cultural research.* Thousand Oaks, CA: Sage.

7

SUBSISTENT AND SUBSTANTIVE COMMUNITIES UNDER ATTACK: THE CASE OF ZOWE IN NORTHERN MALAWI

Mike Njalayawo Mtika

Zowe, a rural community in northern Malawi, Africa, is heavily subsistent. People in the community meet their material and nonmaterial needs mostly through exploiting their natural resources. The people grow food crops—corn, beans, peanuts, millet, sweet potatoes, pumpkins, etc.—on small pieces of land and consume most of what they produce themselves. A family is food secure when it harvests enough crops to last until the next harvest time. Economic status is improved mostly through the sale or bartering of surplus food crops. To generate more income, some families grow cash crops, mainly tobacco; others engage in small-scale income-generating activities or go to seek employment at commercial farms, in urban Malawi, or outside Malawi.

Zowe's economy is not only subsistent but also substantive. Polanyi (2001) views such economies as instituted processes in which economic activities are driven by non-market-based reciprocity, redistribution, and exchange rather than market-driven, rational-choice decision-making processes that are responsive to price mechanisms. Polanyi points out that under substantive economic processes, people follow traditional means of livelihood rather than choosing from a wide variety of alternatives. Not surprisingly, there is little surplus production.

Socially, people in these substantive economies have networks of ties that encourage *helping behavior,* with people's actions solidly aligned to group norms. Their culture is collectivist (see Triandis and Trafimow 2003; also Wilson, chap. 6 in this volume). Politically, social order in substantive economies is guided by traditions and customs that form a binding, unwritten constitution through which rulers are accountable to their subjects. Governance follows gerontocratic processes in which age (until one's seventies), the concern and care one has for others, and wisdom (judicious judgment) in ensuring group solidarity and well-being guide how those in leadership positions rule. Under such an economic, social, cultural, and political system, the use of natural resources is guided by usufructural rights (i.e., the right to use a resource but not necessarily own it). Land, for example, can be used by an individual as long as he or she needs to use it; the individual has no authority to sell it, as it belongs to the family lineage or community (Ayittey 1998, 96–99).

Life in these subsistent and substantive communities is characterized by *ubuntu,* a Zulu term (Tutu 1999), or *umunthu* in the Malawi languages Chichewa and Tumbuka (Musopole 1994). People with ubuntu (umunthu), remarks Tutu, are

> open and available to others, affirming of others, do not feel threatened that others are able and good, based from a proper self-assurance that comes from knowing that they belong to a greater whole and are diminished when others are humiliated or diminished, when others are tortured or oppressed. (1999, 25)

At the risk of overgeneralization, life in subsistent and substantive communities like Zowe, when unadulterated by modernity, exemplifies umunthu. Economic activities, social relations, cultural practices, and political processes under umunthu tend towards what Triandis et al. (1985) and Triandis and Trafimow (2003) term "allocentric behavior," in which people's actions focus on the well-being of both others and themselves. Its opposite is idiocentric behavior, in which people's actions focus more on their goals and less on others' needs (ibid.).

At present, allocentric behavior in Zowe is under attack. It is undergoing significant change with the onslaught of modernity, which is ushering in rationalist lifestyles. People are becoming more idiocentric. They prefer self-reliance, understood as making their own decisions without worrying about what others think. Furthermore, they tend to increasingly engage in cutthroat competition with each other.

I grew up in Zowe and started outreach and community development work there in 2005. In this essay, based on a contrast of the 1960s with the 2000s era, I explore how modernity is fostering idiocentric behavior. Noting that change is inevitable, I argue for helping such subsistent and substantive communities to engage in change that would entail not only improving the socioeconomic status of individuals but advance collective well-being as well. Such change needs to draw on *use-value production activities*; i.e., the production of goods based on their value in using them to meet people's needs. The change should also advance the production of goods that could be exchanged with other goods people need, but in ways that build social ties and relationships rather than tear them down; I term this *relational exchange-value production activities*. Such change should focus on facilitating entrepreneurial creativity founded on relationships of love, informed by biblical principles, with the goal of attaining spiritual, physical, social, cultural, economic, and political security. I start with a description of how Zowe husbands in the 1960s got pushed into modernity by colonialism and capitalism, which are increasingly undermining umunthu.

ZOWE IN THE 1960s

It is 1965. My grandfather has seven sons (my uncles) and two daughters; one of them is my mother. One day, early in the morning, my youngest uncle's wife is pounding corn in a mortar. With her pestle moving up and down, intermittently hitting the corn in the mortar, she sings aloud. Singing helps to relieve the drudgery of pounding, but it also has messages on various issues. The song she is singing has a powerful meaning for her husband, a message that confirms his breadwinning role and demands that he fulfill that role. The lyrics are rich. My other uncles' wives join her. One joins to specifically help her in pounding the corn. Others are making arrangements to pound their own corn. They all sing in a chorus; she leads the song, and the others join in at appropriate points in the singing, making a wonderful melody:

Amama imwe!	Hey, mother!
Manyi nivwalechi naŵo	Will I ever dress well with
ŵanalumi aŵa?	this husband?
Maye maye nthengwa yane.	Oh this marriage of mine!
Aŵo ŵakwenda ku ntchito	Those who go look for work
Ŵakugula suti	They buy suits
Maye maye nthengwa yane	Oh this marriage of mine!
Aŵo ŵakukhala m'kaya	Those who stay home
Ŵakujima mbeŵa	They dig mice
Maye maye nthengwa yane	Oh this marriage of mine!

The song is telling my young uncle to go and look for work, get income, and buy clothes. Laughter follows during breaks in their singing and pounding of the corn. There is significant discussion of various other matters. They share information on how best they can take care of their husbands and children, get their husbands to go look for work, and relate to in-laws—an important part of married life in this patrilineal and patrilocal community. They also discipline one another whenever one is wrong on any expectation or role.

My young uncle has been married for about four months. He is twenty-one years old and his wife is eighteen. A pounding song like this is announcing that the wife is now pregnant and it is time for the husband to go and look for work. There is no paid work in the community; looking for work means going away to commercial farms, to urban Malawi, or to other countries, especially South Africa. There seems to be a cultural prescription. He has performed his conjugal responsibilities: he got married as everyone expected, he has made his wife pregnant (he is indeed a man), and now it is time to get into the crucial breadwinning role. He must leave and seek work away from home.

In this community, a husband is expected to play a critical role in generating food and income for the household. In the 1930s and 1940s, as the elderly recall, a good husband was one who worked hard on the farm to make sure that he had enough food for his household. During the rainy season, good husbands woke up very early in the morning and went to the farm, working until late in the evening. A household with such a hard-working husband/father generally harvested enough food. Any extra food crops produced could then be bartered for other goods or exchanged for other commodities a household needed. While husbands were expected to fulfill breadwinning roles, household chores (e.g., cleaning the house and its surroundings, childcare, food processing like grinding corn into flour, and cooking) were the responsibility of the wife.

Food production was indeed a main breadwinning role for husbands, especially prior to colonial times. Since the colonial era,[1] income generation has become increasingly important and a preoccupation of husbands. Colonialists introduced a cash economy and the resultant capitalism into Malawi in the late 1800s (Phiri 1983). They instituted a hut tax that was supposed to be paid in cash by male adult members of a household. This led to men going out to look for work to pay the tax. They worked at the commercial farms the colonialists had created, they worked as domestic servants in colonialists' homes, and they went to work in the mines. Generally, they were paid little but offered all the labor colonialists needed in their farms, mines, and homes. The tax system was the worst abuse of colonial rule, because it mercilessly exploited the local labor. Phiri remarks that, through compelling Malawians to work on European commercial farms, "the

---

1   The British colonized Malawi in 1891. The colonialists built roads and railways, introduced cash crops, and started commercial activities all geared towards providing raw materials for industrial activities in Europe. They paid little attention to the well-being of Malawians. This led to the nationalist movement that began during the period between the World Wars and ended when Malawi became independent in July 1964.

hut-tax collection introduced a level of violence and insecurity which rivaled that at the height of the slave trade" (1983, 269).

Since colonial times, a husband's income-generation role has received more weight, because income has the dual role of enabling families to produce more food and also meeting other non-food needs. Over the years, many husbands have engaged in the income-generation breadwinning role through not only the growing of cash crops, engaging in small-scale trading activities, and learning an income-generating skill like carpentry or bricklaying, but also going to look for work in distant places like South Africa, which is over two thousand miles away from Zowe. Husbands who go looking for work in South Africa end up in circular migration; they go work for a year or two, or even three, returning to reconnect with their families for a short period of time (ranging from a few weeks to three months), and going back to these places of work (Chirwa 1997; Lurie 2000; Lurie et al. 2003; Mtika 2007). Migrant work has been a main factor in improving the economic status of rural families in Malawi (Read 1942; Chirwa 1997, 1998).

All of my uncles went to work in South Africa or Zimbabwe—when the economy in that country was much better than Malawi's—at one point in their lifetime. Most of my uncles left as soon as their wives got pregnant (around three to four months after marriage) and came back for a three-month vacation when the child was two to three years old. They would go back after making their wives pregnant again and would be gone for another two to three years. They were involved in this circular migration until they were in their fifties and would then "retire."

Whatever my uncles earned in their jobs was shared with everyone in the extended family system, with distant relatives, and with friends. To start with, while working in South Africa, my uncles sent money home for their wives, children, and a host of relatives. This money was used to buy clothes and other necessities in the home, such as improved seed, farm implements, and fertilizer, and to hire farm labor. My uncles sent money home not to their wives but to their father (my grandfather). When he received the money, he would take it and in most cases give all of it to his daughter-in-law, telling her that her husband had sent money to help her. He would at the same time bring along a child, or would draw the attention of his daughter-in-law to some other needy household in his extended family, so that the daughter-in-law would help this child or household. For instance, in 1964 my eldest uncle, who was working in Johannesburg, South Africa, sent money to his wife through my grandfather. My grandfather then took the money to his daughter-in-law and brought me along, telling her that I needed a pair of shorts and a shirt. His daughter-in-law took me to a shop and bought these clothes for me. This marked her as a good daughter-in-law, one who cared for the well-being of not only herself and her children but others as well.

When my uncles came back for their three-month vacation, they brought income and clothes again, not only for their wives and children but also for their father, mother, and a host of nieces, nephews (me included), cousins, aunts, uncles, grandparents, in-laws, and friends, especially those who had helped them go to South Africa or find a job there. They also brought admired goods such as watches, radios, bicycles, etc. With their income, they bought furniture, better household utensils, livestock (e.g., goats, pigs, and cattle), and farm equipment like plows, cultivators, and oxcarts, and shared their use with other members of the extended family system. Extended families that had men working in South Africa not only had adequate food, good clothes, and admirable goods and assets, but also enjoyed higher status.

Most young men—some before getting married, but most just after—would try hard to go look for work in South Africa. Such migrant work was a significant factor in the improvement of socioeconomic status, not only for a particular household, but for extended family members as well as distant relatives and friends of the migrant worker. Thus there was extensive sharing of income and of the goods acquired through migrant work. This helping behavior was the same with food. All men from the fourteen households in my grandfather's extended family system would eat together. My uncles' wives would prepare food, one portion for the women and another for the men. Any household that grew more corn, beans, and groundnuts shared with those that produced less. In this way, no household in the extended family was short of food; this sharing was a wonderful example of social immunity or social insurance against hunger, especially because my grandfather was against any of his daughters-in-law not sharing their food. There was a time when one of them decided to cook food just for me. Somehow my grandfather knew that she had prepared food just for me while there were other children who had no food. My grandfather walked over to this daughter-in-law's house and found me eating the food she had prepared. He sternly rebuked her, and, right there, she was "commanded" to prepare food for the others.

Interestingly, farming itself involved a lot of sharing of labor during the growing season from November to May. People would wake up early in the morning (between 3:00 and 4:00 a.m.) to go and work on their own farms, but would later (around 9:00 a.m.) have to go and provide labor to a household scheduled to receive collective help for that day. They would return to their own farms in the afternoons (around 4:00 p.m.) and work until whatever time they decided to stop for the day. My grandfather was responsible for scheduling this collective help. Generally, the older folks would receive help first and the younger ones later. My grandfather reasoned that the younger were stronger than the older ones, and hence could manage to do their farm work much faster. Of course, the younger folks would still receive help. But by the time it was their turn, they would have done much of the work on their farms by themselves, since they were the ones who woke up much earlier and were stronger. The result was that generally younger families would produce more food crops and end up contributing more to everyone's food security and collective well-being.

This sharing of *income, food,* and *farm labor* was common in all the Zowe villages. It was extended to marriage, which involves the paying of bride-wealth. The bride-wealth was mostly in the form of cattle and ranged from three to seven heads. Various households would contribute a cow or bull to a marriage depending on how many cattle the household had. In terms of other daily work, taking livestock (e.g., goats, sheep, and cattle) for grazing was also a collective activity. It involved getting the livestock out of their pens around 9:00 a.m., taking them to grazing fields, and bringing them back around 4:00 p.m. This was the responsibility of children, especially during school holidays. It did not matter whether one's parents owned livestock or not; any child from any household in the extended family system was responsible for herding livestock, as the older folks were busy attending to other demanding jobs like farming.

In the case of my newly married uncle, he left for South Africa after four months of marriage. His brothers helped him with some money. His brothers who had been to South Africa also provided contact people along the way and in South Africa. My young uncle was a regular migrant domestic servant from 1966 to 2000. He contracted AIDS and suffered for a long time, dying from the disease in 2001 at fifty-three years of age. My maternal extended family has annually had an average of seven to nine men, aged twenty to early fifties, working in South Africa. Fathers, upon "retirement" from this circular migration, are succeeded by sons. It has become a common practice that fathers take along their sons, starting with the eldest, to help them find a job in South Africa. Circular migration is a product of "colonialism and capitalism," which "developed hand-in-hand" (Phiri 1983, 270). Colonialism and capitalism have been linchpins for "modern" lifestyles and *rational thinking* characterized by utilitarian beliefs, values, desires, and actions, choices in such a situation inherently aimed at ensuring that one personally gains the most from any given endeavor (Weber 1958; Barker 2005). This change resonates with changes in people's worldview from a peasant (agrarian) type to a modern one (Hiebert 2008; Piot 1999). The change compromises helping behavior. There is significant evidence of such change in Zowe when we compare the 1960s to the 2000s.

ZOWE IN THE 2000s

My grandfather died in 1969. Since his death, allocentrism in his family lineage has declined. There is less concern for collective well-being, less sharing of food, labor, and income. Instead, idiocentric (or self-centered) behavior has crept in. The term "family" no longer refers to the extended system but to a nuclear unit: father, mother, and children; it excludes cousins, nieces, nephews, or other extended family members. Grandparents (my now aged uncles) have become liabilities, an excess baggage, to the nuclear family.

As of 2008, I had only two surviving uncles out of the seven sons of my grandfather. A visit with one of them showed that he was lonely despite having many children and grandchildren. He does not command as much influence over his five sons (all are married) as did my grandfather (his father) over his own sons. One of his sons is into migrant work. He sends money home not to his father but to his wife. He has built a wonderful house for himself, while his father lives in a shack. When he comes home for his three-month vacation, he is focused on taking care of his wife and children. My uncle's other son, poorer than his brother, is not involved in migrant work. Like his brother, he is also very focused on taking care mainly of his wife and children. There is no collective sharing of income, food, and farm labor in my uncle's extended family, and there are many days my uncle goes without food. As he puts it,

> I eat whenever anyone gives me some food. Sometimes I see them eating in their houses. I just watch. What can I do? Go to them and just join in? That would be bad! So I wait and sometimes the food comes, and I eat many times alone. My sons do not join me. What is painful is even my grandchildren do not join me. That is understandable. If their parents do not join me, how can the grandchildren join?

When asked why he thinks this is going on, he blames his daughters-in-law and says that they have confused their husbands (his sons) so much that the husbands do not care about their father's well-being and the well-being of the whole extended family. He argues that the daughters-in-law are rude, pompous, disrespectful, and selfish. "And the reason this is happening is that nowadays, these children do not care about the elders' opinion when it comes to marriage....You cannot tell your son these days that the woman he wants to marry is not good....You risk abuse from your own son!"

In talking with his sons, they seem not to see anything wrong. They argue that they do give him some clothes and that their wives give him the food he needs. Asked whether they helped cousins, nieces, nephews, aunts, and other relatives in the extended family system, my two cousins responded that this was not their responsibility.

My cousin's actions were indeed idiocentric. I set out to find out whether this change was common in other family lineages in Zowe through interviews and observations of a number of households. I operated on the premise that the allocentric caring or helping behavior that characterizes subsistent and substantive communities was being compromised by idiocentric goals and worldviews brought in by modernity. This modernity that is invading Malawi in general, and Zowe in particular, is reconstituting people's behavior into a more idiocentric type.

My interviews and observations explored livelihood activities of households, contrasting the situation in privileged households to that in underprivileged ones on the proposition that privileged households would be less concerned with helping other households, while underprivileged households would be engaging in more helping behavior. The question examined therefore had two parts: The first was how much helping behavior was taking place among people in the community and across households. The second was whether there was more helping behavior among underprivileged than privileged households. A comparison of the 1960s with the 2000s was done, drawing on my recall of helping behavior in the 1960s as described above and the study of the current situation in the 2000s.

A community population assessment undertaken in 2008 showed that Zowe had 2,003 people in 481 households over 17 villages. Based on the quality of a household's house and assets (e.g., livestock, oxcart, bicycles, radios, house furniture, and farmland), 14 percent (69 of the 481 households) were privileged. I conducted the household livelihood activities research in 2009. This research involved quantitative and qualitative methods undertaken on a sample of 100 of the 481 households. Because I was interested in contrasting the privileged and underprivileged, I oversampled the privileged households: I had 35 privileged households, or 51 percent of the 69 privileged households in the community, against 65 underprivileged households, or 16 percent of the 412 underprivileged households in the community. Of the 100 households in the sample, 95 were interviewed and observed—35 privileged and 60 underprivileged.[2] Quantitative work was done on all 95 households. This involved documenting age and educational attainment of household members, then inventorying household assets, assessing involvement in migrant work, the amount of farm acreage used for various crops, whether the food they produce in their farms lasts until the next harvest, involvement in income-generating activities, and how much help members of a household give and receive.

Qualitative work involved in-depth, unstructured interviews with questions focused on respondents helping other people and households with income, food, clothes, and farm labor; respondents receiving help (e.g., income, food, and clothes) from other people; opinions on helping behavior; and views on changes in such behavior. Qualitative interviews were done on 30 of the 95 households. Eight of the 30 households were privileged, and the remaining 22 were underprivileged. My analysis of allocentrism and idiocentrism is mainly based on these qualitative interviews and observations.

Of the 481 households in Zowe, 78 (16 percent) were food secure in 2009; they produced enough food to last until the next harvest season. Of these 78 households, 69 (89 percent) were privileged households, and 68 of these 69 (87 percent of the 78 households) had husbands working in South Africa. Stated differently, all privileged households were food secure, and all of them except one household in all of Zowe had husbands working in South Africa. There were also less privileged households with husbands who were involved in migrant work, but only within Malawi, working at commercial farms and in urban areas. Those going to work at commercial farms did not experience much change in their socioeconomic status. Those working in urban Malawi

---

2   I was unable to interview 5 of the 65 underprivileged households because of logistical hurdles—basically, not finding them when I went to their homes.

(very few of them) are generally more educated and take their wives and children along to their workplaces.

From various discussions, it was clear that many young men desire to go to South Africa, but passport and visa processes as well as expensive and challenging travel logistics make it difficult for them to go. When the opportunity arises and they go, they get locked into circular migration until retirement in their sixties, and their behavior in regard to helping others slowly changes.

Of the 95 households that were interviewed, 25 (26 percent) indicated having received help and 53 (56 percent) indicated having given help. To verify the offering of help, respondents were asked to indicate to whom they had offered help and/or from whom they had received it; they were also asked to indicate the type of help they offered or received (income, food, clothing, or farm labor). The 26 percent who indicated having received help identified without any hesitation the people who had helped them and the type of help they had received. Twenty-three of those who indicated they had given help could not tell to whom they had given the help or the type of help it was. A few respondents laughingly asked whether the idea was to check with the person they claim to have helped. Only 20 of the 53 (21 percent of the 95 respondents) helped others. Helping behavior is thus low, with just 20–26 percent of the people in Zowe engaged in it.

Case stories also showed evidence of this declining helping behavior, along with some vile atrocities. Tuje[3] is thirty-eight years old and has been a migrant worker for twelve years. He has built a solar-powered house for himself and his wife and children. He has given "nothing" to Goma and Renda, his father and mother respectively, who are in their seventies. They live in a grass-thatched shack a little distance away from Tuje's house. In talking to them, I learned that Tuje had employed a watchman to look after his house and brought his wife and children to visit him in Johannesburg, where he works, but had done little for his parents. The idea of wives going to their husbands in South Africa is a recent household behavior in Zowe. For Tuje to employ someone

---

3   All names in these case stories have been changed.

to watch over his house when his father and mother are around and could do it for him is strange. Normally parents would just move into the son's good house and keep watch over it, since none would want to break into their shack. On one of his vacations, Tuje quarreled with his father and beat him, a dishonorable thing in this highly patrilineal, patrilocal, and gerontocratic community. Talking about the beating, Goma said,

> You cannot believe it; my own son beat me up. You know I could have taken him and fought back, but the whole idea of a son beating his father or a father fighting with a son is horrible. So I did not retaliate when he punched me. He will face God. Beating me, his father.... Where is the honor?

The practice of wives going to live with their husbands in the workplaces is on the rise. As of 2009, six of my uncles' sons were working in Johannesburg. Of these, two had their wives visit them in South Africa for about six months. Almost a third of Zowe husbands working in South Africa have had their wives visit them while the grandparents cared for the grandchildren. In another family in Zowe, two sons took their wives and children to live with them in South Africa. The result of these changes is that the elderly are left to care for themselves. Even in situations where wives stay home, their care of the in-laws continues to decline. Cell phones have complicated matters. Writing (a main way of communicating with people back home in the 1960s) has declined as husbands in South Africa use more cell phones. They talk to their wives mostly, as parents have difficulties operating the phones. These parents end up learning what goes on with their sons not directly from them but through their daughters-in-law, a reversal of my grandfather's situation in the 1960s, when he was the primary contact for his migrant sons.

There is the interesting case of Muka, who is in his early fifties. He has been involved in migrant work since he was twenty-one. To start with, he went to the work alone at a place within Malawi. After working for a few years, he decided to take his wife, Dewa, to live with him.

Then he went on to South Africa and decided to leave his wife behind to care for his parents, who are now in their late eighties. Muka built a big house for himself and has a diesel engine for electricity, which he only uses when he comes home for his three-month vacations. He introduced his two sons (his other children are female) to migrant work; they are not yet married. Muka plans his vacations carefully. Generally, this involves coming together with his two sons if possible during the sons' three-month vacations.

Muka takes care of his aged parents through his wife, but has decided to marry another wife in South Africa (a South African). His first wife manages their assets in Zowe (a big farm, oxen, oxcarts, farming equipment, livestock, etc.). She also cares for the parents and all the children. Some of the children from the second (South African) wife have come to live with the first wife in Zowe. Muka says, "It is important for the children to know where they come from, that their home is not South Africa but Zowe in Malawi."

Muka is one of Zowe's few rich people. He drives expensive cars to the community when he comes for vacations. He generally comes with his second wife on these vacations, since the second wife has to check on how her children are doing. Muka wants the second wife to view Zowe as her home. He has built a small one-room house for his parents and, through his first wife, makes sure that his parents' food needs are met. He provides clothes his parents need and all the other care. While Muka does help his parents, his help to other members of his extended family is very conditional. In 2009, Muka and Dewa were keeping two other children, nephews of Muka, who were orphans because they had lost both parents to HIV/AIDS. The children were not really regarded as members of the family, but rather as orphans who had no one else to care for them. Muka does not extend much help to other cousins, nieces, nephews, uncles, and aunts. When asked why he was not helping the other relatives in his extended family (many looked poor, malnourished, and lacking in basic materials such as food and clothing), Muka and his wife Dewa indicated that these relatives needed to take care of themselves. They added, "Actually we help them through *ganyu* [piece work] that they do on our farm in exchange

for food or clothes or money when they need it to buy soap or salt."
Indeed, these relatives provide the labor Muka and his wife need on
their big farm. They are paid mostly food. Muka needs most of this
labor at the peak of a growing season (December to February) when
his extended family members have an acute shortage of food in their
households. Because they are providing this labor for Muka, they are
unable to invest adequate labor into their own farms, thus getting into
a food insecurity cycle of increasing inability to produce enough food
to feed their own families before the next harvest.

Mbujo, another migrant worker, has been involved in migrant labor
for nearly twenty years. Like others, he is in South Africa for up to
four years at a time, then comes for a three-month vacation, and then
goes back. His wife lives at home and has never been to South Africa.
Like Muka, Mbujo has a big house and plenty of cattle. He also has
a big farm and produces a lot of food. His other assets are various
ox-drawn implements, work oxen, oxcarts, motorcycle, bicycle, and
many household items. Both his father and mother are dead. Mbujo's
younger brother, Themba, is not involved in migrant work. Themba
not only uses the farm implements and work oxen on his and his
brother's farms but also hires them out to relatives and others. He
hires out the oxcart when someone wants to haul things such as corn,
or when people are sick and need to go to the hospital some four miles
away. This latter form of income production is seen as exceedingly
self-centered by other village members. Traditionally he should offer
the oxcart to the sick for free use, but he does not. Themba is very
entrepreneurial and makes money in various ways, including charging people a fee for using his solar power and car battery to charge
their cell phones. Asked whether he offers help to other people, he
responded, "Only to those who are in dire need; the others have to
pay, otherwise people would run us down." We thus find young adults
like Themba, and others not engaged in migrant work, thinking that
the sharing of help should be based strictly on dire need rather than the
promotion of collective well-being.

Tesima is a hardworking young man in his forties. His household
is underprivileged despite his diverse income-generating activities

like growing tobacco, selling mats and various crafts, and growing vegetables, all of which bring in a low income. Asked whether he helps other people and households, he said, "Only my mother, as she is elderly." He explained, "These days, everyone has to take care of himself and his family; the idea of helping others is a thing of the past, except parents.... You can't avoid helping parents."

Talking to those who are in their sixties and older reveals a rather strange situation. Those who have been involved in migrant work see the extension of help to the whole extended family system, which they have done, as taxing. Nizamba, a retired migrant worker in his sixties, indicated that helping others during the many years of his migrant work was not beneficial for his family. "The little you have ends up being shared among so many people.... Your family does not get much; it is not worth it.... It is a thankless endeavor." Nizamba has done well. He has built an improved house, he has plenty of cattle, his household is food secure, and he has introduced his only son to migrant work. For Nizamba, extending help to so many members of his extended family is something that he does not see as worth continuing. He still expects his son to help him and his wife, but not to help a whole contingent of relatives within Nizamba's extended family system.

The elderly who have not been involved in migrant work, or minimally involved in it, expressed concern that the "children of these days have no respect for the elderly and no concern for helping one another," as Vula put it. He remarked that the younger generation does not respect the elderly "these days" and that there is little helping one another even among people belonging to the same extended family. Vula suggested that self-interested motives have increasingly influenced the way the younger generation extends help, and that those who are involved in migrant work and are well-to-do are selfish; they do not want to help others who are needy.

It seems those involved in migrant work do feel the need to help their parents, but not all members of the extended family system. Even the younger people not involved in migrant work reject the idea of extending help to all members of the extended family system (e.g., nieces, nephews, uncles, aunts). Those in their sixties or older, especially those who have not been involved in migrant work, find both those who have been involved in migrant work (young adults as well as older ones) and the younger people (those in their forties and younger) to be selfish.

UMUNTHU IN ZOWE UNDER ATTACK

Migrant work birthed out of modernity has ushered in a significant change in how people help one another. Modernity seems to be developing "habits of the heart" (Bellah et al. 1985) that are increasingly individualistic and disruptive to traditional allocentrism. Modernity encourages a "culture of separation" (277). Bellah et al. (1985) argue that we need to initiate social values that promote a general responsibility to ensure collective well-being through allocentric behavior. Such behavior should be reciprocal and represent *koinonia;* i.e., fellowship and sharing or caring for one another in a group of people, as exemplified in Acts 2:44–47. It should be reciprocal behavior—not in the social psychological sense that entails responding to others' actions based on self-interested motives, with friendly actions receiving friendly responses and hostile actions receiving nasty responses (Fehr and Gächter 2000); rather it should be reciprocal in the "gift economic systems" perspective in which cultural imperatives influence the exchange of goods for the common good (Mauss 1970). We see an example of how this plays out in the Filipino system as discussed by Tan (chap. 4), and an explanation of reciprocity from a theoretical perspective in Meneses' chapter (chap. 1) in this volume.

The point that modernity is bringing in more individualistic and self-centered inequality-generating behavior is not new. Modernity, in its neoliberal, cutthroat, competitive capitalist culture, is riddled with a self-aggrandizing ethos (Giroux 2004). Tutu (quoted in Schmidt 2004, 12) says,

> I loathe capitalism because it gives far too great play to our inherent selfishness. We are told to be highly competitive, and our children start learning the attitudes of the rat-race quite early....

We give prizes to such persons, not so far as I know to those who know how best to get on with others, or those who can coax the best out of others.

This rat-race type of capitalism—what is also regarded as free-market or corporate capitalism (characterized by a small state, little regulation, and weak labor unions)—is a form of ideological addiction or delusion. It enchants, enthralls, and captivates individuals (Ritzer 2005). It captures and appropriates allocentric livelihood processes. It sucks people into idiocentric behavior, offering new definitions of success that are materialistic and selfish. It has a kind of triumphalism that births and sustains the cutthroat, competitive, and individualistic drive towards "the good life"; i.e., the accumulation of stuff—the more in quantity and thrill, the better. In the process, it tramples on social harmony, compromises the drive towards the common good, and undermines helping behavior in society. Goodchild (2002) argues that the love of modernity's free-market capitalism is not only causing disharmony but is an expression of a piety in which capitalism becomes a global religion, in practice if not always in belief. The goods that capitalism produces take on a sacrosanct character. Acquiring these goods and seeking to possess them brings along a selfish lifestyle. Concerned about how this free-market capitalism contributes to the worldwide degree of inequality, poverty, and environmental degradation, Trainer (1996) observes that the capitalist economic system is steadily taking us towards a global catastrophe. This capitalism locks us into the "tragedy of the commons," in which our shared resources are depleted by our selfish, individualistic endeavors to accumulate what we can even at the expense of others (Hardin 1968). It is oligarchic in that it serves the interests of a wealthy and small portion of the population (Baumol, Litan, and Schramm 2007).

There are other forms of capitalism than the corporate one that we are now experiencing globally. Cooperative or welfare capitalism (Smith 2003) calls for more involvement of workers in the capitalist process. The state here is more involved in the distribution of the wealth generated from capitalist processes through regulations. State capitalism, a third form (Pollard 2011), involves stronger state intervention in the capitalist process than is the case in welfare capitalism, for purposes of making sure that workers and the state fully benefit from capitalist activities. A fourth form, entrepreneurial capitalism (Baumol, Litan, and Schramm 2007), emphasizes the need to continue motivating entrepreneurs to provide the radical ideas that respond to marketplace demands.

The rise of various forms of capitalism is in response to the inherent selfishness characteristic of free-market, oligarchic, and corporate capitalism. It is also a response to the human quest for collective well-being, of "being human" as God created us. Capitalism, especially the free-market type, is an enemy of collective well-being. The problem in essence is the individualistic drive towards personal success, and the triumphalism that this form of capitalism expresses. The most treacherous element in free-market capitalism is its suggestion that personal material success is the primary good, when in fact such idiocentric behavior is actually a source of a people's collective peril. The way forward for subsistent and substantive communities like Zowe is to engage in production, distribution, and consumption processes that advance both individual *and* collective well-being. This entails encouraging entrepreneurial creativity but also developing a deep desire in people to engage in helping behavior; it entails promoting entrepreneurship of the type that accentuates allocentrism and social responsibility. It demands that people engage in use-value and relational exchange-value production, distribution, and consumption activities. This would advance an umunthu that is God-centered and rooted in the Christian conception of koinonia.

TOWARDS KOINONIA

Acts 4:32–37 tells of a shared life among early Christians, one characterized by relational ties that accentuated helping behavior through which the needs of every member of the group were met. This was a life governed by generosity and otherness, deep concern for the well-being of not only oneself but others. This is koinonia life, a life of inner goodness towards virtue and outer goodness towards collective well-being—a life of true community (Bridges 2012). Bridges explains that this is a life in which people enjoy communion with God and each other, partner with each other in activities through which they help one another, share their possessions for the sake of meeting each other's needs, and are deeply concerned not only about their own well-being but also about that of others in their community. It is a God-centered allocentric life. In such a life, there is little poverty—the household is the center of economic processes (Meeks 1989). Here, God is "creating, sustaining, and recreating households" as nodes in the network of families and communities (4). The household is a site of livelihood or economic activities—"the production, distribution, and consumption of the necessities of life" (3). It is not directed by the market logic where market-driven exchange processes invade every dimension of life and create the highly individualized self of the West, but by use-value economic activities coupled with relational exchange activities. Such a life demands developing the social self. Sedikides and Brewer (2001) identify three aspects of this social self: an individual self, a relational self, and a collective self. In viewing themselves through these three selves, people are more likely to respond to the needs of others in their network of social ties and to contribute self-sacrificially to the construction of koinonia in their groups.

Under koinonia, economic processes are for purposes of meeting the needs of all members of a community, and networks of social ties operate as conduits through which people respond to each other's needs. It is a life in which cultural values uphold the dignity of all people in a community and people honor God as their creator. Such a life engenders what could be considered *moral wealth;* that is, trust among community members, benevolence in community members' network of social ties, respect for one another, empathy, freedom for individuals to be creative and innovative, transparency and honesty, accountability and responsibility, diligence, integrity, procedural efficiency in dealing with concerns, courage, and joy. These lead to community members deeply caring for one another in the pursuit of both individual and collective goals. They also lead to effective, just, and uncorrupt governance processes. Further, this moral wealth is a tremendous resource for the community in dealing with outside forces, some of which may be corrupt. Moral wealth, to sum up, consists of the relationships of power, interdependence, and solidarity (togetherness) that are critical to a community's tenacity and resolve in engaging in activities that improve livelihoods.

Moral wealth is a foundation for change in a community. Change can be beneficial at times, but it may also bring unbeneficial conflict, controversy, or discord. These arise when the demands of the individual, relational, and collective selves are not balanced. This imbalance is the source of current behavior in Zowe, which tramples moral wealth and undermines beneficial cultural practices (e.g., the sharing of labor, income, and food). It is important to balance individual goals and collective ones, personal efficacy and collective efficacy, individual fulfillment and collective well-being. Balancing entails individuals looking beyond their own problems, desires, needs, and interests. "Balanced" individuals have integrity and are trustworthy, diligent, creative, accountable, responsible, caring, willing to share what they have, and respectful of others. They are personally empowered (have the ability, willingness, and desire to act), are engaged in benevolent social network ties, belong to and actively participate in groups, love and care for others, and have faith and hope in collective action.

Empowered individuals confront injustices in a community's economy for purposes of enhancing collective well-being. Their economic activities are fused in the everyday household livelihood activities. They are, of course, entrepreneurial. This needs further discussion.

Schumpeter, explains Swedberg (2006), argued that there are entrepreneurial and nonentrepreneurial people in society. Entrepreneurial people engage in creative deconstruction that arises from intuitive thinking and willingness to take risks. Where nonentrepreneurs see nothing but routine ways of doing things, the creative destructionists (entrepreneurs) find limitless ways of doing things differently. Because nonentrepreneurs avoid taking risks, the risk-taking entrepreneurs end up buying the labor power of nonentrepreneurs and investing it into risky new ventures. By doing so, entrepreneurs convert the nonentrepreneurs' dormant labor into a productive type, and then use it to implement their innovative ideas. Entrepreneurs organize and manage resources to make profits and add value to their enterprises.

Over the years, Schumpeter's entrepreneurial people have come to be known as economic entrepreneurs, but there are also social entrepreneurs whose entrepreneurial activities are focused on addressing social ills. These social entrepreneurs use innovative and sometimes seemingly bizarre ideas to address social problems (Bornstein 2007). Social entrepreneurs have thus been referred to as unreasonable people who shrug off the "business as usual" attitude and engage in activities that "generate paradigm shifts in the way social needs are met" (Elkington and Hartigan 2008, 6). Social entrepreneurs thus engage in activities that create value not just in terms of profit but in multiple other dimensions; they believe that the future can be re-created not only from an economic viewpoint but also from a social perspective. Thus, unlike economic entrepreneurs, who are driven by profit-making interests, social entrepreneurs, though interested in making a profit, are driven by the need to improve people's life chances.

"Social entrepreneurship" has become a popular phrase in academia, but there is no social entrepreneurship theory. Seeking to develop such a theory, Swedberg (2006) draws on Schumpeter's general theory on entrepreneurship, observing that social entrepreneurship "can be translated into Schumpeterian terminology as a form of dynamic behavior in one of the non-economic areas of society" (33). Swedberg theory thus views social entrepreneurship as the dynamic behavior of problem-solving individuals who draw on their creativity to address social ills such as poverty.

For a subsistent and substantive community like Zowe, entrepreneurship should be both economic and social. Through economic entrepreneurship, wealth is generated and accumulated. Through social entrepreneurship, social ills are addressed while upholding collective well-being. In figure 7.1 I propose a model that integrates economic and social entrepreneurship in subsistence and substantive natural resource–dependent communities.

FIGURE 7.1

A model for entrepreneurship in subsistence communities

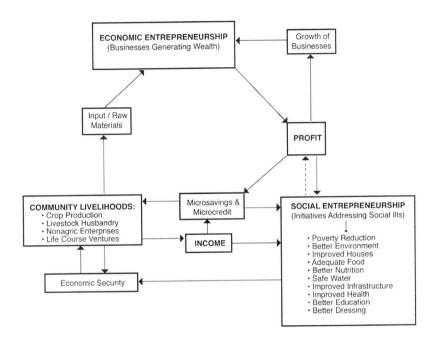

A unique feature of this model is that both economic and social entrepreneurship are founded on backward integration to community livelihoods. Only 14 percent of Zowe households are involved in migrant work, and the remaining 86 percent depend on agrarian livelihood activities. What I propose, therefore, is making these livelihood activities the centerpiece of household use-value and of the relational exchange-value production activities founded on the sharing of labor in all the Zowe households. For lack of a better term, this is "koinonia capitalism"; its foundation is entrepreneurialism engendered by people's togetherness. This should lead to improved and increased production of food crops and cash crops. It should also lead to creative and innovative income-generation activities. The goal is not only improvement in the socioeconomic status of individual households but collective household well-being attained through training and awareness activities that advance individual, relational, and collective selves. As Meeks (1989) admonishes, people's production, distribution, and consumption activities should not be driven by the market logic but by both market processes and social relationships that are concerned with the well-being of the entire community and its livelihood activities.

How will this work? To start with, the model has economic businesses that generate profit. These businesses belong to the community in that any member of the community can invest in them and benefit from the profits. The goal is not just individual but also collective well-being, on the understanding that true joy comes out of relational life (Gergen 2009) and that one's well-being is fully attained when others are not dehumanized (Tutu 1999). The profit from the economic businesses can be appropriated by the investors, further invested into the business, or invested into a microsavings and microcredit facility. This would provide resources that various people in the community can borrow and use in their community livelihood activities or that can be invested in a social enterprise focused on addressing some social ill in the community.

Social enterprises transform the community by addressing social ills, thereby improving life course outcomes (improved health, education, houses, dressing, water supply, food supply, nutrition, infrastructure, etc.), and these then enhance community members' security in life chances. "Life chances," as conceptualized by Max Weber (1978), refer to opportunities for individuals or categories of people to access and utilize resources to improve the quality of their lives. The point here is that social enterprises also produce some profit, generally at break-even levels (hence the dotted line in fig. 7.1), which can be used to address social ills—thus improving people's life chances by investing in the social enterprises—or deposited in microsavings and microcredit facilities, making the money available for use by other members of the community for other social and economic enterprises.

Microsavings and microcredit facilities are critical, not only in advancing entrepreneurship (i.e., economic and social), but also and more importantly for improving livelihood activities that community members engage in. Not everyone will be involved in business or social entrepreneurship, but every family in the community engages in some livelihood activity. In agrarian societies, these livelihood activities mostly comprise agricultural enterprises (e.g., crop production or livestock rearing); nonagricultural ventures such as microscale mining, running a restaurant or food-processing venture; or providing transportation. Through these activities, community members primarily produce materials for consumption (use value), selling whatever surplus they have to make money to be used to meet household needs (exchange value). Some of this income can be saved in the microsavings and microcredit facilities to postpone its use or to save it for some future use, like the buying of farm inputs.

To enhance entrepreneurship in the community, livelihood activities that go beyond meeting basic needs must focus on producing inputs or raw materials for the businesses in the community. If there is a business of packaging and selling mushrooms, most of the mushrooms must be produced in the community. Of course, some inputs for the businesses would come from outside the community, but the kind of businesses a community can start must be based on the ability of the community to produce the bulk of raw materials needed. Another way of enhancing entrepreneurship is for businesses to supply inputs to be used in livelihood activities in the community. The production of mushrooms would require seed, pesticides, etc., that ought to be provided through businesses in the community. Businesses and community livelihoods must be integrated through linking the supply of raw materials needed in the businesses and the supply of inputs needed by community members to produce the raw materials that the businesses need. For example, an orange juice production facility in a community would need oranges (as raw materials) that the farmers would produce. For the farmers to produce these oranges, they would need pesticides (as inputs) that businesses would sell to the farmers. Integrating economic or social businesses such as the orange juice production facility and livelihood activities such as the production of oranges by farmers transforms the community in three main ways. First, it promotes backward integration through which businesses mostly use raw materials produced in the community—this provides a market for the community's produce. Second, livelihood activities provide a market for commodities the businesses produce or supply. Of course the market for products of the businesses can and should also be beyond the community, thus bringing into the community needed resources from the outside. Third, community livelihoods are labor-intensive in subsistent and substantive communities. Whereas the capital needed in these activities is provided through microsavings and microcredit facilities, the labor is provided by the households. When this labor is mobilized across kin lines, its productivity is bound to improve. Collaboration, when members are committed to the common goal, improves group productivity (Brown 2000, 169–84). Such an initiative would restore to Zowe the allocentric behavior that has been lost, because it would create networks of nuclear families.

Getting people to be collaborative, especially those who have been involved in migrant work and are in the younger generation, is a matter of significant training and awareness for community families, who need to appreciate the situation and put collaboration into action. Zowe families need to engage in this awareness training and then mobilize collective labor through social network ties across nuclear families. Revisiting what my grandfather used to do, but this time focusing on creative ways of connecting nuclear families to improve the productivity of their collective labor, is what is needed. To this end, community businesses would play another important role: they would operate as local training institutes for families. A pivotal goal in all this training is to enhance creativity, innovativeness, collective labor mobilization, and change towards engaging in helping behavior. The goal is for households to engage in livelihood activities and enterprises through which not only adequate food for the families (use-value concerns) but raw materials for businesses (exchange-value concerns) would be produced collaboratively (relational ties), thus improving material needs (food) and income needs (to buy other things families cannot produce). Thus production, distribution, and consumption processes under koinonia in subsistent and substantive communities would be based on use-value activities in that production is geared towards the production of commodities for household consumption. It would also entail relational exchange-value activities, in that the focus would be on collective well-being grounded in producing commodities to be used in businesses that directly benefit the community through the building up and use of networks of ties across kin lines.

CONCLUSION

People in Zowe, a subsistent and substantive community, are heavily dependent on migrant work as a way of improving their socioeconomic status in response to the culture of free-market capitalism introduced by colonialists in the 1800s. This culture destroys the humanity in people, diminishes moral wealth in communities, tramples social harmony, and destroys the allocentric behavior of sharing income, food, and labor by helping one another. There is thus less helping behavior in the 2000s as compared to the 1960s in Zowe. Instead there is more of the self-centered, or idiocentric, behavior.

Only 14 percent of Zowe households have been involved in this migrant work. These find little benefit from engaging in helping behavior. The idiocentric ethos has been adopted by the younger generation, for whom helping parents, not to mention cousins, nephews, nieces, and uncles, is a liability; they thus grant just the bare minimum of help needed for survival. This is a modern mindset that espouses rational individualism and is destructive to the community's collective well-being, which is dependent on social relationships (Gergen 2009). As Bellah et al. comment, "Individuals need the nurture of groups that carry a moral tradition reinforcing their own aspirations" (1985, 286). For subsistent and substantive communities like Zowe, this demands dialogue within and across families to bring them back to the critical role of helping behavior that allows the sharing of income, food, and labor through collaborative processes in families' livelihood activities. To the extent that these livelihood activities improve the socioeconomic status of the community through integrating people's activities, economic entrepreneurship, and social entrepreneurship, the importance of migrant work in improving households' socioeconomic status will diminish. To the extent that the use of labor in these livelihood activities is collaborative (making labor synergistically more productive), helping behavior will play a critical role in improving socioeconomic status in Zowe. All of this requires viewing economic activities from a use-value and relational exchange-value perspective grounded in koinonia—the abiding, virtuous, and godly fellowship between people. This demands building relationships of love founded on biblical principles espousing care for each other and sharing what one has (income, food, labor, etc.).

God has entrusted us with what we have, and in sharing we are only fulfilling God's will. Perhaps the point to grasp is that "economy exists for the sake of the human community and its relationship to God and the creation. The criterion of a just economic system will be whether it serves the life and future of the community" (Meeks 1989, 8–9). Abundant life is possible when we work collaboratively.

REFERENCES

Ayittey, George B. N. 1998. *Africa in chaos.* New York: St. Martin's Press.

Barker, Chris. 2005. *Cultural studies: Theory and practice.* London: Sage.

Baumol, William J., Robert E. Litan, and Carl J. Schramm. 2007. *Good capitalism, bad capitalism, and the economics of growth and prosperity.* Yale University Press.

Bellah, Robert N., Richard Madsen, William M. Sullivan, Ann Swidler, and Steven M. Tipton. 1985. *Habits of the heart: Individualism and commitment in American life.* New York: Harper & Row.

Bornstein, David. 2007. *How to change the world: Social entrepreneurs and the power of new ideas.* Updated ed. New York: Oxford University Press.

Bridges, Jerry. 2012. *True community: The biblical practice of* koinonia. Colorado Springs: NavPress.

Brown, Rupert. 2000. *Group processes: Dynamics within and between groups.* Malden, MA: Blackwell.

Chirwa, Wiseman Chijere. 1997. Migrant labor, sexual networking, and multi-partnered sex in Malawi. *Health Transition Review* 7: 5–15, supplement number 3.

———. 1998. Aliens and AIDS in Southern Africa: The Malawi–South African debate. *African Affairs* 97, no. 386: 53–79.

Elkington, John, and Pamela Hartigan. 2008. *The power of unreasonable people: How social entrepreneurs create markets that change the world.* Boston: Harvard Business School Press.

Fehr, Ernest, and Simon Gächter. 2000. Fairness and retaliation: The economics of reciprocity. *Journal of Economic Perspectives* 14, no. 3: 159–81.

Gergen, Kenneth J. 2009. *Relational being: Beyond self and community.* New York: Oxford University Press.

Giroux, Henry A. 2004. *The terror of neoliberalism: Authoritarianism and the eclipse of democracy.* Boulder, CO: Paradigm.

Goodchild, Philip. 2002. *Capitalism and religion: The price of piety.* New York: Routledge.

Hardin, Garrett. 1968. The tragedy of the commons. *Science* 162, no. 3859: 1243–48.

Hiebert, Paul G. 2008. *Transforming worldviews: An anthropological understanding of how people change.* Grand Rapids: Baker Academic.

Lurie, Mark. 2000. Migration and AIDS in Southern Africa: A review. *South African Journal of Science* 96, no. 6: 343–47.

———, B. Williams, K. Zuma, D. Mkaya-Mwamburi, G. P. Garnett, A. W. Sturm, M. D. Sweat, J. Gittelsohn, and S. S. Abdool Karim. 2003. The impact of migration on HIV-1 transmission: A study of migrant and non-migrant men, and their partners. *Sexually Transmitted Diseases* 40, no. 2: 149–56.

Mauss, Marcel. 1970. *The gift: Forms and functions of exchange in archaic societies.* London: Cohen & West.

Meeks, M. Douglas. 1989. *God the economist: The doctrine of God and political economy.* Minneapolis: Fortress.

Mtika, Mike. 2007. Political economy, labor migration, and the AIDS epidemic in rural Malawi. *Social Science and Medicine* 64, no. 12: 2454–63.

Musopole, Augustine C. 1994. *Being human in Africa: Towards an African Christian anthropology.* New York: Lang.

Phiri, Kings M. 1983. Some changes in the matrilineal family system among the Chewa of Malawi since the nineteenth century. *Journal of African History* 24, no. 2: 257–74.

Piot, Charles. 1999. *Remotely global:Village modernity in West Africa.* Chicago: University of Chicago Press.

Polanyi, Karl. 2001. *The great transformation:The political and economic origins of our time.* Boston: Beacon.

Pollard, Vincent Kelly, ed. 2011. *State capitalism, contentious politics, and large-scale social change.* Boston: Brill. doi: 10.1163/ej.9789004194458.i-234.

Read, Margaret. 1942. Migrant labour in Africa and its effects on tribal life. *International Labor Review* 45: 605–31.

Ritzer, George. 2005. *Enchanting a disenchanted world.* 2nd ed. Thousand Oaks, CA: Pine Forge.

Schmidt, Richard H. 2004. *Prophet of forgiveness: Desmond Tutu.* Cincinnati: Forward Movement.

Sedikides, Constantine, and Marilynn B. Brewer. 2001. Individual self, relational self, and collective self: Partners, opponents, or strangers. In *Individual self, relational self, collective self,* edited by Constantine Sedikides and Marilynn B. Brewer, 1–4. Philadelphia: Psychology Press.

Smith, J. W. 2003. *Cooperative capitalism:A blueprint for global peace and prosperity.* Sun City, AZ: Institute for Economic Democracy and Institute for Cooperative Capitalism.

Swedberg, Richard. 2006. Social entrepreneurship:The view of the young Schumpeter. In *Entrepreneurship as social change,* vol. 3 of *Movements in entrepreneurship,* edited by Chris Steyaert and Daniel Hjorth, 21–34. Northampton, MA: Edward Elgar.

Trainer, Ted. 1996. *Towards a sustainable economy:The need for fundamental change.* New York: Jon Carpenter.

Triandis, Harry C., Kwok Leung, Marcelo J. Villareal, and Felicia. L. Clack. 1985. Allocentric versus idiocentric tendencies: Convergent and discriminant validation. *Journal of Research in Personality* 19, no. 4: 395–415.

Triandis, Harry C., and David Trafimow. 2003. Culture and its implications for intergroup behavior. In *Intergroup Processes,* edited by Rupert Brown and Sam Gaertner, 367–85. Malden, MA: Blackwell.

Tutu, Desmond. 1999. *No future without forgiveness.* New York: Doubleday.

Weber, Max. 1958. *The Protestant ethic and the spirit of capitalism.* New York: Charles Scribner's Sons.

————. 1978. *Economy and society.* Berkeley: University of California Press.

FLYING BLIND? CHRISTIAN NGOS AND POLITICAL ECONOMY

David Bronkema

More than thirty years ago, the anthropologist Raymond Firth re-marked on the "thick web of organizations" that had sprung up around the work of development and social change (1981). While he did not have Christian mission efforts in mind, Firth could very well have observed the same thing about them. Already by the 1980s, missionar-ies, their sending churches, boards and agencies, Christian relief and development organizations, and a host of other church and parachurch entities had blanketed the globe, driven by the desires to evangelize, make disciples, and solve social problems (see Bronkema 2002, 2006). In fact, much of the activity and many of the organizations that Firth was observing at the time were a direct legacy of these "faith-based" efforts, even though they were not recognized as such at the time.[1]

In these last thirty years, this "thick web" of Christian mission and ministry organizations of all stripes, seeking to be faithful to their understanding of God's call—many of them interrelated in small and large ways, and many of them at odds with each other theologically, ideologically, and practically—has only increased in size, density, and

---

1   The literature on what are now called "faith-based" organizations in development has grown in recent years. For a good summary of Christian faith-based development literature, see Hefferan and Fogarty 2010.

scope. And as these organizations, entities we will call "nongovernmental organizations" (NGOs) for the purposes of this paper,[2] engage
in their work of evangelism, discipleship, education, relief, care, assistance, development, and advocacy, they are doing so in contexts of
political economy of which they tend to be only dimly aware. In other
words, the way that economies at the local, national, and international
level are created, structured, reproduced, legitimized, run, and resisted deeply impact the people, programs, and projects with which
these organizations are engaged.

There are three main ways in which the question of economics and
economies comes into play in relation to the actions of both secular
and Christian NGOs dedicated to improving the welfare of those in
need. The first and overarching way is that their work itself is of a
deeply economic nature, because NGOs are in the business of providing resources, goods, and services of all different kinds. The second is
the way that the macroeconomy is structured. By "macroeconomy" we
mean the overall economic policies and practices that are promoted
by governments and the role the private sector plays in these.[3] These
policies and practices, as we shall see, have profound consequences
in shaping human thought and action as people are affected by and
respond to both the material effects of the policies and the ideas that
underpin them. In particular, these macroeconomic policies and practices impact not only what is produced and sold, and how, but also
what is available to the population in terms of social services. They
also impact the room NGOs have to operate as governments pay more
and more attention to the resources NGOs are channeling, attempt to
hold them accountable, and try to take advantage of those resources.
Finally, the macroeconomy, as well as the microeconomy, is an arena
in which resources are fought over and distributed—a process labeled
"political economy," manifested in tensions and conflicts around issues
ranging from social services and labor rights to land reform and natu-

---

2   Typologies and definitions of NGOs abound, dating back to the late 1980s and
early 1990s. See, for example, Padrón 1987; Fisher 1993; and Carroll 1992.
3   See Lindblom 1977 for an outstanding analysis of the power and influence of the
private sector in democracies.

ral resource extraction. In short, the macroeconomy plays a significant role in shaping the contexts in which NGOs are operating, and many NGOs are only dimly aware of the implications it has for them and their programs.

The third way that questions of economy come into play for NGOs has to do with the locally based, culturally formulated microeconomies with which the NGOs interact as they engage in relationships with the people of the particular neighborhoods, communities, villages, and cities in which they are working. Oftentimes the people in these microeconomies are in the process of adapting, resisting, and providing alternatives to the prevailing philosophical and material underpinnings of the macroeconomic policies. They do so especially where these macro- policies are undermining the cultural values and meanings of relationships at the local level with family, friends, customers, and the like. These microeconomies tend to be dependent on many factors ignored by policy makers and NGOs. As we shall see, NGOs that do not take the time to attend to the complexities of these factors and relationships and do not adopt a process of mutual learning, consultation, and direction with the local people can and do end up doing significant economic and social harm rather than good.

This chapter attempts to provide an overview of the way that both macro- and microeconomy factors influence the processes and outcomes of the work of NGOs in general and Christian NGOs more specifically, whether they are aware of it or not. It focuses primarily on the macroeconomy level and its ramifications for the micro- level, since other chapters in this book (Meneses, chap. 1; Backues, chap. 5) cover the latter. This chapter starts out by positing that the concept of poverty is at the core of the understanding that NGOs have of their work, whether they are specifically focused on wealth creation or not, and looks at how resource transfer is at the heart of what they perceive themselves to be doing.[4] It then looks at how the global foreign aid process and macro- policy levels of "developing" countries are structured, and the main issues and actors involved. It argues that

---

4   See Lederleitner, chapter 2 in this volume, for insights along these lines.

governments, official development agencies, and the private sector have attempted to lead developing countries through a process of re-production of the path taken by "developed" countries—from rural, agricultural, precapitalist societies to urban, industrialized, capitalist economies. As with the North, this transition has and continues to have significant social consequences, and takes place in the context of interests of governments in both the North and the South that go be-yond simply altruistic motives. This "engineered" transition involves, in short, struggles for power and resources that influence the structur-ing of microeconomies and the lives of the people at the local level in many ways. Whether they know it or not, NGOs are part and parcel of this transition and the struggles that accompany it.

The chapter then goes on to look at the role that NGOs have played in this context, paying specific attention to how NGOs have been a bridge between the macro- and microeconomies. It points to how some NGOs, including Christian ones, have been at the heart of building up local, national, and international processes of resisting and challenging economic policies that are geared towards fostering the societal and market transitions identified above, of proposing and engaging in innovative and creative ways of harnessing the power of the market for social ends as they interface more and more with busi-ness and private sector strategies. It also argues, however, that many other NGOs tend to be caught up in their own agendas and economic survival in a way that can lead them to approaches, projects, and pro-grams that further— unbeknownst to themselves—some deleterious aspects of the agenda of transition.

Finally, the chapter concludes by looking at five pitfalls along these lines that NGOs should take into account as they carry out their work of Christian mission and ministry efforts of care and aid. A greater understanding of the complex dimensions of the economic aspects of NGO praxis will hopefully help us see how Christian mission efforts can and should integrate into their planning and praxis actions that har-ness the power of market-based economies to the Christian mandate to do justice, as well as nurture and nourish macro- and microeconomic relationships that bear witness to Christ.

THE INHERENT ECONOMIC DIMENSIONS OF THE HUMANITARIAN ENDEAVOR: POVERTY AND RESOURCE TRANSFERS

The mission endeavor, whether from a secular, humanitarian perspective or from a Christian one, is based on one fundamental premise that gives it legitimacy: "we" have resources that "they" need, and we can therefore be of help to them. These resources come in various types, and in more recent literature are usually referred to as kinds of "capital": financial capital (money), material capital (actual goods that can be given), human capital (all different kinds of knowledge, including about how things work [scientific] and the best way to do things [technical]), political capital (contacts and influence with powerful actors), cultural capital (an identity that bestows legitimacy), and spiritual capital (favored status with the supernatural, God, as bearers of spiritual truth).[5]

Seen this way, NGOs are engaged in an endeavor that has inherent economic dimensions, and what they do is influenced by, and influences, the economies of which they are a part at the global, national, and local levels. Many NGOs miss this economic aspect of their praxis, since they tend to be more focused on the human face of the problem, on "helping" those in need, and don't necessarily think of the resources they bring to bear as being economic in nature.[6] Many of them also miss the fact that no matter what kind of "help" they are providing, in one way or another they are wielding the most classic economic resource: money. Without money, without financial capital, it would be extremely difficult, if not impossible, for all of the other resources to be deployed—and therefore it is ultimately money that is at the

5   For various forms of capital as applied to development theory, see the sustainable livelihoods literature, especially Department for International Development 1999. For a more recent application of the "capitals" concept to development praxis, see Emery, Fey, and Flora 2006. For the purposes of this chapter, I have taken the liberty of defining and conceptualizing some of the forms differently than do these authors, including adding the area of "spiritual capital."

6   Certainly there are NGOs that are in the business of wealth creation, such as those involved in microfinance and other such actions, and others for whom economics is an important dimension of what they do. However, even these tend to miss aspects of political economy that we go on to review below.

foundation of the inherent power dimension to the donor-recipient relationships through which these resource transfers take place. No matter how much truth there may be to the fact that mutual learning and reciprocity are happening with their "partners," the fact remains that financial and material poverty is central to the equation of NGO work and the relationships NGOs form with the people with whom they are working.[7]

Most NGOs whose ministries involve some kind of help and assistance recognize that poverty is the reason they are engaged in their work in the first place, even if they don't see themselves as being engaged in an "economic" endeavor. But why would they not think about their actions as being intimately involved with the economies of poverty, and why would their analysis and consideration of the way those economies are affected by and affect their work be so lacking, sometimes to the point that they are doing more harm than good?[8] Part of the answer lies in how poverty and its causes have been defined and understood, and it is to this issue that we now turn.

THE PROBLEM OF POVERTY

The definition and causes of poverty, and consequently what policies and approaches should be employed to fight it, have been the subject of much debate in development work. All definitions, however, have included at least implicitly the lack of financial capital, even though other variables such as food, health care, education, shelter, water, and sanitation often take center stage in development work.[9] These "basic needs," enshrined in the UN Declaration of Human Rights as "basic

---

7   See Bronkema 1996 for an attempt by the Committee on Cooperation in Latin America to deal with these power dimensions. Of course, there are some kinds of projects and programs—such as those dealing with conflict and human rights—in which the issue is not one of poverty. In those cases this analysis would not be applicable.

8   The concern with Christian ministries and NGOs doing more harm than good has found its most eloquent expression and analysis in Corbett and Fikkert 2009.

9   The focus on microfinance as a way to tackle these variables is one manifestation of the key role financial capital plays in this debate.

rights" to which all people should have access, have traditionally been the primary focus of NGOs, which have tackled their manifestations in neglected rural and urban communities and among particularly vulnerable groups, such as children, women, and ethnic minorities.

All of these "basic needs" items are "goods" that have to be produced in one way or another; and except in the rarest of cases, the production of these goods, of these "assets," is intimately tied to financial capital (money) and to other goods.[10] For example, not only does access to health, education, and food depend in many cases on having money, but if people do not have access to any one of these, it will affect their overall quality of life and their ability to meet their other basic needs. The "livelihood strategies" in which people, communities, countries, and NGOs engage,[11] therefore, involve complex "economic" decisions around assets and goods, and can be very much influenced, for better or for worse, by any policy or project introduced or engaged in by any of the actors.

Unfortunately, while most NGOs define poverty as a lack of "basic needs" assets and goods, and see the lack of income as an underlying problem, there tends to be little understanding of the complexity of the livelihood strategies and economies by which people are surviving and attempting to build up their assets and financial capital. Moreover, there tends to be little analysis of the overall economic environment in which they are operating, how that environment is created and shaped, and the impact it has on the poverty that exists. In short, they do not think about their actions as involving economies of poverty, and this leads them to flying blind in the two main, interrelated dimensions of these economies. The first is the macro-level dimension, having to do with broad policies and structures over which the national government presides as it attempts to tackle the problem of poverty. The second is the micro-level dimension, which has to do with communities, families, and individuals as they engage in their livelihood strategies. In what follows, we review both of these economic dimensions

---

10 Some exceptions are primarily indigenous communities in which barter and other forms of trade are more common.

11 See the sustainable livelihoods literature mentioned above.

to get a better sense of how NGOs fit into them and what they may be overlooking when it comes to designing and implementing their programs and projects.

POLITICAL ECONOMIES: ISSUES, ACTORS, AND APPROACHES

There are three main kinds of actors at the macroeconomy level that can be roughly categorized as belonging to the public, private, and third sectors: governments (public), with their many different entities that are responsible for governing society and promoting the national interest at home and beyond their borders; businesses (private), large and small, that open up shop at home and all over the world, create jobs and goods and services that people need and want, and make profits for their owners and shareholders; and a host of "civil society" (third sector) organizations that have sprung up for just about any reason one can think of, from holding governments accountable to plugging gaps in services to giving people places that help them shore up identities and have fun.[12]

Seen from the view of "political economy"—a useful term because it reminds us of the particular interests, influence, and actions that each of these sectors brings to bear on the construction and shaping of the economy—the government is in the driver's seat, since it holds the power of regulating any and all actions that take place. One of the main functions of government is to encourage the development and maintenance of the economy, which is generally viewed as being made up of three kinds of productive sectors: the primary sector (agriculture and natural resources), the secondary sector (manufactured and industrialized goods), and the tertiary sector (all kinds of different services ranging from financial services and products to education, health care, tourism, and production and development of knowledge

---

12   The civil society literature dates back to Alexis de Tocqueville's observations on US democracy and society in the mid-1880s; see Tocqueville 2003. See Putnam 2000 for a more recent analysis of the importance of civil society to US democracy and culture. See below for further literature on civil society's role in advocacy and development.

and technology).[13] All of these sectors provide jobs, create products that can be sold inside the country and exported to others, and generate income that can be reinvested in the country to create economic growth and provide resources for the government through taxes for its own functioning and implementation of policies.

The main macroeconomic idea in the development field has been that in order for countries to come out of poverty, they need to follow the path traced by the countries of the North and move from agricultural, rural economies and societies to industrialized, urban ones. The agricultural sector in these economies is seen as backward and inefficient, with low-paying jobs that produce products of low value, while the industrial sector is seen as holding the key to creating good, high-paying jobs and manufacturing products that can be sold for much more value locally and around the world. This means, therefore, that the agricultural sector needs to be "modernized"—including mechanizing production, producing agricultural products that can make the most money (usually export crops), and ensuring that land can be bought and sold freely so that it can be used the most productively— and industries have to be created that will provide jobs for farmers and laborers from the agricultural sector who have been displaced by the processes of modernization. The outcome, in theory, is that resources in the agricultural and industrialized sectors of the economy will be used much more efficiently and will drive a self-sustainable process of wealth generation that will lift countries out of poverty.

This is, in fact, the path that the "northern" developed countries have taken and that more recent "successful" "newly industrialized countries" (NICs) have followed as well.[14] However, significant cultural battles took place and costs were borne as these countries moved from a political economy that placed a higher value on social

---

13 See any economic textbook. The tertiary sector can be further subdivided into the quaternary and quinquenary sectors.

14 See, for example, Haggard 1990 for an analysis of the various "pathways," as well as Fei and Ranis 1975 for a study of the paths taken by South Korea and Taiwan. Singapore and Hong Kong developed slightly differently, but with the same model and idea, making financial services instead of manufacturing their focus.

relationships and responsibilities to one that was driven more by profit making. These battles over values, principles, and traditions continue today in countries that are undergoing a transition to a more "capitalist" political economy as they seek ways out of poverty, and NGOs are caught up in these struggles and transitions in ways that they may not fully realize.

What are the main conflicts that mark these transitions? The overarching one is the conflict brought about by the process of "commodification," where things that were serving a wide range of social and economic functions are transformed into "commodities" that are used exclusively to make money, stripped of their social and cultural value and meaning. Within this overarching conflict, two main flashpoints keep reappearing: land and natural resources, such as water, timber, oil, and valuable minerals; and people's labor. It is no accident that these are the two flashpoints—in agricultural societies, the two key elements needed to produce goods of value are (1) land and natural resources and (2) labor, otherwise known in economics as "the factors of production."

Attitudes towards land and land tenure models vary widely from culture to culture and society to society, but generally precapitalist societies view land as having a sacred quality to it and approach land ownership from a more communitarian perspective, subject to what the Catholic Church itself has called a "social function" or a function for the "common good." One need look no further than the biblical example of the nation of Israel, with the limits on the purchasing and selling of land established by God through the Year of Jubilee (see Lev 25); the manifold indigenous cultures that own the land collectively and link land and natural resources with spirituality;[15] the feudal systems around the world in which the nobles were ethically required to provide land for the poor under their care in exchange for a tithe of

---

15   For this and a host of other insights into the state, beliefs, and issues facing indigenous peoples, see the wealth of material collected and promoted by the United Nations Permanent Forum on Indigenous Issues at http://social.un.org/index/IndigenousPeoples/LibraryDocuments.aspx, especially the *State of the World's Indigenous Peoples* (2009).

loyalty and a portion of the crops produced; the "commons" in Britain, where forests were an open place for the poor to hunt, fish, and gather wood to supplement their subsistence agriculture;[16] the *ejido* structures in Mexico, Honduras, and other Latin American countries, where land belonged to the community and it was illegal to sell it to outsiders; and the myriad land reform laws in Latin America that gave peasants and the state a right to require landowners to forfeit land that remained fallow.[17] This all changed as land and natural resources began to be seen as a way to make money as opposed to being central to a way of life. As peasants are kicked off the land to make way for a more mechanized agriculture focusing on cash crops or to graze cattle to sell on the world market;[18] as the access of the poor to forests and water sources undergoes the infamous process of "enclosure," of restricting their access to or use of these resources so that timber can be harvested and land sold off;[19] and as "agricultural modernization laws" or "free trade agreements" are passed that do away with the "social function" of land and permit or even require individual land titles in *ejidos* or indigenous land tenure systems in order to create land markets,[20] all of this engenders resistance to these processes of transition and triggers a social dislocation as people are thrown into poverty and migrate from the rural areas to cities and other countries, looking for a way to create better opportunities for themselves and their children.

This process of "rapid social change"[21] has deep consequences also in the area of people's labor. In precapitalist societies, in general people have access to productive assets to make their own living, whether by farming their own land or as artisans who by and large make and sell

---

16   For an outstanding history of this transition, see Polanyi 1944.
17   On Mexico and the *ejido* system, see Jones and Ward 1998. On Honduras and land tenure and reform, see Cid 1977. For more on the social function of land, see Losano 2009.
18   For a description of this transition in Central America, for example, see Bulmer-Thomas 1987.
19   For examples along these lines, see Goldman 1998.
20   See Jones and Ward 1998.
21   See below how the World Council of Churches used this term in its worldwide program in the 1950s to help churches understand and respond to these social upheavals.

their own products at what society believes to be a "fair price" based on how long it took to create the product.[22] The main norm, then, is that the person who puts in the work to create the product should reap the lion's share of the profit, and this norm is challenged in the transition to industrialization. As the techniques of mass production put artisans out of work and turn them into wage laborers, and as business owners who employ them try to maximize profits for themselves, the temptation is to pay as low a wage as possible and to skimp on working conditions—a situation that also creates resistance as workers demand a "fair wage" for their labor based on the previous cultural norm, that those who do the work itself should benefit the most. The fact is, however, that local and multinational businesses have the upper hand, since the displaced subsistence farmers and former artisans now have no alternatives other than wage labor. Moreover, even as labor unions gain prominence and power in these times of transition as they battle for a "fair share" of the profits to go to labor and for "living wages," the determination of who gets a job, of who gets to survive and flourish, now lies primarily with the business sector (Lindblom 1977). This transition impacts not only the macro-level of the economy and the corresponding structures, but the micro-level as well. As the "market-based" economy, in which people are encouraged individually to maximize profits, begins to penetrate and dominate local economies predicated more on relationships that emphasize reciprocity and community, and as money becomes more and more the focus, it and the businesses and people engaged in profit-maximizing transactions tend to be branded in spiritual, supernatural, and normative negative terms like "bitter" or "of the devil."[23]

Over all of this stands the government, mediating the transition and mediating between the interests of those pushing for an industrialized, market-based economy and those who are resisting and suffering from it and the legacies it leaves. In the transitions in the North,

---

22 Of course, there has always been wage labor, but in general this has been viewed as less noble and less secure than other ways of making a living.

23 For the concept of "bitter money," see Shipton 1989. For the concept and stories of the devil's involvement in these processes, see Taussig 1980.

governments performed three main functions, functions that are still at the core of what they do today in terms of political economy. First, they created all of the necessary legal systems and norms needed to make sure that the "market" could function effectively, ranging from enshrining the sacred nature of individual private property, to enforcing contracts, to passing antitrust laws designed to create and maintain competition between economic actors. Second, they created projects geared to bring about social stability, tackle poverty within their borders, and promote economic growth by, among other things, enacting laws to provide relief to the population that was being "pauperized" by the enclosure movement. As part of this, they created a host of rules and regulations protecting workers and ensuring the provision of benefits; established extensive educational, health, and welfare systems to provide people with access to opportunities and take care of those who were less fortunate; and supported and subsidized the agricultural and industrialized sectors with an array of programs that are still in existence today.[24] Third, they actively promoted their own economic interests outside of their countries by all means necessary (including military intervention, supporting their multinational corporations [MNCs] and their operations in other countries, subsidizing their own producers, closing their countries' borders to products from others), used their clout to open up the economies of others, and structured the international economy in ways that would benefit them the most.[25]

Finally, starting in the late 1940s, governments of the North, driven by a mix of altruism and self-interest, also helped create and manage the foreign aid "industry" to tackle the problem of poverty and relief in "developing" nations, provide a bulwark against communism and for

---

24   As stated above, Polanyi 1944 has the best account of this transition. For the battles over this transition in the US and the church's role in it, see May's (1949) study. Today in the US, especially since the New Deal after the Depression, extension services, research and development grants, and incentives for new industries, for example, are all part of the US economy.

25   For a good history of the way the "northern" countries have structured the international trade regime, the resistance of the "southern" countries to this structuring, and a proposed alternative, see Stiglitz and Charlton 2005.

democracy, and open up markets for their businesses.[26] This "industry" was driven, and continues to be driven, by four main government-led actors.[27] First, the United Nations, in concert with the northern governments, was the lead "multilateral" actor with its "community development" approach in the 1950s; it continues to exercise significant influence today through the United Nations Development Programme (UNDP).[28] Second, as a desire for increased macroeconomic impact on poverty and development made its way to the fore, first the World Bank and then regional development banks like the Inter-American and African Development Banks wielded tremendous power and leverage through the loans they provided for infrastructure and myriad poverty-related projects. Third, a host of "official" or "bilateral aid agencies,"[29] like the United States Agency for International Development (USAID), played a significant role in funding and implementing "basic needs" projects in education, health, and agriculture, and then in the late 1980s programs geared towards the development of justice and "governance" systems. Fourth, as developing countries plunged into debt in the late 1970s and early 1980s—due to a variety of factors having to do with the increase in oil prices, decrease in the prices of their agricultural exports, and unproductive use of loans— and were unable to repay the development loans they had taken out, the International Monetary Fund (IMF) became a major actor in providing loans to stabilize economies and imposing conditions geared towards "restructuring" the economies to cut costs and meet debt payment obligations. While up until that point government had been

---

26 See Lumsdaine 1993 for a particularly good account of mixed motives in the history of US foreign aid.

27 More recently, and hearkening to the past, when private banks were the major source of loans for the developing countries, the private sector has gained a significant role in its partnership with the government actors. It is beyond the scope of this paper to examine that aspect of the foreign aid regime.

28 See Holdcroft 1978 for a good historical description of this movement. For a history of the United Nations Development Programme (UNDP), see Murphy 2006.

29 In development parlance, "official" refers to government agencies overall, "bilateral" to those government agencies that relate directly to other governments on a one-to-one basis, and "multilateral" to agencies that are made up of representatives of many different governments at once, one example being the World Bank.

seen as the key actor in bringing about development, this new "neo-liberal" philosophy saw government as the problem and sought to create a transition away from government-controlled to "market-based" economies in the belief that the latter held the keys to the generation of wealth and development.

In what became known as the "Washington Consensus," the other development actors, with the exception of the United Nations, joined the IMF in promoting these "neoliberal" policies, which included slashing government spending and programs, privatizing government industries, and doing away with barriers to foreign industries entering into developing countries. They also began to subcontract out their development work to "for-profit" development agencies[30] and to increase their funding to NGOs that were seen as more effective, efficient, and innovative than the government entities, leading to an exponential increase in the number, scope, and presence of NGOs in countries all over the world. In large part pushed by these NGOs, the "official" and "multilateral" agencies also created policies to forgive or drastically reduce the debt burden of the most "Heavily Indebted Poor Countries" (HIPC). However, they also used this process to support the transition to market-based economies, requiring these countries to present "Poverty Reduction Strategy Papers" (PRSPs) that detailed the plans for executing their macrodevelopment policies, which were for the most part along market-based lines. By the 1990s, these neoliberal policies and approaches came in for tremendous criticism for failing to achieve the goals set out for them and for having a severe negative impact in many areas of the world. The consequences included stunted economic growth, increased income inequality within countries, subversion of democracy, and authoritarian, repressive, and corrupt governance.[31] Pressured by protests, governments marshalling the foreign aid regime began to go back to focusing on "basic needs" and tried to coordinate the efforts of the various actors mentioned above to this end. This movement found its most recent expression in what

---

30 In some circles these are known pejoratively as "beltway bandits" because their headquarters tend to be located near the beltways surrounding Washington, DC.
31 See, for example, de Waal 1997, among many other analyses of this nature.

became known as the eight "Millennium Development Goals" (MDGs) to be achieved by 2015, and the foreign aid regime geared its funding towards the achievement of the goals.[32]

Today the foreign aid industry plays a massive role in the economies of developing countries at the local, national, and international levels. Hundreds of thousands of jobs depend on it in the North and the South, and it permeates almost every facet of the life of developing countries. Despite some impressive gains in education and health, foreign aid actors and resources stand accused of creating dependency and meddling in a way that harms societies politically, economically, and culturally rather than aiding their development.[33] It is in this maelstrom of political economy that NGOs are operating.

NGOS AS ECONOMY BROKERS AND BRIDGE BUILDERS

The changes to a more "capitalist" economy have always been met with resistance and adaptation both by governments and local groups, and Christians have been at the forefront of this story. In fact, much of the "Social Gospel" was triggered by Christians trying to make sense of and react to the changes in social relationships and consequences brought about by the transition to a new economic model, and to hold firm to the importance of evangelism and social work. The nonprofit sector (or "third sector") itself in the northern countries was birthed by Christian groups reacting to the flood of people coming into the city and to the corresponding new social problems in England and the United States (Hall 1992). The commodification of labor brought about intense battles in which the Federal Council of Churches in the US participated actively, and the "evils" of business under this new model came in for much prophetic denouncement by a host of Christian pastors and by mission boards concerned over the spread

---

32 See Sachs 2005 for a cheerleading description of this process.
33 For a positive view of the results of foreign aid, see Kenny 2012. For critical views on foreign aid, see the decades-old writings of Bauer (1972) and the more recent critiques of Easterly (2006) and Moyo (2009).

of industrialization to other parts of the world.[34] Globally, the World Council of Churches created its "rapid social change" program in the 1950s as an attempt to help the church and peoples around the world actively analyze, resist, and modify these economic changes at the macro- and local levels, spawning a host of Christian and secular groups working hand in hand in this endeavor.[35] As a result of these efforts and the faithfulness of Christians all over the world, thousands of small and large NGOs and other mission efforts and ministries of care and aid, both through churches and parachurch organizations, are operating across borders and inside developing countries to respond to the problems of poverty. We will first take a look at the praxis of NGOs in general in the local and global economies, and then we will examine the pitfalls to which they are subject. The final section will draw conclusions about what this means for Christian NGOs.

NGO Praxis: Mission, Method, Money

One way of making sense of what NGOs do, of their praxis, is by looking at three key variables that drive their action: mission, method, and money. The first, mission, has to do with why an NGO is formed. An NGO is usually created when somebody, driven by a desire to do good, sees a problem affecting others and wants to help solve it.[36] It is therefore no surprise that NGOs are tackling just about any kind of issue one can imagine. Understanding the mission of an NGO, then, and what drives that mission, is crucial to discerning what the NGO is doing and why it exists in the first place.

Second, despite the tremendous variety of NGOs, there are three basic ways that they can address problems, three overarching methods from which they can choose: (1) they can provide aid or relief directly to the people suffering from the problem—the relief approach; (2) they can help people tackle the problem themselves—the development approach; or (3) they can address the root causes of the problem

---

34 See Bronkema 2006, especially chapter 3.
35 See Abrecht 1961.
36 Of course, there are plenty of examples of NGOs being created to provide jobs for their founders and for other, less noble purposes.

and seek solutions, which usually involves some kind of interface with government and structures of power—the advocacy approach. These three methods are not mutually exclusive, and each of them has myriad techniques associated with it. Many NGOs are created to respond to an immediate problem and do so first by delivering relief assistance. Usually over time, however, they will feel driven to become involved in development in order to make a lasting difference in the lives of the people. A vast majority of them stop at that "second generation" approach[37] rather than moving also into advocacy, either because they do not analyze the underlying political causes of and solutions to the problems they are tackling or because they fear engaging in "political" work and the consequences this might bring.

However, as described in the introduction to this chapter, a significant number of NGOs are engaged in the advocacy approach, a process that most often involves partnerships and intimate links between NGOs working at the international, national, and local levels. These local and national NGOs, such as peasant movements, labor organizations, human rights entities, and academicians, have increased their levels of organization and joint action under umbrella organizations and associations, built bridges with each other, and brought their coordinated power and pressure to bear on government entities and official development organizations in order to protect the rights of, and resist policies and programs that are seen as damaging to, the most vulnerable. They have also advanced alternative economic agendas opposing the "neoliberal," "market-based," "capitalist," "globalizing" agenda. The most public and visible expression of the thick web of "civil society" advocacy organizations lies in the World Social Forum movement, whose first global meeting was in Porto Alegre, Brazil, in 2001. Set up as an alternative to the yearly World Economic Forum held by developed countries' governments and bearing the slogan "Another World Is Possible," this movement has had staggering attendance and significant influence. The yearly forums consistently attract

---

37   See Korten 1987 for the original formulation of the "three generations" insight. Korten later described a "fourth generation" of activity, which was the linking of organizations at the global level (1990).

more than sixty thousand attendees from over 120 countries and are given credit for inspiring and encouraging important alternative policies and movements in countries around the world. As part of this process, they have mobilized massive protests against official events and agendas and spurred changes in foreign policy in the developed countries on a variety of economic and political matters.[38]

As NGOs are driven by different missions to tackle different issues, and as they choose between the methods of relief, development, and advocacy, they are also subject to a third major consideration: money. NGOs are dependent on funding in some form, and the sources of that funding and the demands and pressures that come along with it are a key variable in shaping what NGOs do and how they do it. This can range from the ways they structure their financial accounting and reporting systems and demand that their partners structure theirs, as Lederleitner points out in this volume (chap. 2), to the specific relief, development, and advocacy practices they undertake. Unfortunately, many times the funding and donor pressures and demands lead to poor praxis, as has been well documented in relief and development literature.[39] We will look at this in more detail below when we address the pitfalls to which NGOs are subject. First, though, we turn to the questions that arise from NGO praxis in the context of the macro- and microeconomies.

NGO Praxis: Political Economy Context

As NGOs operate in these complicated international, national, and local contexts of political economies, questions arise about the roles they play. How are their roles shaped by these economies, and what are the consequences and outcomes of their actions? Three factors come to the fore when we consider these questions. The first, an overarching one, is the extent to which NGOs are a useful "pawn" in the transition to and the structuring of a market-based system. The second, related to the first, is the degree to which NGOs are adopting strategies that

---

38 For a history and description of this movement, see Sen 2004 and Santos 2006.
39 See, for example, Minear 2002 on relief and Dichter 2003 on development.

use the power of the market in order to achieve mission and money ends. The third is to what extent NGOs are, on balance, having an impact for good. We will take each of these in turn.

First, what role do NGOs play, whether they are aware of it or not, in the political economy of the structuring of a market-based economy? There are several perspectives on this issue. On the one hand, some who might be called critical theorists have claimed that NGOs arose as part of the transition to a capitalist system in order to specifically clean up its messes, and helped to pacify the local population so as to allow the system to continue to benefit the wealthy.[40] This historically focused argument is echoed today by those who argue critically that NGOs are accomplices in the transition, albeit not necessarily intentionally so.[41] This argument claims that NGOs are not only taking care of those thrown into need by neoliberal policies but also getting governments off the hook by providing services—such as education, health care, and other social services for the most vulnerable—that are the government's responsibility. By doing so, the argument goes, NGOs are part of the system of foreign aid that allows governments and the people within them to siphon off funds and not have to deal with uprisings from a suffering population. This critical argument, however, is in contrast with an opposing "neoliberal" perspective that sees the NGO's role as a positive one. It argues that NGOs should embrace the role of service providers in the transition to a market-based economy, because ultimately that economy will provide the wealth needed to make everyone better off.[42] Moreover, in keeping with this viewpoint, it should be the "voluntary" sector, not the government, that takes care of those who have fallen on hard times, because charity and compassion are key religious and cultural elements that help unite societies and make people better.[43]

---

40 See, for example, Abzug and Webb 1996.
41 See Bornstein 2005, especially chapter 4.
42 The clearest expression of this position is by a Christian author; see Sherman 1992.
43 For the strongest argument along these lines, see Olasky 2008.

There are two additional perspectives critical of the role NGOs play in the structuring of political economies. First, some see NGOs as potentially being or becoming part of the state apparatus to control local populations and reduce their ability and desire to participate actively in democracy building. In this view, by adopting "apolitical" relief and development approaches, NGOs dampen at the community level an analysis of power structures that keep people in poverty in the first place and limit democratic participation in changing those structures of power.[44] This critique is mostly reserved for NGOs that do not integrate an advocacy approach into their work. Second, some say that since many NGOs push for the continuation of foreign aid, from which they receive substantial funding, they share responsibility for the international aid system that perpetuates international dependency, diminishes creativity, and fosters corruption.[45] In summary, the consensus is that NGOs are playing a significant role in the transition to a market-based economy, whether they are aware of it or not.

The second factor having to do with NGO practice is the degree to which NGOs are adopting methods that use the power of the market in order to achieve mission and money ends. This is important because more and more NGOs are engaging in business endeavors for a variety of purposes. This turn to "social entrepreneurship" has been driven by four main considerations. First, for several decades now, NGOs at all levels have been concerned about their own sustainability, and one of the ways to ensure access to funds is to create businesses that will provide the resources needed for their projects. Second, NGOs have more and more seen the creation of businesses or involvement in business endeavors as a way to accomplish the missions to which they feel called. So, for example, NGOs have created businesses, or trained and helped people create businesses, that employ the vulnerable populations with whom they are working to provide them with jobs and sources of income that give them economic opportunities for a better life. This has been particularly prominent in the work with

44 See especially Shaw 2007.
45 See Barry-Shaw, Jay, and Engler 2012. For a polemic in this vein, see Maren 1997.

women rescued from trafficking, but has grown exponentially in other areas as well. Third, NGOs have also created businesses or helped to strengthen businesses to market products created by local peoples, as a way to stabilize and increase their sales. Examples of this range from the marketing of handicrafts by organizations like Ten Thousand Villages, which purchases handicrafts from local artisans all over the world and markets them in the United States and beyond, to the Fair Trade movement, which does the same for coffee, cocoa, and other products grown by small farmers. And finally, NGOs have created businesses or become involved in creating businesses to provide services to those who cannot otherwise access them, ranging from water and health to the whole sector of microfinance, which helps people gain access to capital, savings, and insurance. This focus on using business for development is part of a wider movement of using business for social ends, one that is sweeping the developed countries as well and in which the private sector itself, not just NGOs, is very much involved. "B corporations," for example, have sprung up in the United States as a way for corporations to legally designate workers, community, and environment as "bottom lines" along with profit; "impact investment" is a growing field where entrepreneurs with a social vision are active in creating products needed for development; and "business as mission" is all the rage in the field of Christian missions.

While there is much to be said for this approach, notes of caution are also being sounded. The adoption of Western business approaches and mindset, an approach that encourages profit making even in the context of positing social ends as the main purpose of the business, can have a deep impact on microeconomies and cultural norms. Recent books and articles have begun to explore how these kinds of business approaches may, in some situations, actually dispossess local artisans of power over their own productive processes and eliminate some of what they find most valuable about the productive process itself.[46] In addition, some aid agencies may be tempted to change their strategies away from support for advocacy approaches to more "business" approaches,

---

46 See Elyachar 2005 and Adolina 2012.

in what I have called elsewhere "the economization of social justice" (Bronkema 1998). Nevertheless, this "business" approach is important to explore, since the material impact can be significant. One need look no further than, for example, Paul Polak and his International Development Enterprise, in existence since 1981, and their strategy of jumping over the complexity of the problems causing poverty to focus simply on helping small farmers make more money off their farms. The improvements in appropriate technology and marketing of products that they support increase income, which by itself can lead to more opportunities for the farmers and their families (Polak 2008).

This brings us to the question of whether, in the balance, NGOs operating in this complex situation of political economies are having an impact for good. This calculation is a bit difficult and risky to make, given both the dangers of generalization and the fact that NGOs have come in for both significant criticism and praise. On the one hand, in relief and development situations, for example, NGOs have been shown to have little knowledge of the situation; be driven by money and resources; exacerbate conflict through their programs; engage in competition, deception, and manipulation; adopt approaches that create dependency as opposed to self-sustainability; reproduce cultural patterns of discrimination; and not reach the poorest of the poor. On the other, however, NGOs are still seen as being more in tune with local needs, more relational, more effective in channeling resources, and more able to adjust to local situations and to learn from their mistakes. They continue to be seen as sources of innovation in methods, approaches, and programs that have been picked up by the larger official agencies. They have also, perhaps even more importantly, been seen as brokers and bridge builders between the communities and the government programs in terms of making sure that the population is attended to, and of forming the backbone of civil society, on whose knowledge the government and its agencies depend to move the political economy towards where it should be. As such, NGOs are both influencing and being influenced by the range of political economies that exist, whether they know it or not.

In summary, despite the problems identified, the literature continues to treat NGOs kindly, as opposed to constant criticisms dating as far back as the 1970s that eviscerate the government and official agencies in terms of their performance.[47] The overall perspective appears to be that on the whole they are doing more good than harm and represent significant potential.

PITFALLS FOR NGO PRAXIS

Given the important contributions that NGOs make, what are the potential pitfalls in their praxis? Five stand out from the analysis above.

First, NGOs' reliance on donor money may lead them to poor relief, development, and advocacy practices. The fact that they rely on money from funders means that the vagaries of the economy have a huge effect on what NGOs are led to do in order to secure that funding. The state of the various northern economies will affect the amount of support that NGOs get, both from governments and from private donors, which means that NGOs will always be tempted to tailor the nature, location, scope, and methods of their programs to attract donations. Increasingly donors are looking for and demanding rapid, clearly identifiable results, with an emphasis on efficiency—defined as minimum money dedicated to "overhead" and an adoption of Western accounting practices. All of this has led to a host of methods in planning, monitoring, evaluation, and financial controls that tend to drive NGOs away from best practices in development methods and approaches. As several authors have identified, these financial pressures, coming directly from a scarcity of funds over the years due to economic difficulties and to the competition among NGOs, have also led to much institutional isomorphism, in which NGOs begin to mimic both in structure and in practice the approaches of the donors.[48]

---

47   For an early critique, see Paddock and Paddock 1973.
48   For a treatment of isomorphism, see Verbruggen, Christiaens, and Milis 2011. Leiderleitner in this volume (chap. 2) makes similar observations. For a hard-hitting, sarcastic analysis of how northern NGOs reproduce satellite operations at will, reproducing colonial relationships, see Kruijt 1992.

The main culprit in this is perhaps the time factor. Development and social change methods require many years of patient, inclusive, and mutual learning relationships, which are not accomplished by the drive for quick results. While many development agents recognize deep down that succumbing to the pressure to try to produce quick results with more top-down approaches does not lead to sustainable results, they feel that they have little choice. As a result, as many authors have documented, much of development practice, driven by the question of the economy of funding, has been less than effective and at times downright harmful.[49]

The second pitfall, related to the first as examined above, is that NGOs tend to eschew collaboration. As an overall sector of the foreign aid industry, NGOs have a tremendous impact on the political economy of societies because of the massive cash inflows that they introduce, which provides them with independence from the government and from other agencies. This, coupled with the time factor and competitiveness, leads them to dedicate relatively little time to developing wide partnerships. As such, NGOs can create difficulties for—and even pose a threat to—governments that are attempting to design development policies for their countries, and that are also concerned about their image and power and want to control the kinds of information and organizations operating in their societies. As a result, governments have been passing more and more NGO laws, not only to ensure coordination and transparency within their own countries, but also to protect the public from fraudulent and corrupt NGOs formed by those with less than altruistic motives, and in order to capture some of the funds going to NGOs for their own government projects.[50] NGOs resist these kinds of laws, alleging that they should be free to operate as they feel led and seeing them as attempts by the government to restrict freedoms and prevent challenges to their power and

---

49 The majority of this documentation, as stated above, is on the official aid agencies.
50 See the International Center for Not-for-Profit Law's reports for updates on some forty countries and their legislation in the Global South (http://www.icnl.org/about /reports/index.html) as well as the overview reports as part of their *Global Trends in NGO Law* publication (http://www.icnl.org/research/trends/).

authority. In all of this, the pitfall is one that is common to the foreign aid industry as a whole: NGOs may be tempted to go it alone, without consultation or coordination with the government, other NGOs, or other development actors, and in so doing work at cross-purposes and waste a significant amount of their own and others' resources.

Third, NGOs can have a significant impact on the local economies in many ways that are harmful, especially if they are not mindful of them. For example, by bringing in gifts in kind, such as textiles, food, and other products, NGOs can destroy local businesses and the livelihoods that depend on them. While this problem has been documented well in relief efforts, to the point that the Sphere Project standards for relief practice address it specifically by advocating purchasing products on the local markets as opposed to bringing in materials from the outside (Sphere Project 2011), striking a balance between needs and the impact on local economies is still a difficult one. Purchasing products on the local market may drive up local prices as well, putting goods beyond the reach of people who depend on them. At the same time, NGOs have a significant impact on the local economy in terms of driving up rents, salaries, and other prices, since they can and do pay significantly more than the local going rates. How NGOs balance this is a constant source of deliberation, since many local economies depend on NGOs as a main source of jobs and income.

In addition, in the communities themselves, NGOs many times will monopolize and compete for the time of local leaders, especially those who are the most capable in their eyes, which can lead the local people to set aside other productive activities, including farming and services, in order to work for the NGOs. This can have an effect that strongly skews both the productive and cultural relationships in the community as people vie for good NGO jobs, introducing competition and division and changing the types of goods and services that are available in the community. Usually those hired by NGOs have skills that were previously being used in other places in the community. Of course, the NGO presence may bring many more opportunities for all in the community as well. In short, the pitfalls here are many, and a conscious and deliberate attempt to identify the impacts NGOs have on the local economies is important to be able to make informed decisions that will reduce the potential harm and bring about the most good possible.

Fourth, beyond the strictly material effects listed above, NGOs may introduce and push new forms of economic behavior and relationships through their programs and the "implicit ethical messages" contained in them (Anderson 1999). NGOs at the community and national level are entering into a cultural terrain with dimensions that are important for them to take into account, but which more often than not are not on their radar screen. This is true not only for international NGOs but for local ones as well. It is not always the case, given the rural/urban cultural and economic divides, that local NGOs are as in tune with cultural issues as might be expected, although the odds are that they are much more aware of them than international NGOs. There are several issues that generally come to the fore in this arena, ranging from the valuing of time to the role of gender in local economies, to the pushing of the idea of wealth generation as an individual initiative that needs to be encouraged for progress to occur. Although some authors advocate the importance of doing away with cultural barriers that stand in the way of economic progress,[51] it is extremely important to make sure that one has done an in-depth analysis of what cultural changes sought for economic progress might imply in the noneconomic realm, as Eloise Meneses so eloquently points out elsewhere in this volume (chap. 1).

Fifth, NGOs may be used by the state and local power structures to extend, perpetuate, and legitimize their power, to support the political economy policies and transformations they seek to introduce or maintain, and to put a lid on the participation of people in deciding their own future. Avoiding this pitfall requires that significant attention be paid to the political dimensions of one's own work and context. Techniques such as conflict and gender analyses are helpful in considering the NGO's role from this perspective. It may be that the NGO and its programs are not able to make much of a difference in the "structural" issues of power that exist, or they may not be called

---

51 See, for example, Harrison and Huntington 2001.

to attempt to do so in each situation.[52] But it is important for NGOs to make these decisions intentionally and consciously as opposed to flying blind in contexts where there can be a lot at stake and where the impact of the NGO is pronounced, whether they know it or not.

IMPLICATIONS FOR CHRISTIAN NGOS

What does all of this mean for Christian NGOs and ministries of care and aid seeking to be faithful to God's command to love their neighbor, do justice, and share the gospel? Two dimensions are important for Christian organizations to take into account. The first is very brief and straightforward: each and every one of the observations and elements of the analysis above pertains completely to Christian NGOs and ministries of care and aid. All Christian NGOs and ministries, no matter what they are doing, are part and parcel of the political economies described above and are subject to the pitfalls. Second, Christian NGOs have something to offer that others do not in terms of the political economies—this is not only absolutely essential to take into account, but is the foundation for all successful, sustainable progress and quality of life, no matter how it might be defined in different cultures: they have the spiritual element, the good news of Christ. As such, there is one additional pitfall to which they are subject.

Before analyzing the pitfall, it is good to detail the importance of the spiritual element. While the history of Christian ministries is replete with their battles with each other over the primacy of evangelism or development,[53] there is a growing recognition of the fact that the two must go hand in hand. Recent books from those committed to evangelism, for example, analyze how a neglect of the material di-

---

52 A helpful distinction along these lines is made by Moser (1993) in differentiating between "practical" and "strategic" interests, in her case looking at gender-related projects. Practical interests deal with the symptoms of the deeper problem, while strategic interests have to do with the structures of power that need to ultimately be tackled to end the problem itself.

53 See Bronkema 2006 for a detailed description of this battle as it related to missions in Latin America.

mensions has hampered the Holy Spirit in bringing people to Christ.[54] Moreover, there is a significant recommitment by well-known evangelical churches, pastors, and mission agencies to integrate development with their evangelism and church planting programs, giving evidence of the healthy reestablishment of the mandated synergy that Scripture points to time and time again (e.g., Gal 2:7–11). Ironically, at times it is non-Christians and atheists who present the clearest analysis of the importance of the spiritual element for the positive process of transformation of communities and peoples. For example, Erica Bornstein (2005), a Jewish anthropologist who researched World Vision and Christian Care in Zimbabwe in the late 1990s, came to the conclusion that because of their commitment to evangelism they were the only development agencies that were able to help people get over their fear of witchcraft and clear the way for important progress to occur. More recently, Matthew Parris (2008), a self-avowed atheist, made a similar argument, speaking out in support of Christian evangelical groups and their impact on development. Any attempt to separate the verbal proclamation of Christ's power from the actions of care, aid, development, and advocacy, even if one has to choose carefully how and when to share the good news, not only does a disservice to Christ's mandate but also sets up the projects and programs for eventual failure in more ways than one.

Finally, the pitfall. There may be a temptation for Christian NGOs to support, intentionally or not, the preaching of the "prosperity gospel" in the proclamation of Christ, promising those who convert to Christ the rewards of development progress. This is a particularly difficult pitfall to navigate, because oftentimes when people convert there is in fact an immediate economic benefit, given that money previously spent on things that are now forbidden or frowned upon is suddenly available.[55] Care has to be taken in this realm of spiritual political economy: the process of "making disciples" must communicate

---

54 See, for example, Suttle 2011.

55 See Sherman 1997 for an analysis of the impact of evangelism on culture and economy. See Annis 1987 for a slightly different take on the effects of evangelism on culture and economy.

that following Christ goes far beyond expecting economic rewards for doing so. It is a matter of faithfulness and enjoying the abundant life he has given us, even if it is not in the material realm.

REFERENCES

Abrecht, Paul. 1961. *The churches and rapid social change.* New York: Doubleday.

Abzug, Rikki, and Natalie J. Webb. 1996. Another role for nonprofits: The case of mop-ups and nursemaids resulting from privatization in emerging economies. *Nonprofit and Voluntary Sector Quarterly* 25, no. 2: 156–73.

Anderson, Mary B. 1999. *Do no harm: How aid can support peace—or war.* Boulder, CO: Lynne Rienner.

Andolina, Robert. 2012. The values of water: Development cultures and indigenous cultures in highland Ecuador. *Latin American Research Review* 47, no. 2: 3–26.

Annis, Sheldon. 1987. *God and production in a Guatemalan town.* Austin: University of Texas Press.

Barry-Shaw, Nikolas, and Dru Oja Jay. 2012. *Paved with good intentions: Canada's development NGOs from idealism to imperialism.* Winnipeg: Fernwood.

Bauer, P. T. 1972. *Dissent on development: Studies and debates in development economics.* Rev. ed. Cambridge, MA: Harvard University Press.

Bornstein, Erica. 2005. *The spirit of development: Protestant NGOs, morality, and economics in Zimbabwe.* Stanford, CA: Stanford University Press.

Bronkema, David. 1996. The São Paulo process: North-South donor-recipient relationships, power, and identity among Christian development NGOs. PONPO Working Paper 230. New Haven, CT: Program on Non-profit Organizations.

———. 1998. Economizing social justice: Leveraging foreign funding in peasant unions in Central America. Paper presented at the 21st International Congress of the Latin American Studies Association, Chicago, IL, September 24–26.

————. 2002. Firm foundations: Christian development NGOs, civil society, and social change. In *Local ownership, global change: Will civil society save the world?*, edited by Roland Hoksbergen and Lowell M. Ewert, 234–59. Monrovia, CA: World Vision.

————. 2006. Development as a political gift: Donor/recipient relationships, religion, knowledge and praxis in a Protestant development NGO in Honduras. PhD diss., Yale University.

Bulmer-Thomas, Victor. 1987. *The political economy of Central America since 1920.* Cambridge: Cambridge University Press.

Carroll, Thomas F. 1992. *Intermediary NGOs: The supporting link in grassroots development.* Hartford, CT: Kumarian.

Cid, Rafael del. 1977. *Reforma agraria y capitalismo dependiente.* Tegucigalpa, Honduras: Editorial Universitaria, UNAH.

Corbett, Steve, and Brian Fikkert. 2009. *When helping hurts: How to alleviate poverty without hurting the poor … and yourself.* Chicago: Moody.

Department for International Development. 1999. Sustainable livelihoods guidance sheets: Introduction. Emergency Nutrition Network. Accessed October 13, 2014. http://files.ennonline.net/attachments/871/dfid-sustainable-livelihoods-guidance-sheet-section1.pdf.

Dichter, Thomas W. 2003. *Despite good intentions: Why development assistance to the Third World has failed.* Amherst: University of Massachusetts Press.

Easterly, William Russell. 2006. *The white man's burden: Why the West's efforts to aid the rest have done so much ill and so little good.* New York: Penguin.

Elyachar, Julia. 2005. *Markets of dispossession: NGOs, economic development, and the state in Cairo.* Durham, NC: Duke University Press.

Emery, Mary, Susan Fey, and Cornelia Flora. 2006. Using community capitals to develop assets for positive community change. *CD Practice* 13: 1–19.

Fei, John C. H., and Gustav Ranis. 1975. A model of growth and employment in the open dualistic economy: The cases of Korea and Taiwan. *Journal of Development Studies* 2: 32–63.

Firth, Raymond. 1981. Engagement and detachment: Reflections on applying social anthropology to social affairs. *Human Organization* 40, no. 3: 193–201.

Fisher, Julie. 1993. *The road from Rio: Sustainable development and the nongovernmental movement in the Third World.* Westport, CT: Praeger.

Goldman, Michael. 1998. *Privatizing nature: Political struggles for the global commons.* London: Pluto.

Haggard, Stephan. 1990. *Pathways from the periphery: The politics of growth in the newly industrializing countries.* Ithaca, NY: Cornell University Press.

Hall, Peter Dobkin. 1992. *Inventing the nonprofit sector, and other essays on philanthropy, voluntarism, and nonprofit organizations.* Baltimore: Johns Hopkins University Press.

Harrison, Lawrence E., and Samuel P. Huntington, eds. 2001. *Culture matters: How values shape human progress.* New York: Basic Books.

Hefferan, Tara, and Tim Fogarty. 2010. The anthropology of faith and development: An introduction. *NAPA Bulletin* 33, no. 1: 1–11.

Holdcroft, Lane E. 1978. The rise and fall of community development in developing countries, 1950–1965: A critical analysis and an annotated bibliography. MSU Rural Development Paper 2. East Lansing: Department of Agricultural Economics, Michigan State University.

Jones, Gareth A., and Peter M. Ward. 1998. Privatizing the commons: Reforming the ejido and urban development in Mexico. *International Journal of Urban and Regional Research* 22, no. 1: 76–93.

Kenny, Charles. 2012. *Getting better: Why global development is succeeding and how we can improve the world even more.* New York: Basic Books.

Korten, David C. 1987. Third generation NGO strategies: A key to people-centered development. *World Development* 15, supplement: 145–59.

———. 1990. *Getting to the 21st century: Voluntary action and the global agenda.* West Hartford, CT: Kumarian.

Kruijt, Dirk. 1992. Monopolios de filantropia: El caso de las llamadas "organizaciones no gubernamentales" en América Latina. *Polémica* 16, no. 2: 41–47.

Lindblom, Charles Edward. 1977. *Politics and markets: The world's political economic systems.* New York: Basic Books.

Losano, Mario G. 2009. *Función social de la propiedad y latifundios ocupados: Los sin tierra de Brasil.* Madrid: Dykinson.

Lumsdaine, David Halloran. 1993. *Moral vision in international politics: The foreign aid regime, 1949–1989.* Princeton, NJ: Princeton University Press.

Maren, Michael. 1997. *The road to hell: The ravaging effects of foreign aid and international charity.* New York: Free Press.

May, Henry F. 1949. *Protestant churches and industrial America.* New York: Harper & Brothers.

Minear, Larry. 2002. *The humanitarian enterprise: Dilemmas and discoveries.* Bloomfield, CT: Kumarian.

Moomaw, I. W. 1966. *Crusade against hunger: The dramatic story of the world-wide antipoverty crusades of the churches.* New York: Harper & Row.

Moser, Caroline O. N. 1993. *Gender planning and development: Theory, practice and training.* New York: Routledge.

Moyo, Dambisa. 2009. *Dead aid: Why aid is not working and how there is a better way for Africa.* New York: Farrar, Straus and Giroux.

Murphy, Craig N. 2006. *The United Nations Development Programme: A better way?* New York: Cambridge University Press.

Olasky, Marvin N. 2008. *The tragedy of American compassion.* Wheaton, IL: Crossway.

Paddock, William, and Elizabeth Paddock. 1973. *We don't know how: An independent audit of what they call success in foreign assistance.* Ames: Iowa State University Press.

Padrón, Mario. 1987. Non-governmental development organizations: From development aid to development cooperation. *World Development* 15 (supplement): 69–77.

Parris, Matthew. 2008. As an atheist, I truly believe Africa needs God. *Times of London,* December 27.

Polak, Paul. 2008. *Out of poverty: What works when traditional approaches fail.* San Francisco: Berrett-Koehler.

Polanyi, Karl. 1944. *The great transformation: The political and economic origins of our time.* Boston: Beacon.

Putnam, Robert D. 2000. *Bowling alone: The collapse and revival of American community.* New York: Simon & Schuster.

Sachs, Jeffrey. 2005. *The end of poverty: Economic possibilities for our time.* New York: Penguin.

Santos, Boaventura de Sousa. 2006. *The rise of the global left: The World Social Forum and beyond.* New York: Zed Books.

Sen, Jai, Anita Anand, Arturo Escobar, and Peter Waterman. 2004. *World Social Forum: Challenging empires.* New Delhi: Viveka Foundation.

Shaw, Mae. 2007. Community development and democracy: Reasserting the connection. In *Democratising democracy: A new social purpose agenda in adult education.* Madingley Hall, UK: University of Cambridge.

Sherman, Amy L. 1992. *Preferential option: A Christian and neoliberal strategy for Latin America's poor.* Grand Rapids: Eerdmans.

————. 1997. *The soul of development: Biblical Christianity and economic transformation in Guatemala.* New York: Oxford University Press.

Shipton, Parker MacDonald. 1989. *Bitter money: Cultural economy and some African meanings of forbidden commodities.* American Ethnological Society Monograph Series 1. Washington, DC: American Anthropological Association.

Sphere Project. 2011. *The sphere project handbook: Humanitarian charter and minimum standards in humanitarian response.* Bourton on Dunsmore, UK: Practical Action.

Stiglitz, Joseph E., and Andrew Charlton. 2005. *Fair trade for all: How trade can promote development.* New York: Oxford University Press.

Suttle, Tim. 2011. *An evangelical social gospel? Finding God's story in the midst of extremes.* Eugene, OR: Wipf & Stock.

Taussig, Michael T. 1980. *The devil and commodity fetishism in South America.* Chapel Hill: University of North Carolina Press.

Tocqueville, Alexis de. 2003 [1862]. *Democracy in America and two essays on America.* Trans. Gerald E. Bevin. London: Penguin.

United Nations. 2009. State of the world's indigenous peoples. New York: United Nations, Department of Economic and Social Affairs, Division for Social Policy and Development, Secretariat of the Permanent Forum on Indigenous Issues. http://www.un.org/esa/socdev/unpfii/documents/SOWIP_web.pdf.

Verbruggen, Sandra, Johan Christiaens, and Koen Milis. 2011. Can resource dependence and coercive isomorphism explain nonprofit organizations' compliance with reporting standards? *Nonprofit and Voluntary Sector Quarterly* 40, no. 1: 5–32.

Waal, Alexander de. 1997. *Famine crimes: Politics and the disaster relief industry in Africa.* Bloomington: Indiana University Press.

GLOSSARY

The following are terms and phrases used in this book as they relate to select aspects of economics, religion, and cultural systems. For items not listed here, readers should consult other reference works for further research or examination.

agrarian economy. An economy in which agriculture is the primary means of subsistence.

allocentrism / allocentric behavior. A set of practices or actions that focus on the well-being of both others and oneself. See also *idiocentrism*.

bahasa Indonesia. "The Indonesian language."

baitulmal. An institution that acts as a trustee for Muslims, looking after assets from which Muslim members can benefit.

basa Sunda. "The Sundanese language."

bivocational. Having two vocations. In the context of Christian ministry, this often refers to ministers who have another source of income beyond the church.

bonding social capital. Social ties that link people together with others who are primarily like them along some key dimension. See also *bridging social capital* and *linking social capital*.

bribe. An inducement in any form offered to a person of power or status to coerce him or her to violate a moral law or responsibility in favor of the giver.

bridging social capital. Social ties that link people together with others across a cleavage that typically divides society, like race, class, or religion. See also *bonding social capital* and *linking social capital*.

business as mission (BAM). The intentional use of business as a distinct form of mission to witness to the gospel.

capitalism. The organization of a society's economics around the accumulation and investment of capital, together with the legitimization of profit-seeking behavior.

collectivism / collectivistic society. A society in which people tend to view themselves as members of groups (e.g., families, ethnic groups) and to prioritize the needs of the group above those of individuals.

civil society organization. See *nongovernmental organization*.

commodification. The process of turning something that was previously not seen as a commodity into one.

commodity. Anything that is or can be bought and sold.

derivatives. A type of financial product designed by investment banks to hedge or protect against the risk of debt and offset fluctuations in interest rates and currencies.

economies. The production, consumption, and distribution of goods and services.

extortion. An act of coercion and intimidation in order to compel another person to give the coercer services or other things of economic value.

factors of production. The types of inputs needed to produce any kind of good. In economics, the factors of production have traditionally consisted of land, labor, and capital.

falah. The Muslim notion of prosperity in this world and in the hereafter.

fiduciary. Related to money and finance.

fitrah. A mandatory tax for all Muslims to contribute as part of the observance of Ramadan, the Muslim month of fasting.

gotong royong (gotong rojong). "Mutual cooperation" or "mutual assistance"; denotes a complex constellation of expectations that often frame Indonesian images of "neighborliness."

hakikat. (Indonesia) Derived from Arabic; usually rendered "essence."

idiocentrism / idiocentric behavior. A set of practices or actions that focus more on the personal goals of an individual and less on others' needs. See also *allocentrism*.

ijara. An Islamic financial instrument that entails leasing or lease financing.

iqtisad. An Islamic definition of economy that connotes thrift, frugality, providence, and moderation.

Islamic banking. Any form of banking or financial transaction that is run in accordance with principles of Islamic law. Such transactions include but are not limited to borrowing, lending, buying, debt finance, mortgage, insurance, and bank and stock transactions.

jizya. A poll or head tax levied on subjugated Jewish and Christian minorities during the Islamic empire in the Middle Ages.

kampung. (Indonesia) A hamlet or village; the former if constituting a borough on the fringe of an urban center, the latter if based as a community in a rural context.

khoms. A tax levied annually on the net income of Shiite Muslims whereby the wealth is paid to Shi'a scholars for religious work.

lagay. A Filipino term for "grease money." May also mean either a bribe or an extortion.

laissez-faire. French, "let them be"; in the context of economics, the term refers to a form of free-market capitalism in which it is believed that the market and economy function best when unhindered by burdensome state regulations or policies. See also *neoliberalism*.

linking social capital. Social ties to those with power that provide one with access to resources from beyond the community. See also *bonding social capital* and *bridging social capital*.

mabait. A word used to describe a person who is both kind and good in Filipino society.

macroeconomics. The branch of economics that studies how overall financial policies and practices promoted by governments and the private sector influence the functions of an economy as a whole, rather than just specific markets. See also *microeconomics*.

market. An arena of economic exchange in which buyers and sellers interact to negotiate with one another and thereby set prices.

market exchange. An economic exchange in which, ideally, the parties negotiate the terms of the exchange according to the principle of self-interest.

mayaman. A Filipino term meaning "affluent" or "rich."

microeconomics. The branch of economics that studies the practices by which people influence the production, distribution, and consumption of goods and services within a macroeconomic context. See also *macroeconomics*.

mudarabah. An Islamic financial instrument that entails profit sharing, wherein an investor (such as a bank or person) provides the capital and an entrepreneur works for and exercises complete control over the business venture. Akin to a limited partnership.

musharaka. An Islamic financial instrument that entails profit-and-loss sharing, wherein an investor (such as a bank or person) may earn a return on invested funds provided the investor shares in the risk of the investment and bears a loss if the project fails.

mutawalli. A *waqf* manager or trustee. See also *waqf*.

neoclassical utility theory. A theory that posits that the best price or financial transaction is determined based on a series of rational choices that seeks to optimize market forces to one's economic advantage.

neoliberalism. A set of economic policies, and an accompanying philosophy, that advocates a reduced role for the state in the economy, with a minimum of regulation and involvement. A neoliberal policy holds that a free market produces the best outcome in terms of economic growth and welfare. See also *laissez-faire*.

nongovernmental organization (NGO). An organization that is not officially associated with the state (or government) and is usually dedicated to providing a service to a local community. The term is usually reserved for organizations engaged in relief, development, and advocacy activities. Also known as "private voluntary organizations" (PVOs), "nonprofit organizations" (NPOs), and "civil society organizations" (CSOs).

OPEC (Organization of the Petroleum Exporting Countries). An organization that seeks to coordinate the amount of oil put onto the market by its member countries in order to maintain oil prices at a level that maximizes profit for its members.

pak. Abbreviation for *bapak,* "mister" ("Mr.") or "father" in Indonesian, Sundanese, and Javanese.

Pancasila. The official philosophical foundation of the Indonesian state. The term derives from two Javanese words of Sanskrit origin: *panca,* "five," and *sila,* "principle" or "foundation." The five principles of Pancasila are (1) belief in one supreme being, (2) a just and civilized humanitarianism, (3) national unity, (4) wise government based upon consultation and consensus, and (5) social justice for all.

pangajian. A Sundanese term for ritualized Qur'anic recitation events.

paternalism. A policy or practice of treating or governing people in a "fatherly" manner, especially by providing for their needs without giving them rights or responsibilities.

patron-client relationships. Mutually obligatory arrangements—informal, hierarchical, and generally lifelong—between individuals (the patrons) who have authority, social status, wealth, or some other personal resource and counterparts (the clients) who benefit from the support, influence, and protection provided by the patrons.

pembangunan. A common Indonesian term for "development," derived from *bangun,* "to build." Carries transitive, subject-object connotations of building, construction, or assembly. See also *perkembangan.*

perkembangan. Another common Indonesian term for "development"; appears in national rhetoric much less frequently than *pembangunan* and derives from the root *kembang,* "flower," implying a more organic, natural, intransitive development process.

PKI (Partai Komunis Indonesia). The Indonesia Communist Party.

political economy. The intersection of politics and economics, in which the policies, practices, and opportunities for the management of goods and services are constructed.

precapitalist societies. Societies that are not based on the accumulation and investment of capital, where profit-seeking behavior is not the core organizing or motivating principle of the economy.

reciprocal exchange. Economic exchange in which, ideally, the parties negotiate the terms of the exchange according to the principle of concern for the other.

riba. Islamic prohibition of interest in financial transactions, in particular those of the predetermined or fixed-return variety.

Rukun Tetangga (RT). Indonesian, "Neighborhood Conviviality Unit." The smaller of the two lowest tiers of Indonesian governmental structure; usually consists of ten to twenty houses/households. Quasi-governmental in nature, since administrative heads for these units are not officially on the government payroll. See also *Rukun Warga.*

Rukun Warga (RW). Indonesian, "Citizenship Conviviality Unit." The larger of the two lowest tiers of Indonesian governmental structure; usually consists of five to ten RTs. Quasi-governmental in nature, since administrative heads for these units are not officially on the government payroll. See also *Rukun Tetangga.*

sadaqa. An Islamic freewill offering of money.

shariah. Islamic law; spelled *syariah* in some countries, such as Malaysia.

social entrepreneurship. A business approach that seeks to be socially responsible by helping to solve problems in a community; e.g., by creating a business to alleviate poverty or using business methods in a nonprofit project.

social gospel. Teachings and practices of Christianity based on a theology that emphasizes Christ's ministry as primarily focused on poverty and social justice. Term often used pejoratively to indicate a one-sided approach to the gospel that ignores evangelism.

Soeharto (Suharto). Indonesia's second president, serving from 1965 to 1998.

Soekarno (Sukarno). Indonesia's first president, serving from 1945 to 1965.

subsistent/subsistence economy. An economy focused on the production of goods and services for basic needs rather than on producing surpluses for other uses.

suhol. A Filipino term for "bribe"; usually refers to an act in which the giver intends to coerce a person of power or status to violate a moral responsibility in his or her favor.

sukuk. Islamic bonds or corporate securities that provide an investor with ownership in an underlying asset, usually based on the balance sheet of the issuing company.

takaful. Islamic insurance.

ubuntu. See *umunthu*.

umunthu. (Malawi) A term that refers to the character of desiring and acting to attain the very best for others; based on the belief that one is a person only as he or she is involved in acting to advance the ultimate advantage of others, and thus defines the essence of being human. Known as *ubuntu* (a Zulu term) in South Africa.

usufructural rights. The right to use a resource but not necessarily to own it.

waqf. An Islamic trust or foundation established under Islamic law for the provision of a designated social service or charitable or religious purpose. In modern times it is usually a corporation.

Washington Consensus. A set of ten neoliberal policies promoted by the major, official international development actors in the late 1980s and beyond.

zakat. One of the five pillars of Islam, which stipulates almsgiving as a required observance. Comprises 2.5 percent of one's income.

zakat al-fitr. See *fitrah*.

INDEX

H

hadiths, 45, 51
hakikat, 130
Harris, Marvin, 102
helping behavior, 180, 185, 187, 189–91, 197–98, 205–7
Heryanto, Ariel, 119
Hiebert, Paul G., 90n3
Hofstede, Geert, 150–51
home buying, 60, 63–65
honor, 78, 99–101, 103, 106, 108, 192
hospitality, 97n8, 159, 177
Hu, Jin-Li, 99
humiliation (of Malian pastors), 164–65
hut tax, 183–84

I

Iannaccone, Laurence, 78
Ibrahim, Salman, 63
idiocentric behavior, 180–81, 187, 189–90, 197–98, 206
ijara, 62
imagined community, 123
income/income generation, xxii, xxvii, 20, 99, 150, 217, 219, 225, 231, 233, 236
  in Islamic economics, 46–47, 51, 56, 60–61, 63
  of Malian pastors, 152, 155–58, 164, 166–69, 174–75
  in Zowe, Malawi, 179, 183–88, 190, 194–95, 200, 203–7
India, market women of, 2, 16–18
individualism, 7, 14–15, 70, 72, 77n, 81, 104, 150–51, 196–99, 206
Indonesia, 12, 43, 53n, 113–35, 137, 142

Industrial Revolution, 61, 76
industrialization, 135–36, 214, 219, 222–23, 226–27
inheritance, 44n3, 46, 58n
Institut National de Prévoyance Sociale (INPS), 165
insurance, 59, 66, 68, 232
  social, 100, 186
interest, 16, 21–22
  biblical attitude toward, 76–77
  interest-free financing, 44, 59–70
  Islamic prohibition of, 43–44, 55, 59–70. *See also* riba
International Islamic University, 70
International Monetary Fund (IMF), 224–25
investment, 18, 47, 54, 59, 61–64, 67–68, 80, 232
Iskandar, Dadi J., 122
Islam, xxviii, 43–81, 130, 133, 152
  Islamic banking and economics, xxviii, 43–70, 80
    as a mirror for Christian mission, 70–78, 80–81
    theological foundations for, 45–46, 48
  Hadhari, 69n
  See also specific financial instruments, concepts, and aspects
Islamic Relief, 51
Israel, 14, 73, 76, 137–39, 140n, 220

J

James (epistle), xxv, 32
jangkrik, 132–33
Java, xxix, 113, 115–17, 121n11, 122n13, 126–27, 131n25, 132, 135
jealousy, xxiv, 10, 50, 58